GOVERNMENT CONTROL AND MULTINATIONAL STRATEGIC MANAGEMENT

GOVERNMENT CONTROL AND MULTINATIONAL STRATEGIC MANAGEMENT

Power Systems and Telecommunication Equipment

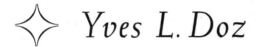 Yves L. Doz

PRAEGER SPECIAL STUDIES • PRAEGER SCIENTIFIC

Library of Congress Cataloging in Publication Data

Doz, Yves L
   Government control and multinational strategic
management.

   Includes bibliographical references and index.
   1. International business enterprises--Management.
2. Industry and state. I. Title.
HD69.I7D69   658.1'8   79-11793
ISBN 0-03-049476-1

Published in 1979 by Praeger Publishers
A Division of Holt, Rinehart and Winston/CBS, Inc.
383 Madison Avenue, New York, New York 10017 U.S.A.

© 1979 by Praeger Publishers

9 038 987654321

Printed in the United States of America

To my father, Felix Doz

ACKNOWLEDGMENTS

This book is addressed primarily to those interested in the management of multinational companies. It should also be of interest to people directly affected by the telecommunication equipment and power equipment industries, to potential regulators of these industries, and to government officials. The goal of the study is to develop a framework to describe and conceptualize competition and firms' management within these two industries.

The first version of this study was completed as a D.B.A. dissertation at the Harvard Business School in November 1976. I am particularly indebted to Joseph L. Bower, who was of great help during my studies, guided the dissertation version of this work, and encouraged me to undertake this revision. John H. McArthur and Michael Y. Yoshino were also valuable advisers for the dissertation. Several fellow doctoral students and colleagues have helped me improve and clarify many aspects of the research. C. K. Prahalad contributed much to the definition of the research design and the interpretation of the data. Richard Hamermesh was a constant encouragement and his advice was helpful throughout the research program.

I am most grateful to the managers of the three companies that agreed to be studied in depth: Brown Boveri & Cie, General Telephone and Electronics, and LM Ericsson. All managers were generous with their time and offered fascinating insights into the issues I was studying. The cooperation of these three companies was critical to the success of the research. Officers in many other organizations also contributed their time, and I am grateful to them as well.

A number of institutions provided me with support during the research. The Ford Foundation provided generous financial support. The Centre d'Enseignement Superiéur des Affaires sponsored my application to the Ford Foundation European Doctoral Fellowship Program and provided complementary loans. All logistic expenses associated with this research were covered by the Division of Research of the Harvard Business School.

The staff of the Harvard Business School was most helpful. Mini Chazen was extremely efficient in helping me with all sorts of administrative matters and typing the correspondence required by the research. Karen Steuber helped with the final dissertation version. Cathi O'Hara handled the final manuscript preparation and Rose Giacobbe and her staff did most of the typing. I thank them.

I have reserved my warmest thanks to my wife, Nicole, who accepted the practical and psychological tensions that came with several years of studies and research work and my several long trips to Europe. She has been most helpful in encouraging me throughout the research.

Despite the many contributions I was fortunate to receive in this research, I alone am responsible for any shortcomings.

CONTENTS

LIST OF TABLES

LIST OF FIGURES

LIST OF ACRONYMS

BBC	Brown Boveri & Cie
BWR	boiling water nuclear reactor
CCITT	Comité Consultatif International des Téléphone et Télé-graphe
CEM	Compagnie Electro-Mécanique
CGE	Compagnie Générale d'Electricité
EdF	Electricité de France
EEC	European Economic Community
EFTA	European Free Trade Association
GE	General Electric
GEC	General Electric & Company
GTE	General Telephone and Electronics
IBM	International Business Machines
ITT	International Telephone and Telegraph
KWU	Kraft Werke Union
LED	light-emitting diode
LME	LM Ericsson
LMT	Le Matériel Téléphonique
LWR	light-water reactor
MHz	megahertz
MNC	multinational corporation
MWe	megawatt
P&T	Posts and Telecommunications
PABX	private automatic branch exchange
PBX	private branch exchange
PCM	pulse-code modulation
PTT	post, telegraph, and telephone
R&D	research and development
SFTE	Société Française des Téléphones Ericsson
SLE	Société Laonnaise d'Electronique

GOVERNMENT
CONTROL AND
MULTINATIONAL
STRATEGIC
MANAGEMENT

1

INTRODUCTION

      This is a book about the management of some multinational corporations (MNCs). It deals with companies that find themselves in a particularly difficult predicament. On the one hand, they are active in industries that attract much host government attention and in which host governments can exercise much influence and demand adaptation to local conditions along a variety of dimensions. On the other hand, within these same industries, the evolution of technology, the changes in production economics, and the constraints of a worldwide oligopoly structure create tremendous pressures for rationalization of manufacturing operations, standardization of products, and integration of research and development activities across boundaries into centrally managed multinational networks. In short, these companies face political imperatives as they sell heavy high-technology equipment through large contracts with government-owned customers; they also face demanding economic imperatives because of the technology and economics of their products and the difficult dynamics of competition in their industries.

      The starting point to the research described here was provided by the intriguing contradiction outlined above: how could multinationals in industries characterized by very high levels of government involvement and, simultaneously, by economic and technological pressures for worldwide rationalization and integration of MNC operations be managed?

THE NEED FOR ADMINISTRATIVE RESEARCH

The Inadequacy of Simple Structural Answers

      Most researchers who have studied the management of multinational enterprises have developed a contrast between two different types of companies. First are corporations managed as holding companies in which each national subsidiary enjoys considerable autonomy and managerial independence. A significant example of this approach would be Nestlé. Nestlé's operations in various countries are primarily run locally with no overall operating integration.[1] The only integrated activities are the management of research and development (R&D) and the treasury function. Operationally, in terms of planning, budgeting, marketing, and manufacturing, each subsidiary enjoys much autonomy.

Second, there are companies whose operations are integrated across boundaries in centrally managed networks; International Business Machines (IBM) falls within this category. IBM runs many of its operations on a more centralized basis. For instance, all product development activities are run on a worldwide basis to avoid duplications or dispensable product differentiation. Specific development programs are carried on in various locations and basic research is also carried out in several countries.[2] Manufacturing is also specialized internationally within IBM. For instance, plants in Germany provide printers, and all electronic microcircuits are manufactured in France for the whole of Europe.[3]

Clearly, for companies manufacturing telecommunication equipment or power systems and other heavy electrical equipment, neither extreme provides a satisfactory answer. The strong economies of scale involved in telecommunication equipment or turbogenerator equipment, as well as the heavy R&D needed for their development, call for rationalization, integration, and central management, à la IBM. Conversely, the influence of governments calls for national autonomy and responsiveness, à la Nestlé. In short the companies studied have to fall between the extreme ideal types and are likely to incorporate some characteristics of both. Such ambiguous adaptation must be administrative in nature, with a centralization-decentralization mix that is appropriate to specific decisions or functional tasks.

An Administrative Interface

Furthermore, the interface between host governments and companies is administrative in nature. First, on the host country side, decisions affecting MNCs are the output of complex administrative processes. Several key players are involved: the users of equipment (electrical utilities or telecommunication services), various ministries and specialized state agencies (for instance, telecommunication research centers or nuclear energy agencies), and other interests (the national industry, various customer groups, and so forth). Policies generally emerge from ad hoc consensus among key players. The process of policy formation over time usually makes a clear, enduring country strategy impossible unless one key actor dominates the others. In France, for instance, Electricité de France (EdF), the national electrical utility company, had long dominated the policy process. With the shift from fossil fuel power systems to nuclear ones, other key players took a more active role and EdF's prominence was eroded. Similarly, in large, complex, multinational companies, decisions at the subsidiary level emerge from complex managerial and administrative interfaces between managers. Coalitions can develop on specific issues between, say, corporate functional staffs and subsidiary managers, or top management and product division management. The attractiveness of particular coalitions to individual managers will depend on how they perceive certain situations, on what information they get, on how their units' performances are measured, and on how they are rewarded or punished. This has three important consequences:

1. Any particular decision made in a subsidiary can only be understood by looking not only at its analytical components, but also at the way in which specific administrative procedures, such as the formal reporting relationships, the planning and budgeting systems, the information flows, the measurement criteria, and the personal incentives systems shape the perceptions and premises of individual managers when they reach decisions. [4]

2. Because the decision processes span several levels within the organization as well as several functions, the result from the formation of particular coalitions, the importance of power phenomena needs to be recognized. [5]

3. To a large extent, top management can influence decisions by controlling the administrative procedures that shape perceptions and interests and confer or withdraw power. [6] Administrative procedures become administrative tools when they are used purposefully by top management to shape decision premises.

In short, it is not possible to assign to companies an economic rationality or to consider their specific decisions outside of the internal administrative context in which they were reached.

Administrative Context
and the Literature on the MNC

The available literature on the management of the multinational company does not illuminate administrative interface well. General theories are based on broad conceptual approaches and empirical generalizations. Interesting and insightful as they are, they offer little administrative content and provide little assistance in understanding specific situations. Most of these theories have been derived from aggregate data that do not incorporate much managerial content. The most notable efforts to take account of managerial content are works by John M. Stopford and Louis T. Wells, Lawrence G. Franko, and Michael Y. Yoshino that review the structural evolution of a large sample of MNCs.[7] But again, because these studies only cover broad strategic variables (product diversity, foreign growth rates, search for resources or markets) and general organizational firm classifications (looking only at one level below corporate management), the managerial content remains fairly limited.

Beyond these general theories, one can find two types of administrative research dealing with the MNC. First, one can find isolated clinical glimpses at individual companies. These range from purely descriptive, very detailed company histories, such as E. P. Neufeld's study of Massey Ferguson, to refined conceptual essays illustrated by abstracted examples from one company, such as C. K. Prahalad's study of the international operations of a large petrochemical company or Michel Ghertman's study of an industrial gas company.[8] Second, one can find detailed studies of one issue in international management. Sometimes such studies are quite rich and fascinating, for instance, Henri de Bodinat's study of "influence" in the manufacturing function of MNCs.[9] Most often, however, these studies suffer from several limitations and take issues out of context. For instance, researching managers' patterns of transfer between subsidiaries within MNCs is almost meaningless unless this is put in a broader managerial framework. Conversely, studies of individual companies, or of a few companies, are not revealing unless these companies are carefully selected as deviants, as potential countercases to enrich or dismiss an existing theory or paradigm or to challenge conventional wisdom.

Conclusion: Territory and Scope

This research began with the intention to inquire into the apparent paradox of strong successful multinationals operating in industries of much salience to host governments. The lack of a rich administrative literature on the management of MNCs added a second starting point: the realization that the interface between MNCs and host governments was administrative in nature and thus required a methodology that would capture much administrative and managerial content. The interaction between these starting points guided the choice of a research territory: the conditions under which the management of MNCs was likely to be most difficult, and its clinical description and

TABLE 1.1

Political and Economic Imperatives

Political	Economic
Government-owned customers	Large scale of industry
Quasi monopsony power	Economies of scale in production
Strategic products and technologies	Economies of aggregation in research and development
Small number of large contracts	Importance of production experience effects
Intrinsic difficulties in shifting from one supplier to another due to interface problems and product technology	Increasing scale and technological complexity of products
	Worldwide oligopoly industry structures

Source: Compiled by the author.

conceptualization most rewarding, were found in industries where the political and economic imperatives would most directly conflict. Such conditions prevailed in the telecommunication equipment and power system industries.

Table 1.1 summarizes the elements of the political and economic imperatives that made these two industries particularly fascinating. In addition, both the telecommunication equipment and the power system industries are going through significant technological changes. Telecommunication equipment is shifting to electronic technologies, and power systems to nuclear-driven technologies. In both cases the new technologies add pressures for multinational integration by driving up the minimal efficient scale of operations and attract more government attention as they are particularly salient for strategic, military, and social reasons. The conflict between political and economic imperatives is thus made more acute by the new technologies. This dimension of change, with the contradictions it implies, made these two industries all the more fascinating as a research territory.

FIGURE 1.1

Research Scope

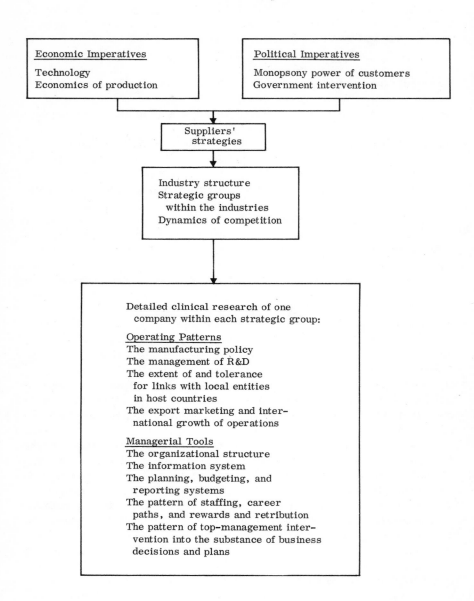

Source: Compiled by the author.

In order to provide integration between the broad theories and models purporting to describe MNC behavior in general terms and specific clinical glimpses, one had to adopt a medium-level methodology and an exploratory approach. An external look at MNCs and the popular view of their management assume a dominance of their environment by the MNCs and a monolithic management.[10] Concretely, the popular view of MNCs is one of companies seeking maximum profits through a number of ways that undercut the sovereignty and independence of individual countries. It includes visions of governments begging companies for new plants, of executives shrewdly manipulating transfer prices to minimize taxes and exploit financial market differences, and of companies trampling over the needs of people and governments.

Insiders' views project a very different image: they see almost powerless companies trying to cope with difficult environments. Their understanding is functionalist and reactive, conceiving the MNC as an adaptive system reacting to changes in its environment.

A missing link between these two views is probably at the origin of most genuine misunderstandings about MNCs. MNCs neither dominate, nor do they merely react to, their environment; they do some of both. Few MNCs find themselves in a dominant enough position in almost any country to determine their environment or to afford ignoring it. Some historical examples from lesser developed countries (for instance, the U.S. food companies in Central America) sustain this view but many other examples show the limits to MNC influence on host country environments.[11] Conversely, few MNCs simply react to their environment. Most companies have some kind of strategy to deal with the environment that is not rooted in dominance or reactiveness, but rather rests on some assessment of the company's strengths and weaknesses with respect to its competitors and some measure of bargaining power vis-à-vis host government. Strategy is thus a mediating variable between the company and its environment. Strategy also provides guidance to the implementation of specific tasks and the use of administrative systems as management tools.[12] Strategy also provides a central relational concept between the industry structure, the individual posture of a firm in an industry, and the management of that firm.[13] This concern with strategy as a mediating variable and a relational concept led to the research scope depicted in Figure 1.1.

METHODOLOGY AND DATA

The territory and scope of the research, as outlined in the above section, called for an exploratory research scheme combining industry

analyses with detailed administrative clinical studies of selected companies. Through this combination of industry analyses and detailed
case studies, the goal was to develop a framework that would relate
characteristics of the management of the firm (the managerial tools
being used to run it) to its posture within its industry and the strategy
it followed. In other words, the objective was not to establish general propositions of the type usually found in natural sciences but to
develop a language and broad general framework that would make it
possible to treat each organization as an individual entity. Studying
how individual companies responded to the conflict between economic
and political imperatives was expected to reveal more about the administrative management of multinational companies.

Any empirically developed framework of this kind will have
counter-examples or will be reduced to the broadest level of generality. Here the counter-examples are accepted. The test of validity is
not statistical empirical applicability but logic and usefulness. Therefore, the framework is helpful only if it helps one to illuminate, describe, and understand individual situations. Further work in the
same research area would involve the search for deviant cases and
inquiry into whether the framework helps to understand these cases.
In summary, the way to "validate" the conceptual scheme presented
here is to apply it to other in-depth clinical studies of companies facing difficult conflicts between political and economic imperatives.

Concretely, the research involved two main levels of analysis:
industry studies and clinical management-process case studies.
Sources of data were accordingly quite different. The two industry
studies combine three sources:

1. A variety of articles published largely in specialized trade
publications (Electronics, Telephony, Electrical Engineering, and so
forth) and to a lesser extent in general business publications (Business
Week, Fortune, Management Today, European Business, l'Expansion,
The Economist, and The Financial Times).

2. Industry and market studies or statistics published by such
organizations as the United Nations (UN), the European Economic
Community (EEC), and the Organization for Economic Cooperation
and Development (OECD), by consulting companies, research institutes (Atlantic Trade Center and others), and individual researchers.

3. Interviews with officials in most of the companies involved,
consultants, government advisors, bank officers, and other experts
in government, business, and academics.

Well-structured information was generally available on the heavy
electrical-equipment industry, so published sources could be used
more reliably. For the telecommunication industry study, a more

TABLE 1.2

The Three Major Research Sites

	Brown Boveri &Cie (BBC)	LM Ericsson (LME)	General Telephone and Electronics (GTE)
Headquarters	Baden, Switzerland	Stockholm, Sweden	Stamford, Connecticut (United States)
Major products	Turbogenerators, transformers, rolling stock, circuit breakers, motors industrial system, electrical apparatus, electronic components, microwave systems, radars appliances, medical electronics	Main exchange telephone switchgear, private switchgear, transmission equipment, radio communication equipment, electronic components	Telecommunication equipment, consumer electronics, military systems, electronic components, data transmission, radio systems[b]
Total sales, 1974 (dollars)	Approx. 3.4 billion[a]	1.46 billion	Approx. 5.60 billion[c]
International sales (dollars)	Approx. 2.9 billion[a]	1.21 billion	Approx. .86 billion
Personnel			
Worldwide	96,000	77,320	198,000
Nondomestic	77,000	46,250	34,600
Profits[a] (dollars)	–	48 million	366 million
Production centers abroad	Approx. 40	Approx. 70	Approx. 48
Countries where manufacture is undertaken	16	17	15

[a]BBC does not consolidate financial statements on a worldwide basis.

[b]GTE also operates large telephone networks in various regions of the United States; about half of its billing comes from telecommunication services, not products.

[c]Including revenue from telephone networks.

Source: Compiled by the author.

complex puzzle had to be assembled from numerous interviews and bits and pieces of anecdotal information found in newspapers and trade publications.

The clinical company studies rely mostly on direct interviews. An average of 25 interviews (lasting from one and a half to four hours) were conducted in each of the three companies. Though the sample of managers interviewed could not be decided with precision, it was possible in all three companies to talk to four broad categories of executives: corporate line managers and staff experts, product-oriented managers, area-oriented managers, and national subsidiary general and functional managers. In each company, I visited at least one national subsidiary, spending from one day to a week there. In virtually all cases cooperation by individual managers was complete and dedicated, with all of them volunteering for further interviews if needed. Companies also provided much written information about their activities, administrative processes, plans, financial results, and so forth.

The choice of the three companies studied in depth was guided by their belonging to three distinct strategic groups. The choice was also partly fortuitous, however, since these companies were the first to agree to cooperate fully. Two further companies were approached, one in each industry, but each declined to cooperate fully.

The three companies studied in depth were among the major MNCs and were clear leaders in both industries. Table 1.2 sketches a comparison between them, in broad terms.

Detailed analysis of the management of the three companies made it possible to relate the posture of these firms within their industry to the way in which they were managed. Though the trade-offs between the requirements for economic success and adjustments made necessary by the demands of host governments were the same among all the companies, their strategic, structural, and managerial responses were quite different. Differences in response could be explained primarily in terms of differences between firms in technology and market positions. This clearly constituted the central finding of the research, around which other conclusions could be developed.

Since further chapters do not depict in detail the development of these three companies, a short historical background to acquaint the reader with each of them is appropriate.

Brown Boveri & Cie

Brown Boveri & Cie (BBC) was created in 1891. Baden (in the Swiss canton of Aargau) was chosen as the location of the new firm because the town promised a first order for a power station. Founders Walter Boveri and Charles Brown had both gained experience in the use of electricity at the Oerlikon company in Zurich. The technical genius of Charles Brown and the managerial expertise of Walter Boveri quickly made the firm successful. Before 1900, BBC sold power stations to several towns in Germany. The town of Mannheim requested the company to maintain a repair shop close by for immediate repairs in case of failure. This plus high duties, insufficient protection against patent violation, and lack of skilled manpower and raw materials in rural Aargau led to the establishment of BBC's first foreign manufacturing operation in Mannheim.

By the turn of the century, BBC had become an integrated supplier of electrical equipment. BBC developed electrical traction equipment for mountain railroads and suburban tramways. Charles Brown invented the oil bath circuit breaker and made high voltage current safe enough for widespread use. In 1900 the company acquired the Parsons licenses for steam turbines, recognizing that water wheels had little potential outside of mountainous Switzerland. Combining these steam turbines with Brown's high speed generators gave BBC a clear technological lead. In order to take advantage of that lead and overcome customs barriers and preferential purchasing, BBC quickly entered agreements with other European companies to join in common ventures and become a shareholder. By World War I, BBC had manufacturing affiliates in Germany, Italy, France, Norway, Spain, Austria, and the Netherlands.

During World War I each company had to operate separately to survive in the warring countries. Political unrest and economic instability in many European countries then led to a growing autonomy of the various national companies. The Swiss company, in Baden, remained the clear technological leader of the group, and the other companies steadily acquired licenses from Baden. Their royalties enabled the Swiss company to invest in further important developments. During the whole interwar period BBC maintained a clear technological lead. A short-lived agreement with Vickers in 1919 failed to give access to the British market but resulted in a takeover by BBC of the Westinghouse operations in continental Europe. The BBC companies in the various countries diversified on their own and found their own ways to weather the storms of the Great Depression and World War II. Links between the companies were technical and financial, with scarcely any managerial exchanges.

Postwar reconstruction, followed by the boom in the 1960s, was extraordinarily favorable to BBC companies, particularly in Germany and France. Relative to the Swiss company, the French and German companies gained in prominence. By the mid-1960s some difficulties began to emerge. Most BBC companies were smaller, individually, than their domestic competitors, and the BBC group as a whole did not take advantage of its multinationality. Changes consequent to these difficulties are described in Chapters 8 and 10.

LM Ericsson

   LM Ericsson (LME) had modest beginnings when Lars Magnus Ericsson opened a telephone repair shop in Stockholm in 1876. The company rapidly developed a telephone system not only in Sweden but also in Russia, Hungary, the United Kingdom, Italy, France, and several other countries. By 1890 more than 90 percent of the equipment made in Sweden was exported, mostly to the captive market of LM Ericsson-owned telephone operating companies in various countries. Early in the twentieth century LME further expanded into Latin America. Except for the adjoining fields of radio transmissions and military communications, the company was almost single-mindedly devoted to acquiring and maintaining a position in the telephone business. Though Sweden was less affected than most other countries, the turmoil of the depression in the 1930s, followed by World War II, wrought havoc on the LME companies abroad. After World War II, LME relied on the Crossbar technology, developed and perfected in Sweden, to spearhead a new drive into foreign markets. The drive was quickly successful. During the same period MNCs came under growing criticism and LME quietly withdrew from telephone network operations, usually able to transfer ownership smoothly to national bodies and receive adequate compensation. By the early 1970s LME was manufacturing equipment in 17 different countries and exporting from Sweden to scores of others.

General Telephone and Electronics

   General Telephone and Electronics (GTE) did not start as an industrial company but as an independent telephone operating company, when the founders bought a local firm in Richland Center, Wisconsin (United States), in 1918. Rapid expansion followed with the assistance of the bankers, Paine, Webber & Company (now Paine, Webber, Jackson & Curtis). The company was named Associated Telephone Utilities following the acquisition of Automated Electric, a manufacturer of telephones since 1892. Automated Electric, in addition to its domestic operations, also conducted manufacturing operations in Canada, Belgium, and Italy. Expansion followed rapidly and the company was renamed General Telephone Services. Further acquisitions took them into microwave transmission equipment (Lenkurt, in 1959) and into a whole range of professional and consumer electronics after the merger with Sylvania (also in 1959). The company was then renamed General Telephone and Electronics, to reflect its twin vocation. Telecommunication manufacturing operations were located in Canada, Belgium, Italy, Brazil, Mexico, and Venezuela, in addition to the United States. New factories were being built in Taiwan and in Iran, following large orders from these countries.

SUMMARY OF FINDINGS AND IMPLICATIONS

This section summarizes the key conclusions of the research from a managerial point of view and presents the major articulations of the framework as it was developed after extensive field work and conceptualization. A first subsection explores the difficulties of managing in government-influenced industries, and a second subsection presents a set of strategic, structural, and administrative responses developed by companies. These responses are configurations of administrative systems and operating patterns adapted to specific postures of companies in given government-influenced businesses.

Difficulties Faced by Management

Against the background of managing in industries characterized by free trade and relatively free investment, the management of government-influenced businesses raises a more complex set of issues.

A major difficulty management must face is the complex relationship that develops between the MNC and its customer. The world world market most often takes the form of a set of separate national oligopolies. Success in becoming part of such an oligopoly flows from the overall efficiency of the MNC. Success in remaining part of it depends on the responsiveness of the local subsidiary. In new markets, economic criteria such as technology, price and financing, reliability, delivery delays, and training programs are used to select suppliers to national customers. Also, commitment to local production is an entry ticket in developed countries as well as in developing ones. Once the market matures and closer relationships develop between the management of the local subsidiaries and the national government administration, the emphasis shifts to balance of payments surplus, joint product design, increased employment and production, local development, and integration into the local economy in accordance with national policies.

Thus, for a corporation to maintain its existing positions in well-established markets, a high degree of local responsiveness is required. Usually an organization that runs along worldwide product lines will tend to favor overall efficiency and overlook local responsiveness. Moreover, an integrated system does not readily provide for a variety of responses to diverse market conditions.

It remains true, however, that in order to compete successfully for new markets, the MNC must have some superiority over local companies in technological and economic terms. Such superiority is not easily achieved by a set of autonomous subsidiaries existing without tangible central support. Thus, an organization run along separate, national company lines will find it difficult to maintain a competitive edge over local companies.

This contradiction frames the dilemma faced by the managers of government-influenced businesses. How to achieve both overall efficiency and local responsiveness and how to integrate different cognitive orientations into the same management processes are questions that lie at the crux of the difficulty.

All decisions, however, need not be made with both orientations aligned in the same perspective. In fact there are relatively few decisions that require such duality. What is critical is the ability to shift from one orientation to the other, almost immediately from one decision to another: not globally through painful reorganizations, but flexibly and locally, with a sensitivity to national differences.

Beyond this central dilemma and the flexibility required to manage it, government-influenced businesses raise several difficult issues that must be reflected in the management processes. First, there is a need for awareness of the complex web of possible consequences flowing from apparently simple decisions. Management must know that a shift toward stronger product divisions in the United States may affect the company's relationship with the government in Spain. Any significant decision made by management will be perceived as a signal by the many government officials who watch MNCs' activities.

Second, it is probably impossible to retain full managerial control. Top management must accept some ambiguity and the loss of direct authority. Formal authority needs to be replaced by more informal, less visible means of influence. The head of each local subsidiary must be recognized, not only as an emissary of the corporation, but as a link between the company and the national coalition that ensures the existence of the subsidiary in the country. Instances where local managing directors ally themselves with local interests against the wishes of the corporate headquarters are bound to multiply as governments demand joint ventures and as local citizens are promoted to leadership positions.

Third, information is indirect and not always confirmable. It is usually possible for corporate managers to check on the assumptions underlying the plans of subsidiaries. But when local managers claim that their plans rest on the word of local intermediaries and on their relationships with local officials, it is difficult, at best, to determine the soundness of the assumptions. Similarly, when subsidiary managers protest that a decision made at the corporate level is going to jeopardize their relationships with local customers, there is most often no way to assess whether or not they are right.

The impact of government involvement is not something that can be grasped analytically, nor does it lend itself easily to the normal strategic planning procedures. One can only succeed by encouraging alertness at all levels in the corporation and by designing the administrative processes to foster cooperation and loyalty inside the company as well as sensitivity to the specific conditions outside. Government-influenced businesses need to be managed with a dual orientation: global efficiency and local responsiveness. The uncertainties surrounding government influence require this dual orientation to be built into the management processes so that both the local and the global interests are given due consideration when key decisions are reached.

The management of government-influenced businesses is sufficiently different to be segregated administratively from other businesses within an MNC. In fact, in all of the diversified multinational companies observed, the government-influenced businesses were little affected by the tighter procedures developed to integrate the activities of different subsidiaries along product lines. In most cases they were segregated and left to develop their own administrative procedures. The sweeping changes witnessed in many MNCs in the relative importance of the subsidiary managers versus worldwide product division managers, in favor of the latter, usually did not take place in government-influenced businesses. The strategic planning orientation did not swing to global product planning but evolved into more complex forms of strategic management rooted in administrative arrangements that lacked the simplicity of pure product or pure country orientations.

Managing for Responsiveness and Efficiency

Combining the local responsiveness and the global efficiency orientations is not equally important for all decisions. For some activities it is critical, largely because the way in which these activities are conducted globally affects the equilibrium reached locally in a number of countries.

Foremost among these critical activities are exports and R&D. Judicious allocation of export orders among national companies enhances both local acceptability and overall success by reconciling the demands of each country for increased exports with the need for efficiency in serving new foreign markets. Thus, the flexibility of shifting export orders from one source to another to reflect the specific needs of each order is a strong competitive tool. Companies such as International Telephone and Telegraph and Brown Boveri & Cie, thanks to their several full-fledged national companies, can play that game particularly well.

Similarly, R&D is another critical area for reconciling the two orientations. One difficult trade-off is balancing the demand for differentiated products to meet the specifications of each particular national customer, with the need for a sufficiently high technology to appeal to new customers. The difficulty of that choice is compounded further by government demands to have some "real" R&D carried out locally instead of the minimal product adaptation done by most MNCs. Answers to such dilemmas vary widely between companies. For instance, International Telephone and Telegraph (ITT) developed a number of variations of its new electronic telephone switching equipment, with the responsibility for each variation assigned to the national subsidiary where it would be most suited. At the same time LM Ericsson, its main direct competitor, built much versatility into a single type of switching equipment developed entirely in Sweden.

More generally, top management has to differentiate the degree of influence accorded to each orientation depending on the tasks and functions at hand. At one extreme, marketing in well-established markets can be left entirely to the local management; at the other, procedures for quality control need to be developed centrally. The management of both technology and export marketing require much coordination between the two orientations.

The orientation that is generally favored in each MNC depends upon the strategy of the company in relationship to its previous development and the maturity of its markets. Technology and existing mature market position determine the balance between the orientations in all of the companies studied. The interactions of these elements have led to the development of three distinct configurations of administrative systems and operating patterns. These are called "managerial modes" to emphasize that they derive more from a concept of management than from a particular organizational form. These elements are sketched in a simplified format in Figure 1.2.

FIGURE 1.2

Choice of Managerial Modes as a Function of the Firm's Market
Position and Technology

Existing Market Positions of the Firm

		Strong	Weak
Technology of the Firm Compared with Competitors	High	Mixed posture Power-balance mode	Proficient posture for expansion into new markets Centralized mode
	Low	Responsive posture for maintenance in mature markets Decentralized mode	Weak posture for retrenchment in domestic market

Source: Compiled by the author.

Managerial Modes

A detailed analysis of each managerial mode is developed in
Chapters 7, 8, and 9 respectively. For each mode the administrative systems used and their interactions with operating patterns are
reviewed in detail. These complex administrative descriptions and
conceptualizations do not lend themselves easily to summarization;
still, the most salient features of each mode are mentioned briefly
below and the section is concluded by a comparative table outlining
the differences of emphasis between them.

A business that utilizes the centralized mode is characterized
by a clear leading company, which is usually in the parent company's
country of origin. The tasks of developing new products and penetrating new markets are clearly assigned to this leading company.
National companies are geared exclusively toward their domestic
markets and do not participate in an internationally integrated network. These subsidiaries are clearly inferior in status and dependent

upon the leading company in the group. This arrangement has been relatively successful for companies that have expanded rapidly into new markets by relying on a strong technology. New manufacturing subsidiaries can be set up and developed rapidly with much assistance from the center. Furthermore, the production processes often can be split between parts manufacture done in the center and product assembly done locally. However, as markets mature and the scope of government demands increase, severe tensions develop between the subsidiaries and headquarters. National governments have grown increasingly resentful of the secondary role given to the local subsidiaries and their dominance by a foreign country, and this mode of operation has come under strong criticism. In 1976 it was not clear how acceptable it would be in the future.

The decentralized mode leaves extensive operational, managerial, and financial autonomy to the affiliated companies. The required coordination tasks (for instance, allocation of export orders) are assigned to a corporate marketing staff. A series of international product-line committees are set up. Committee membership includes the product division manager (or department head) of the various national companies manufacturing the product line, and a member of the corporate marketing staff. The task of the committee is to formulate corporate-wide objectives, develop worldwide business plans, and exploit opportunities for rationalization and coordination. It remains clear, however, that extensive cooperation among the national companies develops only when convenient for the national managers. In fact, without strong support from top management, these committees are no more than useful forums to explore the acceptability of common solutions in light of the short-term interests of the national companies.

In some cases further coordination is facilitated by the administrative systems; in others, it is not. For instance, it is hindered by disparities among internal structures, budgeting and control systems, and modes of reward and punishment within the national affiliates of BBC. Conversely, similarities in these mechanisms were used to bring the telecommunication subsidiaries of ITT more closely together. Despite these variations, in both ITT and BBC the predominance of the major national affiliates remains well established.

The decentralized managerial mode has been very successful for both ITT and BBC because each has a big enough market share to support a full-fledged company in many countries, and because centrally coordinated export sourcing and technology provide a recognizably useful flexibility. In their dealings with public administrations, national companies can alternately argue both their autonomy and their ability to tap into corporate technology and the corporate export network. However, in businesses where government involvement is low,

TABLE 1.3

The Managerial Modes Compared

	Centralized Mode	Decentralized Mode	Balance-of-Power Mode
Managerial tools			
Structure	Primarily functional with daughter companies and product coordination units.	Set of national companies, corporate staff in coordinating role.	Product-area matrix.
Information flows	Between daughters and functional managers at headquarters.	Primarily within each national company, secondarily in worldwide product committees.	Multidirectional between area and product management units.
Planning, budgeting, and reporting	Detailed overall procedures tightly controlled and integrated by functional managers at headquarters.	National.	Interactive between area and product management units.
Career paths	Commitment to center, high mobility between countries.	National, no exchange between countries.	Multiple, exchange between product and area, lenient reward and punishment systems.
Operating patterns			
Manufacturing	Tightly planned and integrated assembly abroad, extensive assistance and control from the headquarters.	Nationally decided.	Interactive between area and product management units.
Research and development	One large central R&D program developing standard products with little local adaptation.	Coordinated between national companies by corporate staff.	Centrally coordinated, initiative to product management units.
Local cooperation	Centrally decided on a case-by-case basis through daughter company's board.	Nationally decided.	Mostly national, but central guidelines and control.
Export marketing	From the center only.	Coordinated between national companies by corporate staff.	Interactive initiative to product management units.

Source: Compiled by the author.

19

such as small electrical motors or private telephone exchanges, the relatively loose structure of coordinating committees makes it difficult to compete effectively against internationally integrated suppliers.

The power-balance mode uses a matrix organization to incorporate both the local responsiveness and global efficiency orientations. In GTE, corporate product line managers have been appointed and given some top management support so that an overall business strategy could be developed among a set of previously autonomous national subsidiaries. Still, the new product managers did not obtain total support from the top and were left to find outside sources of in-influence, such as export orders or technology transfers, that would be recognized by all subunits as beneficial to the whole organization. These sources of influence have triggered a process of constructive but conflicting interaction between the two orientations.

Preserving the integrity of the balancing process requires a constant effort to prevent one side from gaining ascendence and jeopardizing the cooperative spirit. The division manager is able to do that by constant attention to status and detail in the key administrative processes such as bids and proposals, allocation of export orders and factory loading, and the appropriation of capital expenditures. Critical business and country planning decisions emerged from the constant interface between the two orientations. Since the division manager constantly advocates one orientation to the other, understanding of the dual logic can take place at lower levels in the organization. The overall planning guidelines, as well as the impetus for global strategic thinking and coordinated product development, come from the product managers; but no important plan can be articulated without going through multiple interfaces between product and national managers. This ensures that no significant decision will be made without consideration of its impact on relationships in a variety of countries. Interpersonal cooperation and positive use of influence are fostered by the leniency of the reward and punishment system. Cognitive disagreements can be used positively to enrich the perception of the division's environment and lead to creative conflict solving rather than degenerate into hard bargaining as might occur with tight reward-and-punishment schemes.

NOTES

1. "Nestlé at home abroad," Harvard Business Review, November-December 1976, pp. 80-88.

2. Robert Ronstadt, "R and D Abroad: The Creation and Evolution of Foreign Research and Development Activities of US-based Multinational Enterprise" (D.B.A. diss., Harvard Business School, 1975).

3. Christopher Tugendhat, The Multinationals (London: Eyre and Spottiswood, 1971), chap. 9; also, for an excellent short typical description of the policy of an integrated MNC, see "Ford Thinks European, " The Economist, August 14, 1976, p. 67; for a more complete and theoretical presentation, see, for instance, the comparison between "close" and "open" relationships between headquarters and subsidiaries in Michael A. Brooke and H. Lee Remmers, The Strategy of Multinational Enterprise (New York: American Elsevier, 1970).

4. For the foundations of this argument, see Herbert A. Simon, Administrative Behavior (New York: Macmillan, 1945); also see Joseph L. Bower, Managing the Resource Allocation Process (Boston: Harvard Business School Division of Research, 1970); and Graham T. Allison, Essence of Decision: Explaining the Cuban Missile Crisis (Boston: Little Brown, 1971).

5. See, for instance, Michel Crozier, The Bureaucratic Phenomenon (Chicago: University of Chicago Press, 1967); see also Abraham Zaleznik and Manfred Kets de Vries, Power and the Corporate Mind (Boston: Houghton Mifflin, 1975), particularly chaps. 2 and 6.

6. See Bower, Managing the Resource Allocation Process; C. K. Prahalad, "The Strategic Process in One Multinational Corporation" (D.B.A. diss., Harvard Business School, 1975); and Joseph L. Bower and Yves Doz, "Strategy Formulation: A Social and Political Process, " Business Policy: A New View, ed. Dan Schendel and Charles Hofer (Boston: Little Brown, forthcoming).

7. John M. Stopford and Louis T. Wells, Jr., Managing the Multinational Enterprises (New York: Basic Books, 1972); Lawrence G. Franko, The European Multinationals (Stamford, Conn.: Greylock, 1976); and Michael Y. Yoshino, Japan's Multinational Enterprises (Cambridge, Mass.: Harvard University Press, 1976).

8. E. P. Neufeld, A Global Corporation: A History of the International Development of Massey Ferguson Ltd. (Toronto: University of Toronto Press, 1969); Prahalad, "The Strategic Process"; Michel Ghertman, "Enterprises Multinationales et Prise de Decisions Strategiques, " mimeographed (Jouy en Josas, France: Centre d'Enseignement Superieur des Affaires).

9. Henri de Bodinat, "Influence in the Multinational Enterprise" (D.B.A. diss., Harvard Business School, 1976).

10. Richard J. Barnet and Renold E. Muller, Global Reach (New York: Simon and Schuster, 1974).

11. See, for instance, Charles S. T. Goodsell, American Corporations and Peruvian Politics (Cambridge, Mass.: Harvard University Press, 1974).

12. Kenneth R. Andrews, The Concept of Corporate Strategy (Homewood, Ill.: Dow Jones Irwin, 1971).

13. See Michael S. Hunt, "Competition in the Major Home Appliance Industry, 1960-1970" (Ph. D. diss., Harvard University, 1972); and Michael Porter, "Market Structure Strategy Formulation and Firm Profitability: The Theory of Strategic Groups and Mobility Barriers," in <u>Marketing and the Public Interest</u>, ed. John Cady (Cambridge, Mass.: Marketing Science Institute, forthcoming).

2

GOVERNMENT INTERVENTION AND MNC STRATEGIC RESPONSES

A story is told that while an investment application was pending for Heinz to buy a French mustard manufacturer, a question was put casually at a dinner to President Pompidou: "Mr. President, what do you think about the French mustard industry being controlled by foreigners?" The president, who knew nothing about the pending application, answered, "I don't see why it should not remain French." This comment was quickly relayed to the officials in charge of approving the specific investment proposal. They interpreted it as the president's position and issued a stark rebuff to Heinz. Puzzled, because everything had been going so well till then, the company management decided to no longer consider investment opportunities in France.

Whether or not the story is accurate, it reflects the often hazardous and unpredictable character of government intervention. Though our example is somewhat extreme, it remains that there is not always a clear-cut logic to government interventions into the activities of multinational corporations. A variety of arguments can underlie government interventions and justify specific government decisions affecting individual industries and companies. Moreover, intervention is usually the outcome of the combination of several different processes in complex government bureaucracies.

Despite this intrinsic murkiness, many authors have examined the relationships between nation-states and multinationals in recent years.* Many arguments have been developed, but fairly basic questions on the economic usefulness (to whom?) of multinational companies remain without definite analytical answers. This lack of clear-cut answers leaves the door open to all judgmental or ideological answers.

---

*A bibliography published in 1971 listed over 700 references to relationships between nation-states and international corporations. Since then a few hundred more publications have come out.

In a careful analysis recognizing the difficulties and avoiding judgmental answers, Raymond Vernon stresses that the economic consequences of the activities of multinational corporations are difficult to assess and that any assessments are directly influenced by assumptions about alternative courses of action.[1] There always remains the nagging question: As compared to what? Moreover, the difficulty of measuring variables like human skills or technology transfers make such assessment more difficult. Given the fuzziness of the facts, Vernon then stresses that the breadth of choices open to the MNC in terms of location of activities gives governments a feeling of inferiority and dependence, which is one of the exacerbating elements of the relationship. Vernon also sees other causes for tension. Prominent among them are the threat to local elites and the challenge to local ideologies and policies for economic development presented by economic and cultural characteristics imported from more developed countries to less developed countries. Companies from more developed countries also sometimes present the possibility of imposition of foreign cultural attitudes.

Vernon later developed a more theoretical argument in which he refutes the applicability of the assumptions of classical economic theory to the MNCs.[2] He argues convincingly that oligopolistic competition, worldwide behavioral characteristics, and the easy transferability of production factors (available at costs different from the costs incurred by local companies) result in locational distortions for production and development activities. In summary, Vernon establishes that the activities of MNCs do have consequences that matter to national governments.

Governments, in the self-interest of their countries, can thus be expected to take action to blunt the negative consequences of MNC activities and to foster positive consequences. In some cases, particularly for well-defined projects of limited scope in developing countries, it is possible to carry out a social cost-and-benefit analysis of the MNC project activities in the country.[3] In developed countries analyses are often much more murky because of the numerous second-order consequences and of the difficulties of evaluating alternatives in a complex and highly interdependent economy. Michael Hodges,[4] for instance, in a pioneering study of the relationships between the British government and foreign companies, states that government intervention is likely to increase with overall government control of the economy, with the level and distribution of foreign investments, and when foreign subsidiaries either lack autonomy or behave in a way adversely affecting national economic goals. He stresses, however, that civil servants think that the degree of autonomy of a subsidiary is not a factor in determining the willingness of a company to cooperate with governments. In fact, the information

available to government officials is not sufficient to scrutinize the activities of MNCs closely enough to provide for selective control and influence. Finally, Hodges concludes that, with the exception of the
automobile and computer industries, foreign investments are a non-
issue for the British government. He suggests several reasons for
such lack of concern, in particular, an overall political consensus
that allows the problem of foreign presence in key industries to be
handled within an administrative context. In this context the government administrative response is conditioned by the fragmentation of
responsibilities among many agencies. Hodges also underlines that
in the two industries that were the objects of much government attention, there were British companies that offered some national potential, but were also threatened by stronger international competitors.
Analytical difficulties, administrative fragmentation, and lack of political salience can thus make foreign investments a non-issue in developed countries.

Yet their governments are far from passive. A major conclusion of a collective study of several industries and countries in Western Europe is that, largely under the influence of the French economic
control and planning system, most countries, to some extent, see control of business as an instrument for the achievement of national
goals. [5] As formal protectionism disappears, the defense of a "national champion" ("an enterprise responsive to its national government's needs and entitled to its national government's support") is developed as a means to maintain control. [6] The development of free
trade within the European Economic Community (EEC) and the European Free Trade Association (EFTA) has provided the MNCs with a
stronger bargaining position, in terms of location of their investments,
than they had previously. The combination of national champions and
lack of clear barriers to trade leads to all sorts of less visible re-
strictions and preferences.

Though the intricacies of government interventions and the idiosyncracies of each situation defy clear-cut analysis, it is possible to
cast government intervention into a comparative framework provided
one recognizes that unaccountable incidents such as that described between Heinz and the French government remain common.

This chapter presents a simple classification framework to review government interventions. First, the origins and goals of interventions and their importance to multinational managers are reviewed;
second, means of intervention are analyzed; and, third, simple scenarios of cooperation and confrontation between governments and
MNCs are outlined.

ORIGINS AND OBJECTIVES OF GOVERNMENT
INTERVENTIONS: THE DESIRE FOR POWER

A broad view of the origins of government intervention into
multinational management must start with the basic societal functions
—protection and maintenance of individual rights through judicial procedures, provision of public services, external protection, internal
economic integration and management—whose performance is usually
entrusted to the governmental administration. Indeed, political leaders—especially in Western Europe, where an interventionist national
state apparatus has become a matter of course—are judged on how
well the state performs these functions. Robbin Murray argues that
it is how these functions are performed, and by whom, that decides
the relationships between states and MNCs.[7] He stresses that the
functions are inherent in all stages of capitalist development. However, states take keener interest in performing these functions well
when international rivalry becomes more acute, when the economic
development of a territory makes these functions more complex, .
when ideologies and labor movements favor strong social measures,
or when capital is scarce and dispersed. Actions by private agents
become of concern to the government when they affect the state's ability to perform these functions, either by directly affecting the means
of carrying out the tasks that collective functions require or by affecting the tasks performed.

Many of these state functions are of little relevance or interest
to the managers of multinational corporations. Yet, the provision of
public services and economic integration and management by the state
can have direct consequences for multinationals. Governments tend
to see three types of activities as falling largely into their preroga-
tives:

1. Control and regulation of monopolies, whether natural (telecommunications) or de facto (tobaccos in France and liquors in Canada, for instance). This becomes particularly important when monopolies are performing basic functions such as transportation, energy supply, or telecommunications.

2. Protection of key problem industries whose disappearance,
recession, or domination by foreign interests might hamper the performance of some state function. Key problem industries are often
protected either because of their growing strategic value or because
their senescence threatens employment. In the first category we find
the new activities, such as integrated circuit industry; in the other,
such industries as textile manufacturing in Europe or pulp and paper
in Canada, which are usually the only large employers in isolated,
semi-depressed areas such as the Vosges in France or the North Shore
of the St. Lawrence River in Quebec.

3. The turnaround and redeployment of an industry to achieve better international competitiveness (improving the balance of payments) and faster growth. This can involve the shift to higher value-added products. For instance, the Japanese government is intervening to promote a shift in the electronics industry from consumer goods to professional equipment and data processing systems.

To analyze which industrial policy would be appropriate for which sector under what sort of circumstances is well outside the scope of this book, and is not attempted here.[8] However, government policies are likely to be substantially different according to the type of goals outlined above: control and regulation of a national monopoly, protection of a key national industry, and turnaround of an industry to improve its international competitiveness.[9] Thus, the first section of this chapter reviews the potential of multinationals faced by government interventions according to these three different goals.

State Control of Monopolies

Most countries resort to state-owned enterprises to run monopolies. Monopolies are not necessarily national, but individual customers have no direct choice between suppliers of telephone service or electrical energy supply, and blame the state if services fall short of expectations. Such state-controlled monopolies leave little room for MNCs except as purveyors of technology, equipment, and engineering competence. For instance, by the 1970s the few remaining private telecommunication networks seemed anachronistic; most had been nationalized in the late 1800s in Europe and in the 1930s or 1950s elsewhere.

Suppliers of equipment to state monopolies are usually subject to tight procedures for public purchasing that are faithfully adhered to by the customers. Usually governments direct utilities in their choice of suppliers and thus determine market structure for the equipment industries. Access to market is effectively controlled by the government even in countries belonging to the EEC or other free-trade areas.

MNCs usually participate in the industry as suppliers, particularly when technology or scale make complete reliance on national suppliers difficult. However, local manufacture is usually required and the government strives for more extensive control over the activities of subsidiaries.

Protection of Key Problem Industries

The evolution of relative factor costs over time between areas of the world, and the changes in barriers to entry (reflected in the product life-cycle models) imply that a country would theoretically have to adjust its portfolio of industries to its relative endowment in production factors over time. [10] Consequently, development of new industries has to be promoted and the shedding of older ones organized. [11]

Particular industries become "problem industries" when, during phases of rapid change, the social perception of the industry is no longer adjusted to its reality. It may well be that the United Kingdom should not produce motorcars anymore and that the erosion of the British car industry's competitive position has been accelerated by the shortsightedness of owners and workers in milking the industry. [12] Still, the complete abandonment of motorcar production is not considered seriously, witness the many rescue plans of British Leyland and the huge amounts invested by the government in their implementation. [13]

More generally, industries that are no longer competitive on economic grounds may be protected for a variety of reasons if, for instance: (1) they are major employers (the automobile industry), (2) they are basic industries (steel or aluminum), or (3) they are important for national security (shipbuilding).

Except for major employers, few foreign companies are likely to be active in older industries. Large heavy industries have been of sufficient interest for so long that the maintenance of foreign positions is unlikely. Small-scale, mature industries that have been characterized by vigorous local competition will probably be unattractive to MNCs. The automobile industry is a case where scale and perceived product differentiation (through separate dealerships) have been high enough barriers of entry to enable MNCs to protect their positions through maturity.

The major preoccupation of government is probably to preserve jobs (automobile industry) or productive capacity (steel industry). This usually involves rationalization plans. Rationalization can take place within the country (cooperation and consolidation between suppliers) or within the MNC (production specialization, common product range between national subsidiaries, and so on).

MNCs are usually in a position to bargain for international rationalization in their operations rather than forced cooperation with other national suppliers, provided employment is the key criterion for success. Employment is also a bargaining chip in negotiations with governments to obtain a bail-out if integration within the MNC is not favored.

Often alliances can develop between any two groups in the triad of MNC management/government officials/workers' union. In such situations the main concern of most government officials is not with who owns the company, or with how independently it operates, but with whether it can go on to provide the same level of employment.

Industry Turnaround

Turnaround situations involve a more complex set of relationships than protection of problem industries for control of monopolies. The objectives of the state may be either to maintain (or regain) international competitiveness (exports promotions) or simply to achieve some local production (imports substitution). The ensuing policies are likely to be different. Moreover, policies in worldwide oligopolistic industries are different from those in industries where competition is more dispersed. Barriers of entry into oligopolies make it more difficult for a government to attempt independent establishment of a national competitor.

A basic choice for government policies is whether to pitch national companies against MNCs and help them succeed on their own, or to cooperate with MNCs and influence them so that the country obtains a disproportionate part of the benefits accruing from MNC activities.

In many cases, calling in an international company provides the most suitable alternative for a turnaround operation, for example, Compagnie Internationale of d'Informatique Honeywell Bull (CII-HB), Georg Kent-Brown Boveri, Poclain-Case Tenneco.[14] In these operations conditions are put forward by both sides and most often lead to a quasi-contractual agreement between the MNC and the government spelling out what shall be done by each to assist in the recovery of the national company (now subsidiary).

It can be hypothesized that the higher the entry barriers, the higher the incentives to cooperate with MNCs. When research and development, scale and experience effects, product differentiation, and availability of raw materials constrain the entry, bargaining with MNCs takes place—provided the government has something to offer (such as market access or R&D grants).

Imports substitution is relatively simpler to achieve, at least when protection is resorted to. For certain differentiated products (culturally bound items, heavy materials, "branded" products) a regional or national position may be established.

Commitments to free-trade areas also weaken the position of governments. So within the categories of turnaround industries the relevant variables become: (1) government objectives—imports substitution and exports development—and (2) barriers to entry and government control. Each of these needs to be qualified. Imports sub-

FIGURE 2.1

Possible Government Policies for Industry Turnaround

Government
Ambitions

Relative Barriers to Entry

	Low	High
	Protection of local industry	
	Increase capability of local firms	Controlled access to market
Imports Substitution	Bargain for local integration and market access	Bargain on structure of MNC operations
	Grants to local firms	Balanced trade
	Product specification and differentiation	Assistance of an MNC to bail out local company
	Incentives for MNC subsidiary to export	Restructuring of industry
	Restructuring of national industry	State-to-state agreement
	Trade policy	Financing
Exports Development	Incentives for domestic companies	Technological development
		Trading agreements on raw materials and end products
		Agreement with MNC to help restructure the industry

Source: Compiled by the author.

stitution and export development are not entirely distinct and there may be a shift over time.

Barriers to entry do not exist in a vacuum. First, they are relative to the national capabilities as seen from a government standpoint. Second, they are a catch-all category that subsumes rather different phenomena; they only exist in relationship to the competencies and resources of existing competitors in an industry and can be circumvented by entry in certain segments only. Finally, they evolve over time as factor costs and availability, as well as the technology and economies of each industry evolve.

Government control over markets may be multifarious. It can directly guide the choice of customers (state-owned enterprises) and limit the choice by price (tariffs), availability (certification), or quantity (quotas). Emergency controls may be imposed when imports swamp national markets, thus resulting in temporary government control.

In broad terms Figure 2.1 presents the possible government policies to make turnaround possible.

Implications

The differences among possible government policies for the supply of national monopolies, protection of key problem industries, and turnaround of industries to improve their competitiveness are sufficient to justify careful examination by MNC managers. MNCs can contribute differently and find themselves in different bargaining postures according to the aims of the government they interact with.

In supplying national monopolies, the MNC usually has little power because the state monopoly usually has to secure government approval to buy equipment from a nonnational supplier. As for "problem industries," it seems that it is only when scale barriers are very high that (1) the MNC is likely to be active and (2) it can propose MNC system rationalization of production as a viable alternative to domestic merger of a troubled company (Case-Tenneco rescuing Poclain, for example) or of a nonintegrated subsidiary. Chrysler U.K. provided an example of the latter situation when it took severe losses and a threat of bankruptcy of Chrysler's British subsidiary to induce the trade unions and the British government to accept an integration of Chrysler's activities in Europe. [15] For turnaround industries the situation is more complex, the key issue being whether to enter a government-sponsored cooperation agreement with a local company.

In any case, and beyond the origin and objectives of a specific intervention, MNC activities raise a general concern that the response of their subsidiaries to almost any policy will be very different from

the response of a national company and thus compromise the effectiveness of the policy. This point is documented by Richard Caves,
who argues that MNCs have at least three distinct economic advantages
over local companies: (1) scale economies derived from concentrating
the operations most affected in one location; (2) lower absolute-cost
entry barriers, thanks to scarce specialized resources and financial
concentration of resources available only to MNCs; and (3) easier
product differentiation. [16] Caves goes on to contend that one cannot
assume a subsidiary will behave in the same way as a local firm, because any local change may result in changes in the overall MNC re-
source-allocation pattern. He also stresses the competitive advantage
gained by specialized production and by a system in which each national company only manufactures a narrow product range. Moreover,
technological advantages provide quasi-rents from foreign markets
and reinforce the advantages of the firm. In what he calls a "limiting
case," Caves defines multinational differences in conduct in the following way:

> Multinational status makes no difference to the conduct
> patterns preferred or chosen by firms in a national
> market. This pattern implies that the member units of
> a multinational firm serve as independent profit centers
> with full autonomy over national price and product de-
> cisions. It suggests that the MNC could affect conduct
> in a given national market because it differs from a na-
> tional firm, but that cross national links in market con-
> duct would not be involved. [17]

The implications for the management of key economic sectors
are important. Since government officials consider the effectiveness
of their economic and industrial policies important, they will attempt
to narrowly control specific industries. This becomes all the more
important as interdependence between national markets and freer
trade and capital flows make traditional macroeconomic demand management policies increasingly inefficient. Supply policies thus take a
new preeminence and the responsiveness of specific individual firms
becomes all the more important. As the interdependencies within the
MNCs make control of local subsidiaries more difficult (because their
behavior cannot be ascertained from the knowledge available to any
individual government), governments will oppose such interdependencies. In other words, governmental demand for autonomous "national
decision centers" in MNCs is no vain rhetoric, but a very real key-
stone for local control.
    The same control argument can be stated in behavioral terms.
The day-to-day management of the societal functions outlined above is

usually entrusted to civil servants and administrators. For reasons that have been explained in many studies of bureaucracies, such administrations tend to behave incrementally and find radical changes difficult to even consider. The separation between the permanent administration and temporary political leaders makes sweeping decisions still more difficult. Problems of strategic decision making as well as career and reward patterns make these government officials extremely risk-averse. All uncertainties are carefully avoided. Consequently, administrative control is highly favored over efficiency. The costs, in personal terms, that are associated with a major crisis in some activity are considerably higher than those that accrue from day-to-day operating inefficiencies. In particular, the relationship with MNCs must not lend itself to widespread public criticism and political ripple effects.

Administrative control of the activities of foreign subsidiaries thus directly serves the personal advantage of civil servants. Forms of administrative control range over a wide variety of characteristics, from a strong preference for dealing with locally trained and schooled executives (from a few universities in Japan and the United Kingdom, "Polytechnique" or "Centrale" in France, for instance) to extensive product regulations and inspections by government experts at each stage of production.

As was noted by John Zysman in a study of the French electronics industry, the fluid nature of many technologies most critical to state-owned enterprises and government agencies makes control more difficult and introduces a considerable degree of uncertainty, which the bureaucracy is ill-equipped to handle. Zysman also points out that the organization of the companies selling to the government agencies tends to match that of the agencies:

> The centralized and functional structure of the state's procurement funding procedures provided strong incentive for the firms not only to retain, but perhaps even to create functional and centralized organizations. . . . In so far as the choices must be made as part of a cohesive political strategy, and not on technical and market criteria the general management is almost certainly in the best position to make these choices. [18]

Further difficulty is due to the lack of a clear frame of reference in the public administration. Much broader preoccupations pervade the policy of government agencies. Pure political factors play an important role both internally and externally. Most analysts of international relations interpret the relationships between nation-states in terms of power. The technologies developed and used by

MNCs, as well as their own economic power, directly impact upon the relative power of nation-states. Stanley Hoffmann makes the point beautifully:

> In an age dominated by the expansion of science and technology . . . the competition between states takes place on several chessboards in addition to the traditional military and diplomatic ones: for instance, the chessboard of world trade, of world finance, of aid and technical assistance, of space research and exploration, of military technology, and the chessboard of what has been called "informal penetration."[19]

Control of foreign companies in many key industrial sectors is thus part of an overall development policy that often resembles war through other means. Some of the key actors do see their actions in such a light. Mr. Esambert, a chief economic advisor to President Pompidou, once explained:

> In the nineteenth century it was only a competition between corporations, either from the same country, or from different countries. Today the scale has changed: whole nations wage economic war between borders, the increasing pace of exchange rate fluctuations testifies to this competition. And each individual company today participates in that great international war; every single well-managed company increases the standing of its country, and the state must unite the energy of all economic actors by creating the framework for their action.[20]

Though few governments are as straightforward as the Gaullists were about the incorporation of industrial policies into foreign relations and the furtherance of the nation's interests or power, all show willingness to resort to extreme protective measures whenever needed, whether it be for jet engines, computers, milk, or wine. So not under the guise of a military-industrial complex once heralded by John Kenneth Galbraith, but under the cover of national economic management, broad and ill-defined arguments often magnify and blur government interests in MNC activities.

In any case, it is important for MNC managers dealing with host governments to understand the positions of the governments. In some simple cases many mistakes or untenable bargaining positions may be avoided by an analysis of the social costs and benefits of a decision for the host country.[21] In more complex cases it is important to understand both the logic pursued by the government and the context of government concern and intervention. The logic can be analyzed in terms of monopoly control and regulation, protection, or turnaround, as discussed above; but often the contextual elements are more critical in bringing intervention than is the logic itself. How fragmented is the state administration, how different are the goals of various agencies, how sensitive are civil servants to risks and uncertainties, how influential are informal "old boys" networks, what is the quality of the understanding of the economics of the industry by civil servants? All of these are key questions for MNC managers in dealing with government power.

GOVERNMENT INTERVENTION:
THE MEANS TO EXERCISE POWER

A government's means to influence MNC behavior are extensive. They range from broad guidelines for foreign investment screening to detailed contracts drawn between host governments and MNCs. Few countries exercise little control, and extensive controls are often found.[22]

From the point of view of managers it is useful to come back to the distinction made in Chapter 1 between operating patterns and managerial tools. A government can try to regulate or circumscribe the outputs of the activities of an MNC, that is, to exercise power on the operating patterns. Local content regulations or export incentives, for instance, fall into that category: they influence the result of MNC activities, not the way in which these activities are performed. Conversely, a government can try to intervene in the managerial tools of an MNC in order to influence its management processes, that is, to act on the way decisions are reached within the company as opposed to circumscribing and specifying the possible scope of the outputs of decision processes.

Another distinguishable difference is that between explicit selective bargaining and overall regulation for incentive and disincentive. For instance, less-than-complete ownership can be achieved by direct negotiations on a joint venture or by a regulation forbidding fully-owned subsidiaries. Developed countries, with abundant cross-investments between them and multiple joint venture partners, usually take the first route, whereas developing ones go to regulations and restrictive laws.

Finally, it is important to distinguish between means and content of influence: governments can use leverage points to bring about specific results in terms of content. For instance, joint ventures are a means to obtain a content (such as nationals in powerful positions on the subsidiary board, transfer of technology or management

FIGURE 2.2

Array of Means of Government Influence on MNCs

Means	Negotiations	Influence	
Operating Patterns	Planning and control agreements Direct instructions "Directives"	Laws Licensing Taxation Regulation Trade barriers Foreign investment screening	Means
Management Tools	Joint ventures Management agreements "Decision centers"	Informal socialization Incentives to have local nationals in management	
	Explicit bargaining	Incentives/disincentives	

Contents	Negotiations	Influence	
Operating Patterns	Location-invest Employment Trade-and-payments balance Market shares Technology—R&D content Local R&D	Invest incentive Regional subsidies Tax exemption Training assistance Import duties Local content laws Hints on screening process Funding sources	Content
Management Tools	Nationals on board Local ownership Local planning Local veto on resource allocation	Specs, standards Socialization Purchasing process Identity development Loyalties People's transfers	Transfers

Source: Compiled by the author.

talent to local firms, government veto on key strategic decisions). Thus, a joint venture agreement can only be understood in terms of the content it provides to the host country or (and) withdraws from the MNC. Similarly, a particular regional development scheme can be implemented by direct bargaining with MNCs or by the establishment of regional incentives in the form of tax exemptions, subsidies, or lower freight rates, applicable to all companies.

Again, as in the case of specific industrial policies, a detailed analysis of the various means of intervention would not lead very far and is easily available elsewhere in particular cases. There are too many different schemes, used by various governments, for various industries, at various times for a generalization to be practical. Yet, it is important in any particular MNC strategic decision-making process to understand the specifics of government power in the particular case. Figure 2.2 thus is more a checklist of possible means of control and the content that can be used to bring about than any formal conceptual scheme.

COOPERATION-CONFRONTATION SCENARIOS

The relationships between MNCs and host countries depend not only on the objectives pursued by governments, but also on their industrial policies and on the means they have available to entice or compel MNCs to abide by these policies. Another key element is the strategy pursued by the multinational enterprise.

As was described briefly in Chapter 1, there are two simple approaches to MNC management: a worldwide product orientation leading to the development of an integrated network of closely managed subsidiaries; and an area (or national) orientation leaving each subsidiary largely autonomous, loosely controlled, and able to be more responsive to its host government.

The complex approaches to MNC management are based on diversification and technology.[23] Faced with intense government attention and frequent intervention in some of their businesses, companies can decide to move their activities to less sensitive countries or to concentrate their resources in industries attracting less government interest.

Most companies active in mass-produced, mass-merchandised, nonculturally-bound items, such as pens or razor blades, are careful to avoid getting into products and businesses that attract exceedingly intense government interventions. In some companies this is an explicit policy. Gillette, for example, had little difficulty buying lighter manufacturers in Europe, but swiftly backed off when tension developed around potential French perfume acquisitions.[24] Similarly, Bic Pen had little difficulty in extending its position in North America.

Moves toward less sensitive industries and toward countries less eager to interfere are complementary: presence in government-influenced industries makes moving to other countries more difficult. For instance, when Philips decided to move the production of consumer goods to low-wage areas in Asia, it ran into trouble from the Belgian administration, which announced that it would no longer buy computers from Philips if the company reduced its payroll in Belgium. Allegedly, the consideration of such difficulties has contributed to Philips's decision to terminate the manufacture of large computers.

As employment becomes a major concern for most countries and as workers gain an increasingly strong say in management, moves toward lower-wage areas where labor laws are more lax, may be stalled. Employment protection has become so critical that it is almost a given: managers of foreign companies (and most domestic ones as well) must live with a fixed work force. Collective layoffs trigger public anger and force government officials to react strongly.

Labor stability works both ways, however. A company can bargain with a government by threatening to withdraw completely, as Chrysler very successfully did in the United Kingdom in 1975. A subsidiary manager made a typical comment:

> The government will never impose too harsh terms
> against us, as we have a good 3,000 workers; closing
> down is impossible. The government would have to
> bail us out! So it is simpler to let us run our business
> in a profitable way than to put everybody into trouble.

In summary, selectively avoiding government interventions has become increasingly difficult, and reorienting the product market portfolio internationally can only be a slow undertaking. Reducing governments' interest in the company's activities is thus a difficult and constraining policy, which most diversified MNCs cannot pursue exclusively. Our interest is with companies where management has decided to live with government interest and intervention. Thus, companies moving to less sensitive industries or more accommodating countries are outside the scope of this book and they will not be studied in detail.

Technology provides another opportunity: to offer such innovative, unique, and desirable products as to be able to sell them on one's own terms. To most MNC managers, this appears the best solution to the problem: restore a monopoly by turning out something so desirable that every country will want it. The ability to remain "at least one step ahead" technologically is a trump card in bargaining with most host governments.

In fact, the technology of many government-scrutinized industries calls for such large resources and such deep and varied competencies that individual national companies can no longer afford a competitive technology either privately or with government funding. International government-sponsored joint ventures have been found subject to many intrinsic difficulties of coordination and management. [25] In the uncertain environment of high technology the ability of the MNCs to mobilize resources, pool knowledge, and carry out complex, heterogeneous sets of tasks is at its best. Yet, since their current technology is likely to provide the key to tomorrow's most important industrial sectors, government attention is highest.

In all likelihood, governments will increasingly resent international companies' dominating technology and will attempt to control them. Pressures to make MNCs cooperate with government-sponsored international projects is bound to increase. What forms such cooperation might take is not yet clear.

In the meantime, maintaining a technical superiority over both local companies and other MNCs is seen by many managers as crucial for MNCs active in manufacturing industries. Moreover, since the demand for high technology products is not very price elastic, some of the difficulties created by the combination of labor unrest and higher wage rates in Western Europe are avoided.

Of course, these four classes of strategy (cooperation and flexibility, development of a worldwide integrated network, movement toward less sensitive industries and more accommodating countries, and being "one step ahead" in technology) are not necessarily exhaustive, but they represent four basic types of strategy that can be followed by MNCs.

Which of these classes of strategies to choose for which purpose depends on a multiplicity of factors. Most of them are difficult to grasp in abstract, let alone to understand their interplay; it is possible, however, to explore how they affect cooperation or confrontation with governments pursuing their own objectives.

Monopolies Controlled by the State

Only an MNC strategy of adaptation and cooperation seems to be feasible in the case of a state-controlled monopoly, as there are strong pressures for the monopoly to internalize transactions with its suppliers. [26] Pressures are particularly important when equipment purchases are very lumpy and far between, a tendency prevalent in both telecommunication equipment and electrical power systems as technological evolution brings about larger unit sizes, as will become apparent in Chapter 3. Monopoly power on suppliers is usually sufficient to prevent them from rationalizing their activities on a multinational basis or to retain proprietary control of high technology products or processes. As we shall see, there still are considerable variations in government power and multinational strategic, structural, and managerial responses.

The higher the technology provided by the MNC, the more it can contribute to the country and be selected as a supplier by the monopoly. So it seems that the best possible agreement here is with companies pursuing a technological competitive advantage.

Protection of Key Industries

For mature, possibly senescent industries, the key question becomes whether to allow integration into an MNC in order to maintain the existence of a national employer or to consolidate the national industry through mergers. The second approach has generally been favored, but not in a systematic way. Companies can also play the support of unions to their own advantage. A fascinating example is provided by the acquisition of Kent by Brown Boveri in the United Kingdom. Kent was the result of a merger between several British instrument manufacturers; one of them was government owned and made classified military devices. Consequently, the British government owned about 20 percent of Kent when BBC let its interest in acquiring Kent be known. At first, a stiff refusal was issued and the British minister of industry called in General Electric & Company (GEC) to take over the ailing Kent. Workers feared the integration of Kent into GEC would reduce employment, and a poll was suggested. Except for the workers of the military division, an overwhelming majority of the workers voted to request that BBC take a share in the equity of Kent. The management of BBC had, in the meantime, detailed its expansion plan to union representatives and let it be known that Kent would provide the hub of the new international group.

The Labour minister of industry (Tony Wedgwood Benn) had to accept the choice of the union and spin off the military division, whose products were too salient for foreign control. More and more decisions to protect local industry or let MNCs have control hinge on employment considerations and on the opinion of the workers, even in countries such as the United Kingdom and France where codetermination does not legally exist.

For newer industries, MNCs may be called in in order to transfer technology and quicken the start-up process. Whether a company will want to cooperate depends primarily on its strategic orientation. For instance, in the semiconductor industry, Texas Instruments (a company centrally and tightly managed from Dallas) has always rejected any scheme to cooperate with local companies abroad or to enter joint ventures. It has even managed to negotiate, after a difficult haggle, a fully owned subsidiary in Japan. Conversely, Fairchild, which pursued a more flexible strategy aimed at national markets, joined forces with Società Generale Semiconduttori (SGS) in Italy to set up an Italian semiconductor industry.

Companies that offer very desirable high-technology products seldom expect to cooperate in the setting-up and protection of nascent high-technology industries that might later compete against them. The major interest they can see in such a deal is to penetrate foreign markets very quickly, particularly when they have little or no international experience. A high-technology company aspiring to become multinational could use superior products and technologies as a locomotive and, in a first stage at least, join forces with foreign companies. This can be particularly true when the technical lead can quickly be diminished by followers better established abroad. This was largely Fairchild's predicament when it cooperated with SGS to penetrate European markets.

Turnaround Industry or Company

The development of a "national champion" is a key element in a government turnaround policy, the expectation being that one day the national company will be able to stand on its own among the MNCs. The practicality of nurturing a national champion or turning around an ailing company in an internationally competitive industry has been criticized by many experts of salient industries. The forced mergers and consolidations necessary to foster a national champion require industrial realignments of such magnitude that social turmoil is almost inevitable. For instance, industrial rationalization was not implemented either in the creation of British Leyland in the United Kingdom or of Aérospatiale in France; both companies were lame ducks draining the budgets of their countries. While tendering selective help to a few companies at critical points is seldom criticized, the systematic search for a national champion in each and every industry in the wake of supranational economic integration is considered pointless by many experts.

Whether or not a turnaround is successful, it results at best in tense and shaky relationships with MNCs. Unless these companies are willing to play the government game and enter into all sorts of technical assistance, licensing, or management contracts, their position in the country is threatened in the long run.

The higher the barriers to entry, the more desirable the MNC cooperation becomes and the less threatened it is in the long run. So in some cases the national aspiration for import substitution or even export development is probably better than trying to build up a potential champion.

FIGURE 2.3

Cooperation and Conflicts between Host Governments and MNCs

<u>Government Policies</u>

Company Strategy	Control of national monopoly	Protection of national industry		Turnaround
		Nascent	Senescent	
1. Development of an integrated network	Conflict	Conflict	Cooperation / Conflict	Cooperation / Conflict
2. Good relations and responsiveness	Cooperation if can bring proprietary knowledge	Possible cooperation	Conflict	Likely conflict
3. High-technology unique products	Cooperation if some flexibility	Possible if not multinational yet	Irrelevant	Conflicts

<u>Source</u>: Compiled by the author.

The discussion above is summarized in Figure 2.3. Again, this table should not be interpreted as an empirical generalization but more as a way to think about individual situations.

NOTES

1. Raymond Vernon, Sovereignty at Bay: The Multinational Spread of U.S. Enterprises (New York: Basic Books, 1971).

2. Raymond Vernon, "The Location of Economic Activity," in Economic Analysis and the Multinational Corporation, ed. John H. Dunning (London: Allen and Unwin, 1974).

3. Louis T. Wells, Jr. and David N. Smith, Negotiating Third-World Mineral Agreements (Cambridge, Mass.: Ballinger, 1975).

4. Michael Hodges, Multinational Corporations and National Government (Lexington, Mass.: Lexington Books, 1973).

5. Raymond Vernon, ed., Big Business and the State: Changing Relations in Western Europe (Cambridge, Mass.: Harvard University Press, 1974).

6. Ibid., p. 11.

7. Robbin Murray, "The Internationalization of Capital and the Nation State," in The Multinational Enterprise, ed. John H. Dunning (London: Allen and Unwin, 1971).

8. Alain Cotta, "Reflexion sur la politique industrielle de la France," Le Redéploiement industriel (Paris: Documentation Francaise, 1977).

9. Christian Stoffaes, La Grande Menace Industrielle (Paris: Calmann-Levy, 1978).

10. Louis T. Wells, Jr., ed., The Product Life Cycle and International Trade (Boston: Harvard Business School Division of Research, 1972); Christian Stoffaes, "Une analyse 'multicriteres' des priorités sectorielles de redéploiement industriel," Le Redéploiement industriel.

11. The Boston Consulting Group, "The Dynamics of International Competition" (Boston: The Boston Consulting Group, 1970).

12. The Central Policy Review Staff, The Future of the British Car Industry (London: Her Majesty's Stationery Office, 1975).

13. Sir Don Ryder, British Leyland: The Next Decade (London: Her Majesty's Stationery Office, 1975).

14. Jacques Jublin and Jean Michel Quatrepoint, French Ordinateurs (Paris: Editions Alain Moreau, 1976); "George Kent/Brown Boveri—Anatomy of a Marriage" (A), (B), & (C). Harvard Business School Cases ICCM nos. 9-277-017-9-277-019 (Cambridge, Mass.: President and Fellows of Harvard College, 1976); "Poclain: Borrowing Knowhow from Its JI Case Partner," Business Week, July 24, 1978: 170, 173.

15. Stephen Young and Neil Hood, Chrysler U.K.: A Corporation in Transition (New York: Praeger, 1977).

16. Richard E. Caves, "Industrial Organization," in Economic Analysis.

17. Ibid., p. 131.

18. John Zysman, Political Strategies for Industrial Order (Berkeley: University of California Press, 1976); idem, "French Industry between the Markets and the State" (Ph.D. diss., Massachusetts Institute of Technology, 1973).

19. Stanley Hoffmann, "International Organization and the International System," International Organization 24 no. 3 (Summer 1970): 401.

20. Interview to Les Informations (text communicated privately).

21. Louis T. Wells, Jr., "Negotiating with Third World Governments," Harvard Business Review, January-February 1977: 72-80.

22. Richard D. Robinson, National Control of Foreign Business Entry: A Survey of Fifteen Countries (New York: Praeger, 1976).

23. C. K. Prahalad and Y. L. Doz, "Some Emerging Issues in the Management of Diversified Multinational Companies," (Paper prepared for the International Institute of Management Multinational Management Conference, Berlin, West Germany, November 16-18, 1978).

24. "Gilette," L'Expansion, April 1974, pp. 78-83.

25. See, for instance, Milton S. Hochmuth, Organizing the Transnationals (The Hague: Sijthoff, 1973); and Henry R. Nau, National Politics and International Technology (Baltimore: Johns Hopkins University Press, 1974).

26. Oliver E. Williamson, Markets and Hierarchies: Analysis and Antitrust Implications (New York: The Free Press, 1975).

3

THE POLITICAL IMPERATIVE: STATE-OWNED UTILITIES AS CUSTOMERS OF HEAVY EQUIPMENT

Among various industries whose products are used by government agencies or state-owned customers, electric power systems and telecommunication equipment are of particular interest. They are subject to intense government interventions on various grounds, yet the major competitors are prominent international corporations. The very names of leaders in these two industries, like Brown Boveri or ITT, evoke images of large, sprawling, powerful groups that some see as archetypical international corporations. These two industries are under constant scrutiny by government services because they serve public utilities that affect the everyday lives of millions of citizens and because they require complex technologies fully available only to a handful of international companies. Given this posture, it is not surprising that governments frequently attempt to influence their structure and performance.

This chapter focuses on how the public status of state-owned customers influences their purchasing practices and the management of national subsidiaries within these industries.

TELECOMMUNICATION EQUIPMENT AND POWER SYSTEMS: INTRODUCTION AND OVERVIEW

Both electric power and telecommunication equipment industries are of significant size and rank among the major industrial sectors in most developed countries. Moreover, a faster than average growth rate steadily augments their relative weight in many economies. This important position is further bolstered because their finished products are used for basic public-service networks whose orderly growth is essential for successful economic development. Finally, the energy and communications industries have been thrust into the political limelight following the 1973 oil embargo and energy crisis.

TABLE 3.1

Telephone Market and Growth of Demand in Selected Countries

| | As of January 1, 1975 | | | Market Forecast, Lines to Be Installed During the Year (measured in thousands of lines) | | |
| | Existing number of (in thousands) | | Sets | | | |
	Sets	Lines	per 100 Population	1975	1980	1985
European Countries						
Belgium	2,667	1,724	27.3	112	186	267
Denmark	2,184	1,603	42.5	107	148	205
France	12,405	6,126	23.5	890	1,466	2,415
Germany	18,767	13,118	30.2	1,320	2,120	3,403
Italy	13,695	9,163	24.6	962	1,585	2,615
Netherlands	4,679	3,050	34.4	265	400	600
Spain	7,043	4,035	20.0	390	615	975
Sweden	5,178	3,796	63.3	133	160	190
United Kingdom	20,342	12,244	36.3	650	1,430	2,114
Yugoslavia	1,143	822	5.4	130	270	565
Asian Countries						
Hong Kong	989	817	22.7	130	287	612
India	1,690	1,275	0.3	110	168	256

46

Iran	806	620	2.4	260	850	1,325
Israel	735	549	21.6	45	64	95
Japan	41,904	31,527	37.9	3,150	5,080	8,200
Korea (South)*	1,120	876	n.a.	136	280	575
Taiwan	901	518	5.7	95	215	480
Turkey	900	598	2.3	76	136	250
United States	143,972	79,182	67.7	2,770	3,290	3,900
Canada	12,454	7,489	55.0	500	600	778
Latin American Countries						
Argentina	2,374	1,745	9.4	145	171	240
Brazil	2,651	2,190	2.5	265	1,670	6,370
Colombia	1,186	846	4.7	95	163	279
Mexico	2,546	1,347	4.3	190	362	700
Peru	333	242	2.1	37	75	150
Venezuela	554	430	4.7	75	160	350
African Countries						
Nigeria	111	80	0.1	32	210	925
Australia–New Zealand	6,495	4,325	40.1	210	250	315

*Estimate.

Source: Compiled by the author from The World's Telephones (AT&T, New York); and various other in-dustry sources.

By 1975, worldwide sales of telecommunications equipment were estimated at close to $20 billion. In that year nearly 15 million telephone lines and more than 22 million telephone sets had been installed around the world. The average cost of a line to the customer was in the vicinity of $1,000, including the public works and construction involved. Demand was growing at an average yearly rate of 10 percent in real terms. Abnormally low telephone densities (lines per 100 individuals) in many countries and the prospects of data communication called for a sustained growth over several decades. Table 3.1 evidences the rapid medium-term growth for telephone equipment markets.

Similarly, the demand for electrical energy seemed insatiable. Sales of heavy electrical equipment (not including boilers and nuclear reactors) were also approaching the $20 billion range and were averaging a 9.1 percent annual growth rate. It was estimated that between 1975 and 1985 an average of 120 new large power plants would be needed every year. Table 3.2 shows demand growth forecasts for electricity in various regions of the world. Like telecommunications, the electrical equipment industry has a very high proportion of value added (about 40 percent). The cost of new power plants and electricity distribution networks was well above $50 billion per year, the bulk of which went for boilers and nuclear reactors.

In both cases the investments for a utility company or a telecommunication network were of such magnitude that outside financing was required. This was most often provided by state-controlled financial institutions whose budgets strongly affected national resource allocation and economic growth. Manufacture of telecommunication gear and production of electrical power plants also required considerable resources on the manufacturers' side. The typical accounting unit was $100 million, both in terms of research and development budgets and plant investments.

Over 750,000 persons in Western Europe were employed by electrical equipment companies. Telecommunication equipment manufacturers also employed several hundred thousand people. Employment figures for North America and the Far East were of comparable magnitude. In summary, both were heavy industries in terms of resources, manpower, and financial needs. The huge, fast-growing market and the heavy nature of these industries compounded to increase the stakes for both suppliers and customers alike.

Technological changes were also playing an important role. In both industries the basic technology had evolved slowly and predictably for decades; but in 1975 many discontinuities were occurring and the implications of innovations were difficult to forecast. Telephone technology, for example, had remained relatively stable since Strowger developed the first automatic exchanges at the turn of the century.

TABLE 3.2

Growth of Electricity Uses (TWh) and Installed Capacity (MWe)
(forecasts)

| | 1975 | | | 1980 | | | 1985 | | | Growth Rates of electricity uses percent per year | |
| | | GWe | | | GWe | | | GWe | | | |
	TWH	Total	Nuclear	TWH	Total	Nuclear	TWH	Total	Nuclear	1975–80	1981–85
EEC (9 countries)	1,200	300	20	1,680	400	62	2,400	500	170	7.0	7.5
Other European countries	400[a]	90[a]	5	604	140[a]	30	860	200[a]	60	8.5	7.5
United States	2,210[a]	520[a]	54	3,185	700	132	4,400	980[a]	280[b]	7.7	6.7
Canada	330[a]	60	3	325	100	7	430	110[a]	15	3.0	3.0
Japan	515[a]	120[a]	9	740	170[a]	32	970	220[a]	60	7.5	5.6
Australia and New Zealand	115[a]	20[a]	0	230[a]	45[a]	1	330[a]	70[a]	2	15.0	7.7
Other countries	210	45[a]	—	327	77	4	450	117	29	8.5	8.5

[a]Forecasts or estimates not based on plans or projected developments.
[b]Assuming no further delays are incurred by the U.S. nuclear power plant construction program.

Sources: Compiled by the author from: Commission of the European Communities, Situation et perspective des industries des gros equipements electromécaniques et nucléaires liés à la production d'energie de la communauté, SEC(75)2770 (Brussels: Commission of the European Communities, 1976); United Nations Statistical Yearbook (New York: United Nations, various years); and United Nations Economic Commission for Europe, Long Term Prospects of the Electric Power Industry in Europe—1970.

But recently there was a series of changes that profoundly affected the nature of the industry. Most prominent among these innovations were stored program control (SPC), that is, computer-directed exchanges; electronic switches replacing rotary, crossbar, or Reed relay switches; digital coding and modulation; time separation; and, further in the future, optical fiber transmissions.

Similarly, power generation and distribution were undergoing drastic changes after years of gradual evolution toward bigger power generators and higher-voltage transmissions. The introduction of nuclear reactors to replace conventional boilers had forced major manufacturers to reorganize their productions and to refurnish or rebuild workshops to handle the heavier equipment required. Whereas a conventional boiler might feed a 600 megawatt (MWe) generator, light-water nuclear reactors have a steam output of 1,300 MWe, demanding a very different type of generator. Changes toward entirely new technologies such as supraconductors and cyogenics, however, possibly would make these new investments obsolete before fully amortized.

Thus, both industries were becoming dependent upon the evolution of extremely advanced technologies of a very critical nature. Telecommunication was expected to become a major user of special-purpose computers and complex microelectronics devices; power equipment was tied to the fortunes of nuclear technology. Problems presented by changes of such magnitude were a serious challenge to management of electric utilities and post, telegraph, and telephone (PTT) services. Electronic switching, for instance, required a very different manpower structure and very different skills—implying certain social consequences if adopted. Utilities planning operations were also disrupted by licensing delays for nuclear reactors caused by site controversies and questions of safety. The United States was even considering a ban on new reactor construction, and European programs were slowed down.

In summary, risks and uncertainties of a technological origin were higher than at any previous time for both industries. Such uncertainties together with the reliance on very critical technologies made the pattern of interaction between administrations and companies less predictable. Moreover, the accelerating demand called for quick decisions and actions; but the uncertainties of the new technologies screamed "slow down." Given the heavy nature of the industries, relatively minor errors in planning or in the choice of equipment might have drastic consequences. As a result, the competitive positions of companies could improve or deteriorate rapidly. Many observers expected a major shake-out in market positions of power equipment and telephone manufacturers.

One key issue for a possible shake-out was that of scale of operations. Traditionally, cozy relationships had developed between customers and suppliers within nationally closed oligopolies. Government control over public customers and their quasi-monopsony positions were the main reasons for such close relationships. National subsidiaries of multinational companies had adjusted to these conditions and found a balance between local responsiveness and multinational integration. But, with much higher unit power, the larger size of nuclear-driven power plants, and the shift to electronic technologies in telecommunications, the balance was questioned. National producers (or for that matter, national subsidiaries of MNCs) could no longer maintain large enough production series to remain competitive. With much higher unit power they had many fewer turbo-generators to build each year. In a rather similar guise, electronic telecommunication switching manufacture required much less manpower than conventional electromechanical equipment and was more sensitive to economies of scale.

Another key issue was that of shifts in market locations. With the slowdown of growth in developed countries and the rapid industrial development of countries in the Middle East, East Asia, and Latin America, most growth for both industries was going to take place in newly developing areas of the world. These technological and market shifts questioned the national orientation of manufacturers and challenged their viability; yet they also created new opportunities and were leading to the development of new strategies.

These issues and the strategic responses developed by multinational companies are reviewed in three chapters. The remainder of this chapter analyzes the behavior of state-owned utilities as customers, the means through which they and their governments influence their suppliers, and the special demands made upon subsidiary managements in these two industries. Chapter 3 focuses on political constraints affecting these industries. Chapter 4 analyzes the products, their technology, the economies of manufacture, and their evolution over time. It also reviews markets and market trends in terms of geographical location and technological changes. Thus, Chapter 4 provides the basis for an understanding of the economic and technological constraints affecting the industries. Finally, Chapter 5 analyzes the development of competitive patterns over time and the strategies followed by individual companies in response to market and technological changes. This analysis allows the definition of classes of strategies and the identification of strategic groups. It also leads to a discussion of the administrative imperatives of companies falling in each of the major strategic groups identified in Chapter 5.

GOVERNMENT CONTROL OF
EQUIPMENT CUSTOMERS

The customers for telecommunication and electrical equipment
are public agencies or state-owned enterprises. They have a broader
set of preoccupations and objectives in dealing with suppliers than
might private corporations or individuals. Most often, the means
available to these customers to control their suppliers are extensive
enough to entice, or to compel, the suppliers to abide by the policies
and decisions of the agency or the company. Over time there develops a phenomenon of osmosis through which the suppliers influence
the customers and the customers become part of the management of
the supplier. The following sections describe the interactions between suppliers and customers—interactions to which the customers,
at least, give a higher priority than the pressures of the economic
imperative.

Public Ownership and Funding of Customers

Telecommunication equipment is sold primarily to PTT administrations. All main exchange equipment goes to PTTs, which have
a monopoly on public telephone services. Long-distance transmission
equipment has a more diverse range of customers but the PTTs still
buy most of the production. Other customers are government agencies such as public television networks, the military, railroads, and
departments of the interior. Only 5 to 20 percent of transmission
sales are made to private customers, usually large oil companies,
banks with their own data transmission systems, and private television
networks. Private automatic branch exchanges (known as PABXs) and
station equipment ultimately go to private users, but are often leased
or rented from the PTTs, which buy the equipment from the manufacturers. Even when direct sales to private users are allowed, the
equipment must always be approved and certified by the PTTs before
it can be linked to the public network.
The administrative arrangements under which the PTTs operate
vary from one country to another. Colombia, France, Great Britain,
and Italy provide good examples of such variety.
Colombia is divided into fairly autonomous provinces, each of
which runs a separate local telephone network. Expansion and purchasing decisions are made locally and each provincial authority may
decide upon different equipments and suppliers. In addition, an inter-
regional long-distance network exists.
In France the telecommunication operations are a ministerial
service belonging to the same organization as the post office. They

are a division of the Ministry of Post and Telecommunication. Historically this allowed telecommunications revenues to be transferred
to offset mail deficits. The result was a general neglect of the telephone, since budgeting was done in a central administrative fashion
with no separate accounting for telecommunications. All purchasing
was decided according to the procedures defined by law for government purchasing. By the early 1970s, in order to accelerate network
expansion the government had created leasing companies whose goal
was to use private funds to buy equipment from suppliers and lease it
to the PTT, thus decreasing the short-term public investment needs.
These companies were largely "shadow" organizations whose only purpose was purely to channel private savings to the telecommunication
network.

Great Britain, plagued by the same financial problems as France,
had decided to spin off the post office from general administrative services and set it up as a separate, financially autonomous, public corporation. Funding remained governmental, but the new management
of the British post office reported to a separate board of directors
functioning in a corporate fashion. The telecommunication network
was managed as a division of this new corporation.

Italy had a more complex set-up. At the end of World War II
both the local operating companies and the former plants of the Siemens company were nationalized and entrusted to the Instituto per la
Ricostruzione Industriale (IRI), which in turn created a new specialized
financial holding company, STET, with the status of a private stock
company. A research institute was also created.[1] The financial
structure of the overall operation is depicted in Figure 3.1.

FIGURE 3.1

Financial Structure of the Italian Telecommunication Networks

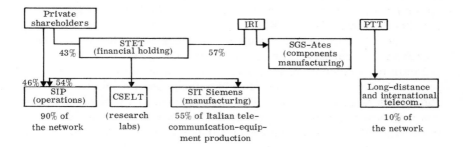

Source: Compiled by the author based on research interviews.

SIP (see Figure 3.1) operates all local telecommunication networks and purchases its equipment either from SIT (ex-Siemens), also owned by STET, or from Italian subsidiaries of international manufacturers (mainly GTE and LM Ericsson). IRI also owns an electronic components manufacturer (SGS-Ates) that supplies components to SIT. Long-distance transmissions are carried out by the PTT ministry directly. Most of the equipment is purchased either from Telettra (partly owned by the Italian automobile industry giant, FIAT) or GTE's Italian subsidiary.

The general class of organization described above is prevalent: responsibility for the telecommunication network is given to a division of the PTT ministry, in some cases with a separate state-owned operating company licensed by the PTT to carry out the operations. In any case, public ownership prevails for network operation. For equipment manufacture, on the other hand, private ownership prevails (either national or multinational) with the exception of SIT in Italy and some similar examples in other countries resulting more from historical accidents than a conscious attempt by the PTT to own its suppliers. The only case of willful PTT ownership is found in Sweden, where the PTT operates its own manufacturing plants to prevent LM Ericsson from enjoying a monopoly position. Furthermore, a research and development joint venture between LM Ericsson and the state ensures the equivalence of technology and production processes between the public and private supplier. In summary, private ownership of operating networks is found only in North America (Bell System, GTE, United Telecom) whereas public ownership of manufacturing facilities is prevalent in socialist countries, with Sweden, Italy, and several developing countries owning some manufacturing facilities.

Whatever their organization, all telephone-operating companies are heavily dependent upon external sources of funds to meet the demand for new services. Growth can be financed from revenues only up to 23.1 percent of the investment needs in Spain, 38.1 percent in the United Kingdom, and 46.1 percent in Canada. A mature network such as Switzerland's still has to rely on external funds for 10 percent of its needs. This reliance on an influx of new funds has prompted many governments to make telecommunications a separate institution, funded by conventional private mechanisms. This has been the trend in Belgium, Germany, Spain, Portugal, and the United Kingdom. To some extent this resulted in more autonomy being granted to the telecommunication operations. In France, M. Valery Giscard d'Estaing, when minister of finance, advocated a similar approach. It resulted in the creation of separate financial institutions to gather funds and lease the equipment to the PTT, but not in more operating autonomy.[2] Despite this growing use of market financing, a large part of the development of telecommunication networks is still financed out of governmental budgets in most countries.

TABLE 3.3

Ownership of Electric Utilities in Selected Countries

Country	Number of Systems*	Extent of Government Regulation
Austria	6	Publicly run, one state holding company
Belgium	1	Nationalized system
Canada	21	75 percent public ownership, mostly state-owned systems at provincial level
England and Wales	1	Nationalized system (regionally owned company)
France	1	Nationalized system (state-owned company)
West Germany	12	70 percent federal ownership (nine companies supply 75 percent power)
Italy	1	Nationalized system (state-owned company)
Japan	10	One government-owned, others private
Sweden	2	Over 50 percent of public ownership
Switzerland	28	Municipal and cantonal control and ownership
United States	1,078	70 percent federal or municipal ownership

*"System" here means an independent electrical supply network.

Sources: Compiled by the author from Barbara Epstein, Politics of Trade in Power Plants (London: Atlantic Trade Study, 1971); Nuclear Power in Europe (London, PA Consultants, 1972); and industry sources.

Similarly, <u>heavy power equipment</u> is sold primarily to publicly owned electric utility companies. In some centralized countries such as the United Kingdom, France, and Italy, a central government board (as in the United Kingdom) or government-owned company (Electricité de France, ENEL in Italy) owns, plans, and operates the electrical network. In all noncentralized countries, local authorities, such as the Swiss cantons or German Länder, control or own local electrical utility companies. Table 3.3 summarizes the situation in selected countries.

The state has granted each of these electric utility companies a local quasi-monopoly on the sale of electricity, and sometimes on its production. In a number of countries there remains a small private market for power plants: large users of electricity such as aluminum smelters and refiners have their own plants. This market seldom exceeds a few percent of the total national market. Financing varies widely but the investment plans of these public electrical utilities are usually submitted for approval, if not decided, at the government level. Funding itself depends upon governmental decisions in most instances.

Staffing of Managerial Positions by Civil Servants

Beyond straight ownership, national government influence on telecommunication networks and electrical utilities is exercised less directly. To a great extent the staffing of both the PTTs and the electrical utilities is similar to that of government agencies, and at high levels there are exchanges between these institutions and other government agencies, often on a political basis. Some countries have engineer corps trained in special schools to run the telecommunications and electricity supply organizations and provide continuity. In certain European countries, engineers and managers have been attracted to public utilities and telephones out of political convictions about nationalized industries. Career paths are well-determined and predictable, except at very high levels. It also happens that in an environment still marked by seniority, civil servants who move to the private sector find themselves being controlled by junior graduates of the same specialized schools. This contributes to the weaving of close links between the utilities and their suppliers.

Technical Capabilities and Control

Yet, in many cases distrust of private-industry corporate suppliers immediately after World War II (when Europe was marked by

collectivist ideologies) led utilities and PTTs to develop strong technical competence in order to feel that they could adequately control
the suppliers. The engineering background of most high-level civil
servants encourages a bias for technological over commercial and
managerial aspects of the operations. The need to quickly reconstruct
the networks after World War II reinforced this bias. As a consequence, many of these agencies are involved in extensive research
projects of their own to keep abreast with the industry and to keep
their large engineering staff busy. Customer research is frequently
done separately from that of the industry, for instance, at the Centre
National d'Etude des Télécommunications in France, and is subject
to criticism from the industry for its lack of practical or feasible applications. In some cases joint research is successfully carried out
by customers and suppliers, as with ELLEMTEL in Sweden, a research company jointly owned and operated by LM Ericsson and the
Swedish PTT. In some others, the PTT forces its various suppliers
to share technical know-how—for instance, in Britain or France. In
France two companies, SOCOTEL and SOTELEC, had been created in
the 1960s to serve as patent clearinghouses. After some initial reluctance, international suppliers (LM Ericsson, ITT, Western Electric)
agreed to participate and share their technical knowledge. With the
advent of electronic switching technology and of a more liberal government in France, the arrangement was abolished in 1975. Allegedly,
a similar arrangement was partly responsible for the relative lack of
sophistication of a new exchange switching system (called TXE4) being
developed in the United Kingdom: the prospects of having to share their
technologies had deterred major international companies from incorporating the most advanced features in their TXE4 submissions.

In addition to their role in carrying out their own research and
disseminating the technical knowledge of leading companies, customers' technical services also certify all equipment and draw up their
own specifications. As interface problems can be important and costly
in telecommunication, there are good reasons for the PTT to ensure
in great detail that all the pieces of equipment procured are going to
be fully compatible. This technical approval and certification process,
of course, is another way to exercise influence.

Rates, Operating Revenues, and Planning

Beyond ownership, staffing, and technical control, government
can also intervene in more managerial questions. First, governments
usually tightly control the rate levels and structures applied by
PTTs and electrical utilities. Both agencies must petition supervisory
ministries and price control boards for rate increases. This often re-

sults in rate distortions. For example, though main exchange switching is by far the most expensive component of a telephone network and is used for local and long-distance calls alike, rates for local calls are usually underpriced and long-distance calls overpriced. Local calls are seen as a social service to the masses, whereas long-distance calls are considered a luxury affordable by corporations or wealthy individuals. Rate distortions of the same nature also develop in electricity distribution, where certain categories of users may be privileged.

Second, the planning of PTTs is often disrupted by government decisions. Many countries have waiting lists for telephone lines, and the PTTs try to decrease this demand in an orderly way. However, the governments often intervene in two ways: through countercyclical spending to suddenly increase PTT investments and through local intervention in response to election promises. These government interventions result in sudden surges in the PTT orders to suppliers, followed by slump periods. Similarly, rate increases usually are followed by waves of new orders.

Dependency Concerns

Finally, broader concerns are often voiced about telecommunications and electricity supply; they can be summarized in the following way: By nature these two industries have a strategic importance to many government services. Obviously telecommunications is important to the military; power generation is important to almost all specialized agencies and to the railroads. The use of computers and sophisticated components in telecommunications and the coupling of nuclear reactors to power-generating units further increases the interest evidenced by the political sphere toward the telephone and power equipment industries. Some government members in European and Latin American countries fear that relying upon technologies in which U.S. firms like IBM, Westinghouse, or General Electric are clear leaders greatly increases their dependence on the United States in general.

In short, governments have both the means and the desire to tightly control the activities of the PTTs and electrical utilities. So in dealing with their suppliers the latter must be extremely sensitive and responsible to a much wider spectrum of concerns than would normally be considered in a business transaction.

CUSTOMERS' PREOCCUPATIONS
IN PURCHASING EQUIPMENT

One might expect the PTTs and electric utilities to have some genuine preoccupations, and also to transfer the broader sociopolitical pressures weighing down on them to the manufacturer. We shall review both these preoccupations and the means available to make the manufacturers bear the brunt of external pressures. The impact of customers' preoccupations differs between developed countries having well-established markets and industry and the developing countries with new markets and no industrial tradition. However, the underlying themes of the preoccupations are not significantly different. They cover technology, pricing and financing, and local manufacture.

Technology

Technology is consistently important to the customer. First, the products have to be highly reliable. This is all the more true with the new technologies. Though electrical distribution networks are interconnected over growing areas, the failure of a major turbogenerator during a peak period has unpleasant consequences for the utility, such as overstress on equipment, power cuts making irritated customers, political complaints, lost revenue, and loss of goodwill. Computer control in telephone switching also raises the fear of a whole set of exchanges going "dead" if a breakdown occurs in the central processors.

The importance of reliability and the overall technical bias of the better-equipped customers results in their insistence on designing their own quality-control criteria and acceptance tests. In fact, all major customers draft their own specifications. International standards define broad categories but the specifics are drafted locally. While forced to follow these different standards, manufacturers have an ambiguous attitude toward them: local standards are both a hindrance to international expansion and a protection for existing positions.

The administrations of developing countries lack the technical proficiency to evaluate equipment, so they rely on specialized consultants and on the references the manufacturers present. Thus, it is important for a manufacturer to sell a new product to a few well-qualified administrations to be able to present these choices as references to other administrations. For example, if telecommunication equipment were purchased by Australia or France, or power equipment by South Africa or Brazil, it would help sales in other countries considerably. A track record of technical excellence, a guarantee of orderly and timely start-ups, and performance exceeding technical specifications are paramount. A single technical mistake or ill-managed project can ruin the image of a supplier for years.

In general, customers are reluctant to accept a new technology because it means taking risks that they are ill-prepared to face. For instance, in main exchange switching, top management of the PTTs had been trained in electromechanical technology. Shifting to electronic technology meant managing operations, the technical heart of which they no longer understood. Reluctance toward new technologies is further reinforced by the lumpy nature of commitments. For instance, to facilitate interfaces, large numbers of exchanges of a given technology have to be procured. However, bias for the latest technology can be found further down the line in the bureaucracy where positions are held by younger engineers and economists. This means skirmishes between purchasing services, which want the latest equipment, and regional divisions, where the operating reliability of proven equipment is given the utmost priority.

Usually, there are considerable delays between the invention of a technology and its diffusion and widespread use in the telecommunication industry. Critics have charged public organizations with some inbred conservatism; in fact, it is more the extremely heavy investments needed, the dangers of technological failure, and the interface problems. Further, the very long useful life of a product (40 years for telephone equipment) and the low return on the investment to the PTT as well as the complete absence of secondhand markets, discourage the early replacement of not fully amortized equipment. For power equipment, on the contrary, European state-owned utilities have often been the driving force behind the development of larger and larger and increasingly efficient turbogenerators, whereas for circuit breakers (where again interface problems are important), the same delayed new technology introduction as in telecommunications has sometimes been evidenced.

The same is true in developing countries where political leaders want to purchase the most technically sophisticated equipment, while the users would rather rely on proven equipment that is easier to operate and maintain. This leads some experts to conclude that technological changes are made when a firm starts to aggressively promote new and more sophisticated equipment to the political establishment of proud countries over the more prudent PTT or utilities management teams.

Pricing and Financing

Pricing and financing are also critical elements to many customers, though they come into play only when choosing between equipment of comparable technical performance and operating reliability. Several mechanisms are at work. First, to avoid being accused of corruption, customers like to purchase the lowest-priced equipment. This decision criterion is easily understood and not likely to be criticized by anyone without a good knowledge of the industry and the specifics of the various offers. Second is to systematically rely on competitive tendering, and never make any private direct contract with a manufacturer. This, of course, applies much more readily to developing countries than to developed ones. In the latter, establishment of close relationships with locally implanted suppliers leads to a predominance of direct private contracts. Similarly, in developing countries follow-up contracts are more likely to be negotiated privately. Third, if the supplier has adequate external low-cost financing, acceptance is easier because less government-budgeted funds are required immediately. Moreover, most developing countries would be utterly incapable of paying for large equipment like power plants or telephone exchanges without external financing. Many of the most attractive financial schemes come in the form of tied-in aid or loans from a developed country to a less-developed one.

Local Manufacture

The useful life of the products is such that a long-term commitment is often required from the manufacturer for maintenance, supply of spares, and expansion of the installations. Moreover, the interface difficulties, at least of telephone switching, mean that once a supplier has been selected and assigned an area of the country, in all likelihood it will receive all further orders for expansion in that area. The same is true of transformers and circuit breakers to a lesser extent. Turbogenerators and transmission equipment of different manufacturers are more readily interchangeable.

Preference for local suppliers dates as far back as the beginnings of industrial development. Initially it was reluctance to depend upon a distant foreign supplier for maintenance that triggered the desire to have local suppliers. Eventually, pressing for local production became a standard behavior to decrease risks. Today such reluctance remains true for products that require extensive specific project engineering. For example, the design of a new telephone exchange (not a whole system but the individual configuration for assembly at a given location) requires an in-depth knowledge of the local equipment and traffic flows. PTT engineers are more satisfied when they can interact casually with manufacturers' designers on the spot rather than from 3,000 miles away. The risk of blockade and severed supplies was another early reason for local production. Though not so relevant by 1975, it had affected thinking throughout most of the twentieth century.

The reasons just mentioned, combined with pressures from some industrialists seduced by the comfort of cartels and market allocations, led to the development of a national production capacity in both industries in almost all European countries during the first half of the century. By the 1960s, despite the free-trade areas developed in Europe, the split into local markets was well defined and solidly defended.

Moreover, a series of other factors compounded to make national preferential purchasing the rule in the industry. Prominent among these was a network of personal relationships. Executives of the PTT or utility who have had good relationships with the executives of a trusted manufacturer find it easier and safer to continue to deal with the same supplier. Also, close personal relationships develop along national lines among engineers who attended the same technical schools and can communicate easily about a common experience. In many cases people who once worked as engineers for the customer join the suppliers in managerial positions. The whole hierarchy of the local manufacturers is organized to match that of the state administration. Consequently, an order to foreign suppliers would break this loyalty and affiliation pattern, and would be perceived as more risky than relying on usual national suppliers unless the latter became unacceptable in terms of price or quality.

Another reason for local purchasing derives from the sensitivity of leftist (and in some cases narrowly nationalist) oppositions in most European and Latin American countries. Buying heavy, expensive, technologically advanced products from foreign sources, particularly from the United States, would invite criticism, and employment questions would be raised. Arguments about free trade and optimal use of resources carry little weight with workers whose jobs are threatened and pressure for local purchasing is powerful when votes are at stake. Few managers of PTTs or utilities relish facing waves of criticism for not supporting more jobs in the country.

With threats of massive unemployment and the inflation/recession economic situation in the 1970s, employment became a major preoccupation of most governments, particularly those who rested on shaky parliamentary coalitions. Typically it was considered better to keep people working in relatively inefficient companies than to resort to more welfare and unemployment compensation. More than ever, market penetration in the industries studied here required the promise of local employment. All managers in the industries underlined the impossibility of entering a market or expanding operations without a commitment to local manufacture.

Most developing countries are especially eager to develop a local telecommunications industry. Most often they require local assembly of switchgear equipment, followed by increasing local integration. In some cases it might be more attractive for the supplier to set up a transmissions plant than a switching one, if labor costs were lower. Small countries might be satisfied with a partial plant; for instance, one that manufactures connection cables only. Besides jobs, the improvement of trade balances is a dearly sought objective, first through import substitution and then through exports. The start of Giscard's presidency, combined with the economic recession in France, resulted in a push for the development of exports—a complete turnaround from the Gaullist "like it or leave it" policy. Similarly, many smaller countries want foreign plants for exports. Often requested are exports to offset the imports made; for instance, a small factory in Ecuador assembled cable connectors for the whole of LM Ericsson's Latin American operations in order to offset imports of other equipments.

Power-generating equipment raises somewhat different questions. The heavy part of it is not amenable to incremental development of a local industry. In fact, many countries have given up the production of turbogenerators. The only country trying to start a heavy electrical equipment industry is Iran, with tremendous resources and full-fledged assistance and investment by Brown Boveri, a world leader.

Transformers, however, can be built easily in most countries. Their technology is more accessible and the investment required is much less. Transformers are indeed manufactured in a variety of countries and a national electric utility might make the construction of a plant for transformers (or smaller equipment such as motors or low voltage breakers) a part of a contract to buy heavy power plants. A somewhat similar situation can develop in telecommunications with a country requesting the local manufacture of a set or small console-type PABX for the export market in exchange for an import order of main-exchange switching systems. A manager of one company summarized the situation:

> Economic elements are a secondary consideration in our
> business, so long as the national PTTs insist upon having
> some kind of national telecom industry, we shall have to
> go by their request. They see not only a need for jobs,
> but also for national technological upgrading, and the tele-
> phone can provide just that, PTTs being an arm of national
> governments. So since our customers always insist on a
> national industry as a means of doing business, we have to
> abide by their demands and undertake to provide some kind
> of local industry.

In fact, formal commitment to the development of a local industry that provides jobs for workers, engineers, and managers, has become an entry ticket to any market. Often the customer is careful to let the supplier bear the brunt of the technical and managerial effort at the outset, as well as supply foreign currency for the investment. Later, a growing proportion of the staff would be local nationals. In time the plant would also be expected to achieve at least an even trade balance, to start developing products and systems locally, and to respond to all shifts in government economic policies.

Conclusion

The patterns of public ownership of the telecommunication and power supply networks, the ways in which their growth is funded and their staffing carried out, and the use of their large technical staffs make them good transmission relays between government objectives and the way in which their suppliers carry out their business. Broader preoccupations than those of most private industrial customers thus affect the behavior of PTTs and electrical utilities when they purchase equipment. In particular, as a way to gain some control over suppliers and thus be protected against possible disruptions, customers are very selective in their choice of technology and very sensitive to low-cost financing, and usually request local investment and assembly—a full-scale operation. The very nature of the products, particularly their complex technology, long useful life, and the importance of reliability also contribute to the development of closer relationships between suppliers and customers.

The close links that develop over long periods of time between customers and suppliers within nationally closed oligopolies (imports of telecommunication equipment in developed countries seldom exceeded 10 to 15 percent of national markets and were mostly specialty products; for power equipment the corresponding figure was about 5 percent) worked to protect already established suppliers and prevent further entries.

DIRECT GOVERNMENT INFLUENCE
ON EQUIPMENT SUPPLIERS

Beyond the indirect, day-to-day influence exercised through the purchasing practices of operating networks' managers, national governments may exercise more direct control on suppliers of heavy equipment. Such control is usually directly and selectively applied to individual suppliers through direct negotiations. These often take

place at a ministerial level whereas the management of day-to-day
purchasing relationships is distributed over the hierarchy of the PTT
or electrical utility. Direct means of control usually involve access
to preferential credit, joint ownership between a multinational and the
state, threats to call in new suppliers, the allocation of research funds,
and support to export sales.

Funding and Ownership Constraints

In many countries very real financial leverage is exercised over
suppliers because the government controls all sources of credit. Special loans can be made to companies by financial institutions at preferential rates; qualification for these loans is decided by a committee
in the Ministry of Finance. Furthermore, conditions of payment on
specific contracts are subject to government budgetary approval, thus
terms may vary between suppliers at the government's initiative.
Control of sources of credit was found to be extremely important in
the control of many industries by governments in general.[3] Most often in developing countries the control is even more direct, with the
government requesting a joint venture between the customer and the
supplier. For instance, the Brazilians requested ITT and LM Ericsson to sell control of their subsidiaries in Brazil to Telebras, the
newly created, government-controlled federation of telephone companies. Similar moves were made in other Latin American countries.
Where extremely critical technologies are concerned such moves are
not uncommon even among developed countries. For instance, the
Commissoriat à l'Energie (French national nuclear research organization) purchased from Westinghouse 30 percent of the shares of Framatome, which had become the only French supplier of light-water reactors (LWR), as a condition for further orders in 1975. Later on,
Westinghouse's holdings in Framatome were further reduced. Allegedly, there was no complete consensus on this move in the French
political sphere. Well-informed observers saw in the move against
Westinghouse a token that the Giscard administration, recently elected
and willing to adopt a more liberal policy toward foreign involvement
in high technology sectors, had to give diehard Gaullists in order to
offset cooperation with international and U.S. firms in other very high
technology industries such as computers and aerospace.

Choice of Suppliers

Besides control of the financial institutions and joint ownership,
many other means of control are available to governments. Threat-

ening to change suppliers is one. There usually are other manufacturers, domestic or foreign, willing to abide by national policies. Allocation of market shares or orders by government agencies through the customers provides the ability to change suppliers at will. Another way to control suppliers is by starving the local subsidiary of a foreign group because it does not export enough. Sometimes bids from new foreign suppliers are solicited to keep local suppliers in line. Sometimes governments are disgruntled enough to actually choose the foreign bid. For instance, shortly after the British post office was made a public corporation both methods were used: when the domestic British suppliers and the ITT subsidiary showed reluctance toward starting the manufacture of a semi-electronic exchange system (TXE4), the post office called in Pye TMC, a British company recently acquired by Philips, and threatened to order the TXE4 from Pye TMC. In due course both ITT and the British suppliers decided to manufacture the TXE4 after all. Slightly later, angered by the inefficiency of the local suppliers (80 percent of its orders were late by more than a year), the post office bought a complete international exchange from LM Ericsson for $60 million. Discontent spread through the British industry, spurring the suppliers to react. In 1975 a new order was awarded to LM Ericsson, but in the meantime LM Ericsson had entered a joint venture with Thorn Industries and the order was granted only under the condition that part of the equipment would be manufactured in Britain. The amount of the second order was $75 million.[4]

The use of such drastic measures as starving a locally established supplier is often tempered by the risk of layoffs. This was not the case in the first order from LM Ericsson as British suppliers could not deliver anyway. Company management can threaten the local authorities with layoffs whenever dissatisfied by strong government policies. In most cases an agreement can be reached before the threats are carried very far by either side, yet the ability to call in new foreign suppliers at will is a strong bargaining chip for national governments or dissatisfied customers.

Research and Development Subsidies

The selective allocation of research funds and contracts is also critical. For instance, the subsidiaries of ITT in France have benefited from government R&D contracts almost as much as purely French suppliers. Less directly, but to a similar effect, government research institutes may lend their test benches and experimental facilities to some companies for R&D work, relieving them of heavy investments.

Assistance for Export Sales

In both industries, government involvement is critical for export sales. All developing countries purchase heavy electrical and telecommunication equipment partly on a political basis. Buying from a friendly country is always favored strongly. For instance, the warming up of British and French policy toward Egypt, after close to 20 years of icy cold following the Suez affair, was a bounty for industrialists in the United Kingdom and France. As one put it: "You have to be on the president's plane during a state visit, have the prime ministers talk about the contract, and get your trade minister to sign it." Moreover, most of the financing for third world or socialist countries is decided by bilateral intergovernmental trade or aid agreements. Financing and governmental support are mentioned as the factors most crucial to success by most managers in the two industries. By selectively granting or withdrawing support, governments can directly influence the success of companies in foreign markets. Moreover, domestic customers, by granting more flexible delivery terms, allow their suppliers to accept foreign orders with very stringent delivery dates. The political support and friendliness of a government toward developing countries is typically a more powerful influence than anything a company might do on its own.

CONSEQUENCES FOR THE MANAGEMENT OF NATIONAL SUBSIDIARIES

The means of government influence above provide for complete control over the local subsidiaries of electrical power and telecommunication equipment suppliers. The success of a supplier depends very much on the ability of its management to play on the internal diversity of customers and governments in order to build stable interlocking coalitions in which the existence and profits of the subsidiaries are not threatened. In other words, because they have to be included in the coalition, government officials and customers' managers have a direct say in the management of the subsidiaries. Under such conditions, long-term viability and financial success depend not so much on conventional measures of economic efficiency as on the maintenance of a viable coalition between suppliers and customers, under the control and protection of the state.

A Negotiated Environment

The coalitions summarized above have been described by Lawrence Franko as the "negotiated environment" typical of European markets in the pre-EEC era.[5] In this type of environment, key decisions affecting the strategy of the firm are not the result of an analysis of economic and competitive pressures, but they emerge in the interaction with the state and state-influenced customers. Comments by a key manager in the French electrical industry reflect that process of interaction:

> Electricité de France (EdF) is a huge, many-sided organization. Its top management is close to the Ministry of Finance and to the Prime Minister. The management of the equipment division is closer to the Ministry of Industry. The regional divisions behave in a more bureaucratic way and evidence some distrust toward private corporations. The president of Compagnie Electro-Mécanique (CEM) is well regarded in the French milieu. He is the chairman of the Association of Electrical Equipment Manufacturers, though CEM is part of the Brown Boveri group. It is absolutely clear, however, that the foundation of CEM's acceptance in France is the technology. If it were poor, CEM would be wiped out right away. The same might be true if there were outstanding French competitors. The position of CEM as a major supplier of turbogenerators has never been questioned and is well accepted by everybody. The government plays a balancing role. At one point the financial plight of Alsthom began to worry the government. Alsthom was trying to free itself from General Electric licenses. Both the Ministry of Industry and EdF's equipment division supported that attempt heartily. It then appeared that Alsthom would receive all 1,300 MWe orders. In the meantime, Alsthom and the Chantiers de l'Atlantique got together without prior consultation with EdF or the administration. The game was open again. Moreover, the former main Alsthom shareholder, Compagnie Générale d'Electricité (CGE), had displeased the government because it unduly pulled out of the boiling water nuclear reactor (BWR) orders given by EdF, and blamed the customer.
>
> Neither Alsthom nor CEM ever had a narrowly defined contract with EdF; EdF's control teams periodically check the implementation of the industrial process supplying them; and inspectors are stationed in their plants to monitor the execution of the general contracts. EdF cares a lot about what is manufactured, and where. I do not know of any state enterprise that does not care about the origin of what it buys. BBC owns 40.9 percent of CEM; the other

holders are not individually significant. Though the Roths-
child Bank still holds a few percent of the equity, it recognizes it cannot significantly influence the management of
CEM any longer. A minority holding enables the French
customers who like what BBC makes to order from CEM
without a loyalty conflict. These elements are never openly
discussed by anyone. The present status quo is satisfactory
for everyone. French competitors highlight CEM's foreign
connections; but, in fact, the present situation is not dis-
turbing—it's a stable equilibrium. Any evolution weakening
the French influence on CEM would result in open threats to
further orders. CEM's Swiss connection is no discomfort
so long as the status quo is not modified in any way! [6]

In some cases the state can lead a more openly competitive
game. For instance, it can nurture a local competitor when all other
suppliers are foreign subsidiaries and try to use that locally dependent company as a wedge to split foreign suppliers and as a tool to influence the whole industry. Telephone prices in France were kept
high for a long time to protect the growth of CIT-Alcatel (a concomitant result being windfall profits for the ITT subsidiaries, the European management of ITT allegedly referring informally to France as
the "golden cage"). When CIT-Alcatel became a mature supplier, it
was then used to impose spectacular price cuts.
    In most cases the ability of management to understand the inter-
nal workings of the customers, to grasp the interplay of various government agencies and officers, and to protect a balanced relationship
are the major requirements for success. Steering a course through
the unclear waters between collusion with local governments (resulting in complete dependence) and adversary relationships (resulting in
eviction or sanctions) is a most difficult task.
    To a large extent the same has been true in developing countries,
as an executive of a telecommunications company commented:

> If we sell something to our customers in Latin America it
> is because we can join their problems, help them work out
> solutions. After a while everybody realizes we are all in
> the same boat, then we come to mutual trustful relation-
> ships. If the capability of the operator is not high enough
> you take the responsibility by yourself. If you abuse it and
> take advantage of your superior knowledge you put yourself
> into bad trouble over the long run. You have to reach a
> delicate balance, to be an honest person. Educating the
> customers is binding them to you in a balanced relation-
> ship; you have to keep them happy all the time, otherwise

they will start to look elsewhere for gear. In that process you have to be careful not to get involved in local politics and lose your independence and diplomacy. You can't exist as a supplier just by being a friend of the minister and the president and assume that the organization will dance to their tune in the long run. It does not work that way; you need to develop relationships early in the career of bright people, show that you respect them.

An executive in another company commented:

The phone-operating company would like to get the best available equipment. This usually means to import it. For financial reasons the phone company would also rather import, because the unit price per line is usually lower on the import market than when the equipment is locally manufactured. Often it is torn between a desire to import for the efficient use of its resources and governmental directives to create local employment, reduce imports, train people, and so forth. The government has a program of localization. They expect a company like ours to come to them and say, "Here, we have this product to satisfy your needs and here is a manufacturing integration program to go with it." European governments are more interested in how many people the factory will employ than in who owns it ultimately. In Mexico and most other Latin American countries no proposal is accepted with less than a local majority of capital.

Obtaining a share of the newer, faster-growing markets not only requires coming up with good offers in an economic sense, but also canvassing the whole administration and committing the company to some local investment usually through a joint-venture agreement.

Shared Management

To operate successfully in salient businesses, companies must not only create local manufacturing operations but also agree to share their management with the local interests, including government agencies, operating companies, and local industrialists.

The desire of most of these local interests to exercise some control over local industry, and the extent of their means of control, puts manufacturers in a weak bargaining position. The existence of a number of large international competitors, each willing to preempt a promising market, allows governments to play the companies against each other in the initial stages of selecting a supplier. Suppliers not only must provide an attractive deal in terms of technology, prices, services, and so forth, but also must be willing to make extensive investments in local manufacturing and to accept local intervention in management.

The long life of the products moderates the temptation for suppliers to make short-term profits and forget their commitments after a few years. Moreover, a few instances of mishandling customers' needs can severely affect the possibility of a manufacturer getting into new markets. For instance, knowledge of interventions by a company in the domestic politics of some countries severely hampers the penetration into new, nationalistic markets. This is perceived very differently from payment to local intermediaries, an accepted business practice in many countries. The building of a trusting relationship with the customer is of critical importance to continued presence, and after a while becomes much more valuable than a particularly advanced technology or extremely low costs. The structure of relationships inside public administrations leads members to avoid uncertainties rather than to take risks (technological or economical) for the sake of economic efficiency. Status quo on both sides is sought for reciprocal comfort.

In such a negotiated national oligopoly the key to success is restraint and avoidance of any drastic change that might upset the local coalition between suppliers and customers. An in-depth understanding of the national administration facilitates the monitoring of changes by the subsidiary and early responses to government policies before any change can become a political issue. In many cases, given vested interests, the need to avoid crisis is tantamount to the maintenance of the status quo. Whereas national administrations usually show much understanding and tolerance for the economic and financial arguments of suppliers in slowly evolving situations, severe reactions are likely when a crisis develops publicly and provides ammunition to political opponents. If a normal incident in an ongoing bargaining between the national customer and an MNC subsidiary causes a break in relations and becomes a visible social issue, it is usually quite detrimental to the company because it locks government officials into publicly known positions that are difficult to back out of.

This pattern of negotiated environment and shared management long prevailed in both industries. After a relatively freewheeling period in the telephone industry that lasted until the turn of the century in Europe and until the 1930s in developing countries, relationships fell into that pattern. For electrical power equipment, such relationships had prevailed almost from the beginning. The two world wars led to minor readjustments (mostly the acquisition of former Westinghouse interests by national companies in the early 1920s and the nationalization of Siemens subsidiaries in the late 1940s), but altogether the pattern showed much resilience.

NOTES

1. The Instituto per la Ricostruzione Industriale (IRI) is a government-controlled public holding company created after World War II to implement structural reforms in the Italian economy and remedy market deficiencies. It became an instrument to deal structurally with key economic problems. See Romano Prodi, "Italy," in Big Business and the State, ed. Raymond Vernon (Cambridge, Mass.: Harvard University Press, 1974), pp. 45-63.

2. For instance, J. P. Anastassopoulos, in a detailed study of several state-owned industrial or service operations in France, found the Direction des Telecommunications most narrowly controlled by the government. See J. P. Anastassopoulos, "The Strategic Autonomy of Government Controlled Enterprises Operating in a Competitive Economy" (Ph.D. diss., Columbia University, 1973).

3. For instance, see John M. McArthur and Bruce R. Scott, Industrial Planning in France (Boston: Harvard Business School, Division of Research, 1969).

4. Electronic News, February 17, 1975, p. 66; and research interviews.

5. Lawrence G. Franko, The European Multinationals, (Stamford, Conn.: Greylock, 1977).

6. Research interview. (Actually the status quo was modified less than two years after these comments were made. Consequences are described in Chapter 5.)

4

THE ECONOMIC IMPERATIVE: PRODUCTS, TECHNOLOGIES, AND MARKETS

Technological changes have affected the telecommunication equipment and power system industries very significantly. Market changes have taken place and there is more market growth to come from developing countries. Technological changes, in turn, have led to significant changes in production economics and conditions for use of the products. This chapter describes the major products within the telecommunication and electrical power equipment industries. Technological changes are then analyzed, as are their consequences on the production processes and production costs. Finally, national markets are reviewed and patterns of international trade are presented.

MAJOR PRODUCTS

Telecommunication Equipment

Telecommunication products fall into four major categories: cables, main-exchange switchgear, transmission equipment, and station equipment. Cables are generally considered a very distinct product. Not necessarily made by telecommunication equipment manufacturers, they are not in the mainstream of the industry.

Main-exchange switchgear accounts for by far the biggest proportion of telecommunication equipment sales. Main exchanges enable connections to be made between individual telephone lines. The principle of the telephone is fairly simple: by lifting the receiver, a caller activates a uniselector that looks for free switches. A dial tone signals the link with a switch. The first digit is accepted and sorted by the switch, which then hunts for a second switch for the second digit, and so on. This is the basic procedure for all telephone exchanges—it has remained the same since the initial Strowger switch was invented in 1889. However, several generations of switches have followed at about 30-year intervals. The rotating arms and contact racks of the initial Strowger (known as rotary switching) were replaced by Crossbar systems, using matrices of wires and a semi-intelligent device, called the register, which store all the digits dialed instead of using a step-by-step approach. Crossbar is much faster than Strowger and reduces the number of switches needed. It was invented in 1919 in Sweden but has been widely used only since 1945. Until World War II, Strowger systems had been sufficient for most networks, but extensive war damages to existing exchanges provided an opportunity for their replacement with more modern equipment.

Semielectronic exchanges, developed by Bell Laboratories in 1965, use tiny switches the size of matchsticks called Reed relays. In them, small magnetic coils activate tiny gold-plated contacts. The process of calling is similar to the Crossbar system but is aided by a computer that contains a real time map of the whole exchange that determines paths between switches more quickly than a step-by-step procedure or a register search. Instead of searching for a path by trial and error, the memory immediately directs each call to an available path. This system is generally called stored program control (SPC), and is faster than Crossbar. Finally, pure electronic systems, which use both computer-controlled stored programs and solid-state devices and contractors, were introduced in 1975.

A further technological distinction can be made between space- and time-division switching equipment. In space-division switching used by Strowger, Crossbar, and the present SPC systems, each conversation needs a separate physical path. In time-division switching, speech is sampled, converted into digital pulses, and interleaved with other conversations. Theoretically, this maximizes the use of transmission equipment with pulse-code modulation (PCM) and allows good transmission with lower-grade equipment (it is less difficult to transmit digital symbols than voice-analog frequencies because greater distortions can be allowed). Most data-transmission systems already use time division to link up computers over long distances. Though digital time-divided telephone transmission networks are superior to space-divided networks, in practice they are very difficult to introduce because they need a costly translator (called "modem," for modulator-demodulator) to interface with space-divided systems. In 1976 no time-divided telephone systems were in operation, except for prototypes in France and the United States.

A major difficulty for main-exchange manufacturers is the need to interface a wide variety of existing equipment of different origins and different standards. To alleviate this difficulty somewhat, the PTT usually assigns the same type of equipment to large areas and uses special regional trunk exchanges for interarea calls. The internationally accepted standards (Comité Consultatif International des Téléphone et Télégraphe [CCITT] for instance) only define general classes of signals and transmissions but do not specify detailed system characteristics.[1] Consequently, international exchanges must have very flexible systems that are able to use several standards simultaneously. The advent of SPC simplified the interface problems, which can be dealt with by software modifications in the central memory and processors rather than by building hardware to different specifications. The equipment of a given manufacturer usually is entirely compatible from one generation to another.

The development of SPC, Reed relays, and solid-state circuitry also brought other advantages. Parts of the circuit can be simply unplugged and replaced, reducing the need for on-site maintenance by 60 percent. Also, central processors are able to test the equipment and locate failures. They can easily track and bill separately all communications and keep complete statistics on traffic. Such information makes network planning much easier and more accurate.

Prices for main exchanges range from $250 to $600 per line. Large-scale production of electronic exchanges would lower the cost per line to $250 for large exchanges (10,000 to 60,000 lines per unit) and $400 for smaller exchanges with less than 5,000 lines per unit. Above 60,000 lines per exchange the unit cost of a line increases moderately. These costs would compare favorably with the average costs for conventional exchanges, which are mostly Crossbar. Prices for conventional equipment vary from $250 to $300 in low-wage countries with efficient large-scale production and up to $600 in smaller markets such as Switzerland or Norway.

Transmission equipment is simpler than main-exchange switching. It includes microwave transmitters, frequency and pulse-code modems, data-transmission equipment, and earth-satellite stations for long-distance communications. This equipment usually relies on straightforward radio technology and involves electronic design and assembly. The unit price of a microwave system varies considerably according to the extent and complexity of the system, but is usually in the million dollar range. Long-distance transmission started in the 1930s with cables. Coaxial cables, developed before 1940, allowed large numbers of pairs of wires to be grouped on one cable without distortions. Multiplexers allowed the use of wider wavebands (up to 12 megahertz [MHz]) to transmit as many as 2,700 conversations simultaneously on a given axis with centimetric waves, which use mountaintop or pylon relays, thus dispensing with cables. Pulse-code modulation and digital coding now allow new densities to be reached with up to 300 conversations per channel. Due to the rapid succession of innovations it is not possible to outline distinct generations of equipment.

Station equipment comprises all the equipment directly used by the customers of PTTs: telephone sets, intercom and loudspeaker systems, extensions, private branch exchanges (PBX) from 50 to 12,000 lines, and other devices such as message recorders and alarm systems. The value of this equipment relative to main-exchange switching is rather low. Though these products did not change much during their first few decades, they evolved more rapidly in the 1970s. In conjunction with the new electronic main exchanges, more advanced sets were introduced, featuring touch-tone dialing, priority listing, and call-forwarding or call-holding circuits. Solid-state electronic technology made the entirely electronic set possible. The generalization of electronic sets could only follow that of digital coding, however. PBX technology followed that of main exchanges, though PBXs are somewhat simpler because they usually have a single interface point and smaller capacity than main exchanges.

Of course, all these products complement each other and all are required in a balanced mix for the development of a telecommunications network. The following is a typical breakdown of capital costs to a PTT administration:

	Percent
Main-exchange switchgear	40
Transmission equipment	6
Station equipment	7
Cables	6
Buildings and grounds	25
Installation of the equipment	16

Nearly half of the total value of the network is not normally supplied by telecommunication equipment manufacturers, or at least not by them alone. Installation is often done by the supplier, but many technically proficient PTTs carry out their own installation work. Cables are supplied by specialized cable manufacturers, which are sometimes subsidiaries or divisions of telecommunication equipment companies.

Electrical Power Supply Systems

Power equipment products also fall into three essential categories: turbogenerators,* circuit breakers, and transformers.

---

*A turbogenerator is a steam turbine coupled to a large, alternating-current electromagnet generator. It is driven by steam from a fossil-fuel boiler or nuclear reactor.

Turbogenerators are large, heavy pieces of equipment. The turbine shaft for a 1,100 MWe generator weighs approximately 300 tons and is about 100 feet long and 5 feet in diameter. The rotors are normally cast in one block and then machined on heavy mills and lathes. Thousands of carefully machined blades are then fitted on the shaft. The unit price of a medium-sized turbogenerator averages $5 million. A large 1,300 MWe turbogenerator of the type developed and ordered in 1975 costs well over $10 million. Though they are sold to many different utilities, turbogenerators are not extremely differentiated products. They are designed around two basic parameters: the conditions of the steam input and the electricity output.

Transformers are also bulky, heavy equipment with well-known technological characteristics. Despite the well-known technology, they differ considerably because of the different safety devices required by various utilities. There are no standardized specifications for voltage and wattage between countries, so product diversity is very high. Transformers are manufactured according to scores of different standards and safety tests, often detailed by customers. Typically, transformers must handle 3.5 times the output of the generators. The average price of a transformer is $150,000.

Circuit breakers rely on a variety of technologies developed in response to the need for higher voltage and better safety. After World War II, bath technology was replaced by air-blast technology, which in turn was replaced by sodium fluoride breakers in the 1970s. Specifications for breakers depend to a large extent on how a network is run, how well a wave of breaks can be tolerated (like the wave that blacked out the northeastern United States in November 1965), and how well a utility company can accept long repair delays—some breakers literally blow up and have to be replaced before power can be restored. Here again, product diversity is extreme, with a range of different standards. Unit prices for high-voltage circuit breakers range from $15,000 to $100,000 according to safety standards and peak-load requirements.

In addition to products aimed at generating and distributing electrical energy for general purpose networks, most manufacturers also make products using the same basic electrotechnical techniques for specialized applications. Most important among these are railroad substations and rolling gear, and industrial systems for large heavy industrial plants. For these special applications, products similar to those used by utilities, but smaller and less powerful, were combined into large systems with other products—mostly motors of various size and power, to drive and control large factories such as steel mills.

TECHNOLOGICAL EVOLUTIONS

Both industries were characterized by rapid technological evolutions. These had required considerable investments from all manufacturers and resulted in significant market shifts. This section summarizes the technical evolutions in both industries and then reviews their impacts on equipment customers and suppliers.

Electronic Switching Development

In telecommunications the most effort has gone into main-exchange electronic switching technology. Electronic switching was developed by Bell Laboratories between 1955 and 1965. The cost to Bell was in the $500 million range for the first SOC exchange (ESS1), which used conventional components (Reed relays) for the switches themselves. This was several times over the initial estimates of Bell scientists. The design and programming of special-purpose computers had presented the major difficulties, and software development had cost ten times more than anticipated.

Bell made the general design of the system available to the public by publishing detailed technical data on ESS1. Various other manufacturers decided to copy Bell and to develop their own systems for electronic switching. The cost of developing a range of electronic exchanges in various sizes and configurations was $150-250 million, even with all that was known about Bell's ESS1 system. A single type of exchange costs at least $100 million to develop, with "small" increments for derivatives. Industry experts thought that it would take a commitment of several hundred engineers working from three to seven years to develop a workable electronic exchange for an experienced telecommunications equipment manufacturer.

The major difficulties stem from the need to combine an indepth understanding of the complex problems of exchange interface and capacity requirements with the ability to adapt and modify electronic hardware and to develop extensive software packages. One major stumbling block is the extremely high level of reliability required of complex, nonduplicated computers (that is, no more than two hours breakdown of central processors over a 40-year period). Moreover, the equipment has to be simple enough to be operated and maintained by normal PTT employees without extensive retraining in advanced electronics. The diversity of PTT requirements and specifications taxes the design capability for flexible and versatile equipment.

Adequate design of components is another requirement. Some of the components used in main-exchange switching systems are "off-the-shelf" standard items produced by a number of suppliers. Others require special design so they can be mass produced at a low cost without intolerable rejection rates. Extremely tight specifications for the overall system lead to component specifications far exceeding what would normally be required of commercially available components.

Industry experts thought that whereas most R&D work in the early 1970s concerned overall system designs, the focus would shift to the design of better circuits that could be mass produced cheaply and at very high standards through large-scale integration.

The expected transition toward digital coding and time separation in telephone networks would somewhat decrease the need for high-grade components and provide computer manufacturers with the opportunity to enter the telecommunications industry. Very few companies, at present, possess both the telephone and computer technologies. The telecommunication equipment manufacturers had been busy developing an electronic capability to counter the threat from computer manufacturers.

Other Technological Evolutions
in the Telecommunication Industry

The technology of private branch automatic exchanges (PABXs) is similar to that of main exchanges, but the development costs involved are smaller. For telephone companies PABX technology is a by-product of main-exchange development. For electronics companies the R&D effort required by PABX is more affordable than main-exchange switching because of a single interface, much smaller processors, and lower reliability standards. Technological entry barriers are relatively low, at least for consoles (5 to 50 lines) and medium-sized PABXs (up to 600 lines).

Telephone sets do not involve much development, except for certain refinements. Entirely electronic sets are being introduced by ITT in Denmark. These are digital and could easily double as data terminals with a few modifications. The phones already include repeat dialing, automatic dialing, light-emitting-diode (LED) display of alpha-numerical calls, and an extra set of buttons for data transmission.

Transmission technology has been evolving much more steadily than either main exchanges or station equipment. Every few years new extensive improvements appear. The magnitude of effort involved, however, is much smaller than for main exchanges: a score of good engineers and a few million dollars per year can keep a company at the forefront of at least one segment of the market (for instance, radio links or satellite stations). Leaders in the transmission equipment field seldom have research staffs of more than 200. Little diversity in standards (there are basically two standards: Bell's in North America and "Comité Consultatif International de la Radio" elsewhere; they are not compatible) makes adaptation to local markets easy. The combination of pulse-code modulation and circular wave guides allows a very high number of conversations to be carried simultaneously. By 1975 several companies were working on the development of optical fiber that would transmit ultra-high frequency pulses of light generated by solid-state devices activated by digital switches.

The convergence of the technology of the three segments of the telecommunications industry is clear: pulse-code modulation, digital coding, and time separation result in simpler, more integrated telecommunication systems with a technology closely akin to computer networks. More and more, a strong competence in electronics will be an underlying requirement for any company in the telecommunications equipment field as technical evolution increasingly depends on the development of better and smaller solid-state devices.

Technology in Electricity Supply:
Higher Input Power, Higher Distribution Voltage

The electrical power equipment industry has not witnessed such sweeping technological changes as telecommunications. Turbogenerator technology has evolved fairly slowly since Charles Brown coupled his fast generators with efficient Parsons turbines early in the twentieth century. Power output and yield of turbogenerators, however, have increased dramatically over the years. In the 1930s the standard output was 25 MWe, though by 1926 Brown Boveri had already developed the first 126 MWe turbogenerator. Steady improvements led to the 600-900 MWe models in the 1960s. When trying to further increase the output power above the 900 MWe level, basic design problems forced the U.S. suppliers to decrease the rotating speed from 3,000 to 1,800 rpm and increase the size of the generators and turbines. The U.S. suppliers were moved to do this sooner than the Europeans because of the different current frequencies (60 Hz versus 50 Hz). The basic technology of the product remained unchanged, however. Unit power soared from an average of 230 MWe for turbogenerators ordered in Europe in 1966 to 780 MWe for orders placed in 1973, to 1,100 MWe for orders placed thereafter.[2] Companies that could not maintain required standards of performance and reliability as unit power went up lost ground to competitors.*

---

*For instance, when Parsons failed to meet contractual performance levels for the TVA in 1965, the result was a complete halt

Research and development work in the turbogenerator business is of an incremental nature over long periods of time. Several types of such work are narrowly intertwined, including research in basic physics on new alloys or blade profiles, product development to improve overall efficiency in manufacturing methods, and experience gained from contract-by-contract project engineering.

Industry experts estimated that a minimum R&D budget of $10 million per year was required just to remain in the turbogenerator business. Being a leader, or freeing oneself from licenses on key elements, costs considerably more. The high cost of technological proficiency and the scattering of research teams during World War II has led European and Japanese companies to rely heavily on licenses bought from Brown Boveri, General Electric, and Westinghouse in the 1950s. Product development expenses average 5 percent to 8 percent of sales volume for a large leading firm with an extra 5 percent for project engineering (usually billed to customers) and 1 percent to 5 percent for corporate research. Licensing fees charged by such leading firms to smaller licensees range from 4 percent to 10 percent of the sales volume of the licensee. [3]

The advent of nuclear reactors did not modify the turbogenerator technology per se, except for the need to increase maximum unit power up to 1,300 MWe by reducing rotating speed and increasing the size. It is believed, however, that the long-term impact might be stronger. The element of light-water power reactors most amenable to improvement is the secondary loop. It is thought that with time it might be possible to design the steam circuit and the turbine simultaneously for better interface. In that case integrated manufacturers designing both the reactor circuitry and the turbogenerators might acquire a technical edge over nonintegrated suppliers.

Transformer technology has also been evolving incrementally toward higher voltage and power, but this does not involve massive research efforts. Product development might cost in the vicinity of $1 million a year to manufacture. The technology for most standard transformers is widely available and the technical barriers are low. The same is true of circuit breakers in the 1970s, except for the need for costly testing to make sure the breakers meet extremely stringent safety requirements. Producing several hundred high voltage breakers per year is seen by industry experts as a minimum for using a testing laboratory efficiently.

---

of orders from the United States to that company. When Allis Chalmers' Ravenswood (Queens, New York) plant had multiple breakdowns, plans to reenter the industry with Kraft Werke Union's help in 1972 were postponed.

*For instance, none of the French circuit-breaker manufacturers owns testing laboratories. Electricité de France, the nationalized

IMPACT OF TECHNOLOGICAL
EVOLUTIONS ON PRODUCTION ECONOMICS

It is clear that economic characteristics of the production process are deeply affected by technological change. The tendency is
toward larger minimum production volumes for turbogenerators and
other heavy electrical products, and also toward larger scale of production for main-exchange switchgear. These changes in the economics of the production process, in turn, created pressures for consolidation and nationalization. This brought into question the fragmented
structure of the European industry, with its sets of nationally independent suppliers. It also raised for multinationals the whole question
of integration of their operations between countries. The first section below analyzes the evolution of production economics with the introduction of new technologies. A second section presents briefly the
fragmented structure of the European industry.

Technological Evolution and Economics of Production

There are significant differences between the production process
of switching equipment and that of electromechanical equipment, with
Crossbar equipment in something of a median position. Electromechanical telephone-exchange switching manufacture consists of two
major steps: parts manufacture and assembly. Strowger equipment
was basically made from steel and iron sheets, cut, machined, sol-
dered, and chemically treated. The key stage of the production process was metalworking for which specialized workers were needed.
Assembly was straightforward and required less highly trained workers. In Crossbar, because of smaller machine-made contactors and
matrices of wire, less labor is needed and assembly is partly automatic. Crossbar production is not very different from circuit board
assembly of the first generation of electronic circuitry. SPC electronic switching is produced by unskilled workers assembling complex
components and integrated circuits. Direct labor hours per line vary
widely from technology to technology.

	Hours
Strowger	15 to 20
Crossbar	8 to 12
Electronic	2 to 4

electric utility company, has one central lab, designed to its own
standards that it rents to individual manufacturers for testing new
equipment.

FIGURE 4.1

Economies of Scale in Crossbar Exchange Manufacture

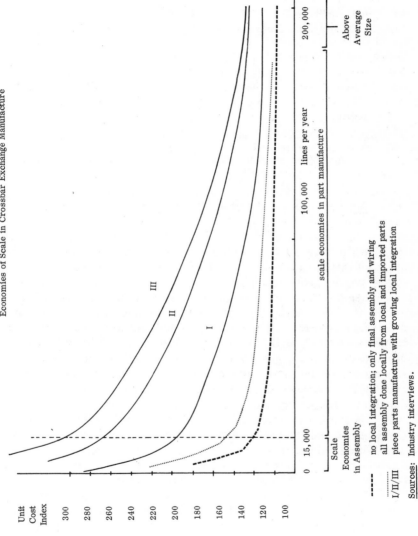

Unit Cost Index

Scale Economies in Assembly

I/II/III

— — — no local integration; only final assembly and wiring
all assembly done locally from local and imported parts
· · · · · piece parts manufacture with growing local integration

scale economies in part manufacture

Sources: Industry interviews.

Above Average Size

83

TABLE 4.1

Typical Factory Costs for the Three Major Switching Technologies
(in dollars)

Costs per Line*	Electronic	Crossbar	Strowger
Direct Labor	15	50	100
Indirect Labor	75	80	100
Materials and Components	120	150	130
Total	200	280	330

*Recovery of such items as R&D costs, amortization, and
overheads is not included here.

Source: Compiled by the author from research interviews.

While direct labor costs are reduced by electronic switching,
quality control and testing costs are high, particularly because of the
expensive apparatus required.

Assembly, a labor-intensive process, is less affected by economies of scale than parts manufacture, which requires heavy investments in machines and surface treatment equipment. As can be seen
from Figure 4.1, little production advantage is to be gained by assembling more than 15,000 lines per year in the Crossbar technology.
However, efficient parts manufacture requires the production of
150,000 to 250,000 lines annually. Also, extensive experience reduces cost levels significantly.

By 1976 it was not yet clear how the production costs for electronic exchanges would compare with those for Crossbar equipment.
The United States, Canada, and Japan had some production experience
in complete electronic exchanges. Table 4.1 gives an approximate
breakdown of factory costs for the three systems.

It was expected that local integration in the manufacture of electronic switching would result in higher costs. Three particular problems arose: the need to use sophisticated and costly testing equipment at several stages of the production process; the difficulty of
using locally manufactured components, even in developed countries;
and the lesser importance of assembly activities. It might be expected that production of 300,000 lines per year would permit a certain

amount of redesign to accommodate locally made components in countries such as France or Brazil with little or no cost penalty. However, in most cases local assembly entails a 10 percent to 20 percent
cost penalty. If local integration reaches a level of 50 percent it
might well result in a 30 percent cost penalty for a production volume
of 120,000 lines per year. Furthermore, the potential for local assembly would decrease. As for other advanced electronics goods, a
shift was taking place from discrete components to integrated circuits.
The first SPC exchange systems used large numbers of discrete semi-
conductors, the assembly of which was a labor-intensive process.
With the growing reliability of large-scale integrated circuits and the
perfection of the metal-oxide semiconductor (MOS) technology, SPC
exchanges would increasingly use integrated circuits instead of discrete components. Low-cost MOS circuits, specially designed for
switching applications but built in very large numbers, made smaller
volumes increasingly costly. In many cases volumes of 500,000 lines
per year or more would be needed to fully exploit economies of scale
in integrated-circuit manufacture. Similarly, electronic switching
tests require costly equipment than can be more easily amortized on
larger volumes. In consequence, though no clear data exist, it seems
that no manufacturer would even consider local assembly and final
testing of electronic systems for an annual volume of less than 20,000
to 30,000 lines. Furthermore, the value added by final assembly of
SPC exchanges is likely to decrease to a few percent of their total
value as integrated circuits come to account for a larger share of the
total value.

Conversely, when electronic switching components and integrated
circuits are mass produced in capital-intensive plants with little di-
rect-assembly labor, costs are less sensitive to labor rate hikes than
in conventional switching manufacture. The lesser impact of labor
rates and the decrease in component prices are expected to make
electronic switching more and more price competitive over time, particularly for large exchanges. Also it is important to note that the
shift to electronic switching leads to significant personnel redundan-
cies in manufacturing unless volume is much higher. Hardest hit are
the qualified metalworkers needed in large number for Strowger or
Crossbar exchanges manufacture, but completely redundant for electronic ones.

Transmission equipment is seldom made in large enough series
to warrant sizable economies of scale. The relatively low price of
transmission equipment and its cost effectiveness, compared with the
revenue generated for PTTs by long-distance communications, result in relatively little cost reduction pressure. Production is undertaken on a set-by-set, job-shop assembly system from components
and parts manufactured in small series. The assembly work requires

TABLE 4.2

Turbogenerator Cost Breakdown
(percent)

	Full Cost	Variable	Fixed
Materials	38	38	—
Direct labor	10	5	5
Indirect labor and factory overhead	28	8	20
R&D amortization	5	—	5
Project design	5	5	—
Amortization, administration, selling, and the like	14	—	14
Total	100	56	44

Source: Compiled by the author from interviews and industry statistics.

more competent technicians than unskilled workers because it is less repetitive. Large PABXs are manufactured in the same way as main exchanges. Small ones and telephone sets are usually manufactured on assembly lines, very much like consumer electronics.

Manufacturers usually stock parts for main exchanges and transmission systems. Assembly starts only when the specific use has been determined. The production cycle of a main exchange takes from 18 months to 2 years, including 9 months for manufacturing parts, 9 months for subassembly, and a few months on site for final assembly and tests. Telephone sets and small PABXs are made in large series, kept in inventory, and sold "off the shelf" just like consumer goods or standard office equipment.

The production cycle in electric power equipment manufacturing is even longer. Turbogenerators are made in very large plants, one by one, over a period of several years. The main rotor shafts are cast in steel ingots up to 300 tons and then machined to shape in huge halls. Next comes cutting, machining and mounting of blades in the turbine, machine stators, wiring the alternators, and so on. All these operations are labor intensive, requiring highly skilled technicians and large numbers of workers patiently machining and assembling the turbogenerators.

Investments required to manufacture turbogenerators are usually well above $100 million. The typical cost structure of a turbogenerator is approximated in Table 4.2.

Pressures for Rationalization

Experience gained is of considerable importance when making between 3 and 12 units of the same type. Economies of design and assembly are particularly possible, but after the twelfth unit costs decrease much more slowly.

Smaller manufacturers are very inefficient compared to bigger ones: R&D costs have become prohibitive, and fixed factory costs unduly high when production series decrease. Till the early 1970s, small multipurpose plants in the 2,000 MWe capacity range could break even. Considerable increase in unit power had been achieved till then through the addition of low pressure stages to the turbine, which could be assembled in the same small plants. Thus, in terms of total MWe, the productive capacity of existing plants was increased dramatically with the shift to 600 MWe (or more) turbogenerators running at 3,000 rpm. So it had been possible in the 1960s to increase the total production of existing plants with almost no new investments.

With the technological change to much larger turbogenerators and 1,800 rpm rotating speeds, the demands on the production process became much more difficult to face. The shift to 1,800 rpm, 1,300 MWe units triggered a massive reequipment of the larger manufacturers and often required new plants to handle the much heavier parts. Between 1969 and 1974 all European manufacturers invested massively (up to $150 million each) to get ready for the production of 1,300 MWe sets. Rapidly rising labor rates also resulted in the quick spread of extremely expensive, multistage, numerically controlled machines in both blade manufacture and turboshaft milling. With these machines requiring long set-up time, the advantage of producing several similar sets on the same order became greater. These various factors compounded to make the old 2,000 MWe capacity plants utterly inefficient compared to the new 10,000 MWe plants. In a few years the critical plant size had increased more than four times in terms of output. A new plant required a minimum of five large turbogenerator orders each year to break even.

Power transformers and circuit breakers have a cost structure similar to that of turbogenerators, but they are not subject to such forbidding economies of scale and minimum critical size. Production, which is done in small batches, is more standardized. A typical plant turns out a few hundred units per year.

In the 1970s most European companies and plants in the two industries were below optimum size given the economics of production

TABLE 4.3

Average Capacity per Manufacturer in the Major EEC Countries Compared with Efficient Sizes of Plants in 1973

	Steam Turbines (MWe per annum)	Generators (MWe per annum)	Transformers (MVA per annum)	Nuclear Vessels (units per annum)
Germany	4,500[a]	7,000	15,000[a]	1
France	2,000	3,000	9,000	6
Italy	3,500	2,500	9,000	3
Belgium	500	1,000	5,000	1
Netherlands	1,000	2,000	4,000	5
United Kingdom	6,000[a]	5,000	10,000	0[b]
Most efficient size of plant	10,000	12,000	10,000	6
Minimal efficient size	8,000	9,000	7,500	5

MVA: megavolt amperes

[a]Several plants per manufacturer.
[b]No LWRs.

Sources: Commission of the European Communities, Situation et perspectives des industries des gros equipements electromecaniques et nucleaires liés à la production d'energie de la communauté, SEC(75)2770 (Brussels: Commission of the European Communities, 1976); Organization for Economic Cooperation and Development, Survey of Power Equipment (Paris, annual issues); and A. Surrey, World Market for Electric Power Equipment (Brighton, Sussex: University of Sussex, 1972).

mentioned above. The situation was particularly striking in the electrical equipment industry as Table 4.3 clearly shows.

The situation was similar in the telecommunications industry. Many countries with small markets for main exchanges nurtured several full-fledged local manufacturers (national or subsidiaries of international groups), most of which were too small to be efficient or competitive. In addition, national markets were not sufficient to support these local producers. In many cases the resulting cost per line was 150 percent or more of the cost to an efficient producer. Also, as we have seen, by decreasing the value added at the assembly stage, the shift to entirely electronic technologies did not facilitate the survival of smaller suppliers or of a nationally independent industry in small countries.

Economies of scale in R&D, and the cost of technology had not resulted in strong pressures for nationalization because the technologies had traditionally been made available rather quickly to all suppliers through extensive cross-licensing. In the 1970s this began to change. First, in the late 1960s the inability of the Europeans to develop commercially competitive nuclear reactors, and the resulting dominance of the market by U.S. firms, suddenly increased government concern. Not only did European governments not allow the U.S. companies to invest locally, they also started a move to free their industries from U.S. licenses, an effort well under way in Germany by 1975, and beginning in France. Second, the potential use of fuel-processing plants for military purposes created some limits on technology transfer. Commercial reactors use enriched uranium that could also be used for the manufacture of the H-bomb.

In the meantime the shock of the oil embargo and price multiplication quickly politicized energy policies. Unanswered doubts about nuclear reactor safety led to further politicizing. This resulted in further government interest, which combined with the growing scale of the industry, brought the relationships between suppliers and governments to higher levels of sensitivity as the traditional patterns of behavior were questioned.

Finally, in a world where rivalry between nations takes place more and more on economic grounds, the importance of heavy capital goods exports is higher than ever and the policy of "national champions" is becoming stronger.

The impact of technological evolutions on production scales is even more important. The survival of individual national companies that were becoming too small to continue efficient production came into question. So far the policy of most governments has been first to consolidate companies along national lines until only two domestic suppliers remain for each product category. Governments use the balance between the two suppliers, and the threat of calling in foreign firms, to extort better conditions from the suppliers. In a later stage there emerged a single national electrical company in each significant country, with Kraftwerke Union regrouping all production under the leadership of Siemens in Germany and Alsthom-Atlantique in France absorbing the heavy equipment division of Compagnie Electro Mécanique, the Brown Boveri affiliate in France. Similar concentration trends could be observed in the United States, where a duopoly was being established between General Electric and Westinghouse, Allis Chalmers not regaining a prime role, and Babcock failing to meet success with nuclear reactors. Also, in Japan a clear national leader emerged with the presence of Hitachi. Finally, in the United Kingdom there were renewed speculations that Parsons would be merged into GEC.

MARKET EVOLUTIONS AND INTERNATIONAL TRADE

In both industries, markets were affected by the change to new technologies and by a different geographical mix, with more growth to come from the developing areas of the world than from the developed countries of the northern hemisphere. The technological and geographical changes in markets were narrowly intertwined, hence they are better described together, first for electrical power systems and then for telecommunication equipment.

Market Shifts in the
Heavy Electrical Equipment Industry

Average market growth in the developed countries had been slow, and with a few exceptions, was almost negligible in most countries during the 1960s. Steam turbogenerators (both fossil-fueled and nuclear-fueled) had grown substantially, whereas hydraulic turbogenerators and transformers had seen almost no growth, as can be seen from Table 4.4.

On the other hand, markets in developing countries grew rapidly, as can be seen from the differences in the growth rate of installed capacity shown in Table 4.5.

Yet, with the importing countries starting from a very low level, and little trade between developed countries for the reasons detailed in Chapter 3, domestic markets accounted for the bulk of production in Europe, with the exception of water wheels where large markets in developing countries and some specialization in Europe led to higher export shares. (See Table 4.6.)

TABLE 4.4

Selected National Markets for Heavy Electrical Equipment

| | Heavy Electrical Equipment Product Categories | | | | | | | | |
| | Steam Turbogenerators (MWe) | | | Hydro Generators (MWe) | | | Transformers | | |
Country	I	II	III	I	II	III	I	II	III
Austria	69	15	—	112	300	5	1,320	1,307	—
Belgium	304	n.a.	n.a.	30	0	0	1,300	1,769	6
Great Britain	3,136	5,910	10	31	80	neg.	10,000	33,262	8
France	1,005	1,765	15	241	480	neg.	8,350	8,750	0
Germany	1,933	2,175	5	91	165	0	12,200	13,000	0
Italy	1,000	1,250	7	255	181	neg.	1,726	1,700	0
Norway	—	—	0	400	660	5	2,435	2,855	2
Spain	592	900	10	325	450	10	n.a.	n.a.	n.a.
Sweden	325	182	20	293	328	neg.	2,770	3,000	2
Switzerland	140	196	20	134	290	neg.	1,711	1,480	neg.
Japan	3,436	3,870	4	600	790	5	12,500	16,500	6
United States	18,215	19,600	6	2,050	2,017	0	82,000	123,000	7

I = Annual average market size during the period 1955-75.
II = Annual average market size during the period 1965-69.
III = Apparent annual growth rate during 1961-69 (in percent), but may be misleading because of cyclicality.

Note: No data were available on circuit breakers.

Source: A. Surrey, World Market for Electrical Power Equipment (Brighton: University of Sussex, 1972).

91

TABLE 4.5

Growth Rate of Installed Electric Capacity per Country, 1969–73
(Annual average compounded growth rate in MWe, in percent)

	Percent
Producers of heavy electrical equipment	
Austria	6
Canada	7
France	6
Germany	6
India	5
Japan	8
Netherlands	6
Norway	4
Spain	9
Sweden	6
Switzerland	5
United Kingdom	7
United States	7
Nonproducers of heavy electrical equipment	
Africa	
Algeria	8
Angola	8
Egypt	12
Ivory Coast	20
South Africa	9
Nigeria	12
Americas	
Brazil	8
Colombia	10
Mexico	8
Venezuela	7
Asia	
Iran	16
Korea	20
Philippines	12
Saudi Arabia	25
Turkey	9
Europe	
Greece	14
Portugal	7
Other	
Australia	8
New Zealand	7

Source: United Nations Statistical Yearbook, 1974.

TABLE 4.6

Sales by European Manufacturers in the Various Market Areas
(in percent)

	Period and Product		
	1955–75		1965–69,
	Turbogenerators	Water Wheels	Transformer
Domestic	58	35	77.0
European	12	21	5.0
North America	14	15	5.5
Other	16	29	12.5

Source: A. Surrey, World Market for Electrical Power Equipment (Brighton, Sussex: University of Sussex, 1972).

A more detailed analysis of patterns of international trade for turbogenerators (see Table 4.7) shows clearly the great predominance of domestic markets, except for Switzerland (Brown Boveri). It also shows the survival of preferred relationship, with the bulk of British exports going to Australia, Canada, India, and South Africa and that of France to Belgium, Spain, and South Africa in the 1955–75 period. Only Germany's and Switzerland's exports are distributed in a large number of markets.

The oil price increase in late 1973 created a new situation. First, it justified a rapid shift from the smaller fossil-fuel-powered power plants to larger nuclear-powered power plants, even when the former were not fully amortized. This shift was most justified in Europe, with no alternate energy sources. Also, the lesser power of environmentalists in Europe would not entail undue delays. Figure 4.2 shows the changes in turbogenerator sizes taking place in Europe.

If all power plants built in Europe after 1981 were to use nuclear reactors instead of conventional boilers, the domestic markets for power plants below 1,000 MWe in unit power would disappear altogether by 1986. In any case no "medium-sized" nuclear reactors are likely to be built after 1986, dooming the market to the 800 to 1,000 MWe range. Since by 1976 no 1,300 MWe plant was in service yet, and since new power plateaus had entailed considerable teething troubles for most manufacturers and the complete disappearance of some, the effect of the size increase is unclear and difficult to anticipate.

An export market remains for medium-sized turbogenerators in countries with abundant oil and coal. The standard size of conventionally heated plants is 600 MWe. Up to the 1970s, the technological

TABLE 4.7

Turbogenerators Installed: Patterns of International Trade
(MWe between 1955 and 1975)

To	From											Percent Share of Market Imports
	United States	Canada	Great Britain	France	Germany	Italy	Sweden	Switzer-land	Japan	Socialist Countries	Others	
United States	344,221	—	3,368	1,650	1,310	—	121	13,499	110	—	—	5.5
Canada	—	3,811	12,057	—	430	—	—	366	100	—	—	79.0
Austria	—	—	—	—	1,056	—	—	320	—	—	—	100.0
Belgium	—	125	—	3,348	661	—	—	1,321	—	—	250	100.0
Great Britain	—	—	62,379	—	—	—	—	—	—	—	—	0.0
Denmark	—	—	—	—	425	—	449	3,002	—	—	389	100.0
France	—	—	—	17,473	—	—	—	—	—	—	—	0.0
Germany	2,505	—	—	—	36,474	15,189	—	770	—	—	—	2.0
Italy	—	—	210	480	696	—	—	—	—	—	—	20.0
Netherlands	—	—	—	418	3,384	—	544	1,820	—	—	2,256	73.0
Spain	5,357	—	787	1,440	1,675	—	—	1,310	330	—	—	n.a.
Sweden	—	—	792	—	1,191	—	2,982	960	—	—	—	50.0
Switzerland	—	—	—	—	—	—	—	1,038	—	—	—	n.a.
Japan	10,081	0	170	—	525	—	—	—	49,305	—	—	3.0
Latin America	1,412	—	700	66	2,357	443	180	946	—	—	—	n.a.
India	2,380	—	450	280	900	0	—	—	307	1,314	1,410	80.0
South Africa	—	—	3,410	2,100	2,850	—	—	3,190	90	—	—	100.0
Australia	—	—	10,095	—	480	—	180	516	760	—	—	100.0
Asia (rest of)	4,090	—	4,255	600	2,777	—	—	—	3,787	—	—	100.0
Percent export share	7.6	3.3	38.0	39.5	39.6	6.0	33.3	96.6	11.6	n.a.	n.a.	

n.a.: data not available

Source: A. Surrey, World Market for Electrical Power Equipment (Brighton: University of Sussex, 1972).

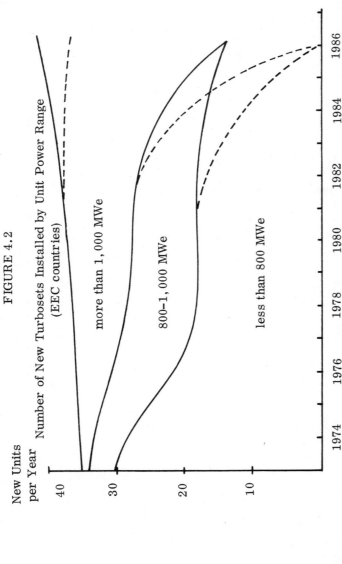

FIGURE 4.2

New Units
per Year   Number of New Turbosets Installed by Unit Power Range
                        (EEC countries)

more than 1,000 MWe

800–1,000 MWe

less than 800 MWe

Note: Dotted lines correspond to a complete shift to nuclear power plants from 1981 onward, considered un-likely, but possible.

Source: Commission of the European Communities, Situation et perspectives des industries des gros equipements electromécaniques et nucleàires liés à la production d'energie de la communauté, SEC(75)2770 (Brussels: Commission of the European Communities, 1975).

95

TABLE 4.8

Size of European National Markets 1970, 1975, and 1980
(in millions of U.S. dollars[a])

Country	Average Growth Rate (percent)	Telecommunications Product Categories																	
		Telephone Sets			PBX Equipment			Main-Exchange Switchgear			Microwave Systems			Modems			Total-by Country		
		70	75	e80	70	75	e80	70	75	e80	70	75	e80	70	75	e80	70	75	e80
Austria	9	3	4	6	3	3	4	29	43	63	1	2	2	1	1	4	36	53	79
Belgium–Luxemburg	8	4	6	8	4	4	5	37	55	79	1	3	2	1	1	5	46	69	99
Denmark	7	3	5	7	4	3	4	32	46	66	1	2	2	–	1	4	40	57	83
France	11	18	26	44	31	37	44	167	350	520	3	7	1	1	7	25	220	366	634
Germany	10	29	55	85	39	37	47	296	500	752	7	6	9	1	12	47	367	610	940
Greece	10	3	5	9	2	3	4	39	59	98	4	6	17	–	1	–	48	74	128
Italy	10	18	29	35	22	18	35	173	300	482	4	7	12	–	3	17	217	357	581
Netherlands	8	7	12	17	5	6	10	62	86	114	2	6	5	–	2	22	76	112	168
Norway	7	2	2	4	2	2	2	16	25	35	1	1	1	–	–	2	21	31	44
Spain	10	11	19	29	7	13	29	100	144	250	4	9	6	–	2	3	122	187	317
Portugal	11	1	2	3	1	1	2	13	21	35	1	1	1	–	1	2	16	26	43
Sweden	6	9	14	19	4	5	8	56	69	78	2	3	4	–	7	24	71	98	133
Switzerland	7	5	8	15	2	3	3	52	70	92	2	4	5	–	–	–	61	85	115
United Kingdom	9	23	31	52	26	26	30	261	430	603	10	11	7	2	24	52	322	522	744
Yugoslavia	18	2	8	24	3	2	2	26	74	134	1	30	12	–	–	1	32	114	173
Total		138	226	357	155	163	229	1,359	2,272	3,401	44	98	86	6	63	208	1,695	2,761	4,281
Annual growth rate[b] (compounded yearly percentages) during preceding 5 years		–	10.5	10.0	–	2.0	7.0	–	10.4	9.0	–	15.0	-1.0	–	-60.0	27.0	–	10.5	9.3

[a]Current dollars adjusted at a discount rate of 3 percent per annum.
[b]All figures are estimates as the exact values of most contracts are seldom made public. Exchange rates used have not been specified.
Note: Figures are generally too conservative and do not take into account the acceleration of equipment programs in 1973-76 in many countries.

Source: National Export Expansion Council, U.S. Department of Commerce, Washington, D.C., 1972.

difficulties and the magnitude of investment had deterred all but the richest and most aggressive developing countries from attempting to manufacture turbogenerators. The possibility of a rapid spread of heavy equipment manufacture is not very likely, but the rapidly growing new markets will in all likelihood require the establishment of plants for lesser capital- and technology-intensive electrical products. With the much higher growth anticipated in electrical power demand in developing countries, this export market is likely to grow, but would increasingly require industrial participation agreements and offsetting imports.

TABLE 4.9

Markets for Electronic Systems, Including the Electronic Parts and Components of Semielectronic Systems, in Europe and Japan in the Telecommunication Equipment Industry

	Europe			Japan		
	1974	1975	1976	1974	1975	1976
Radio communica-tions[a]	517	553	631	347	352	384
PABX and consoles	219	243	302	68	71	70
Main exchanges (MEX)	310	400	585	117	140	172
Carrier and micro-waves	1,017	1,058	1,102	269	332	355
Total	2,063	2,254	2,620	801	895	981
Share of electronics industry sales (percent)	11.25	11.70	12.30	8.5	8.7	8.6
Share of telecom industry (percent)[b]		65			70	

[a]Not normally included among telecommunication products.
[b]Estimate: share for main exchanges is only 12 percent, whereas whereas all microwaves, radio communication, and carrier equipments are electronic.

Source: Electronics, January 8, 1976, p. 98.

Market Evolution in the
Telecommunication Equipment Industry

Growth of the markets for telecommunication equipment was much faster than for electrical power supply systems. Most European annual growth rates in the 1970s were in the 10 percent range, as seen in Table 4.8.

In developed countries the move in telecommunications to electronic technology for main-exchange switching was rapid, as can be seen from Table 4.9; though by 1976 only a small proportion of new exchanges installed was using purely electronic or even SPC technology. The shift was expected to speed up until electronic exchanges accounted for more than half the number of new lines by 1981. France was committed entirely to electronic technology from 1978 onward and Germany had similar plans, whereas the United Kingdom was lingering with semielectronic Crossbar systems.

There were many elements, however, that were working to slow down the change as an industry expert noted:

> Everything will be built from electronic micromodules; industrially it is simpler and makes sense, but the networks are reluctant. The reasons to go to electronic switching have little to do with customers. An electromechanical factory is filthy, smoky and noisy; workers do not want that any more. You also need well-trained people to machine the parts well; you don't find them or they ask huge pay. Our environment has evolved in such a way that, soon, we would not be able to keep such factories operating. The customers are reluctant. The public is used to low-grade service and there is no demand for sophisticated services. An argument is that electronic switching requires 60 percent less maintenance, but how on earth could government agencies, such as PTTs, lay off people? This will slow down the transition; PTTs need to retrain their people, decrease their clerical staffs, find operators for electronic systems. . . . That is going to take time, particularly as PTT executives themselves are still used to thinking electromechanical. From our point of view (that of a supplier) electronic switching is socially easier to manufacture, but the change will be slow.

But despite this dampening factor, the shift was in process toward electronics technology, and by the 1980s main exchanges were to become the major electronic segment of the telecommunication industry.

Similar to power supply systems, trade between developed countries was rather limited, with only a few European countries being

TABLE 4.10

Telecommunication Equipment: Pattern of Trade among Europe, the United States, and Japan, in 1970

From:	Importers											
	Austria	Belgium	Denmark	France	Germany	Italy	Nether-lands	Norway	Spain	Sweden	Switzer-land	United Kingdom
Austria	—	57	—	—	414	51	—	61	—	53	262	111
Belgium	—	—	445	466	4,525	469	12,640	1,078	235	—	815	657
France	—	968	—	—	1,284	477	1,376	239	417	—	73	2,246
Germany	3,933	5,619	6,250	3,629	—	3,028	7,740	2,357	1,577	2,922	4,153	1,693
Italy	285	262	122	1,738	397	—	110	216	1,853	346	409	1,618
Japan	—	146	238	380	638	—	367	91	—	131	199	462
Netherlands	—	660	2,451	837	520	167	—	264	366	431	337	805
Norway	—	—	345	259	256	—	80	—	53	578	71	254
Spain	—	—	—	—	—	—	—	—	—	344	—	60
Sweden	115	216	7,277	635	703	1,920	3,889	1,780	1,206	—	678	1,016
Switzerland	939	70	256	327	204	304	1,447	—	—	508	—	549
United Kingdom	683	101	126	1,141	934	1,917	669	344	436	553	90	—
United States	—	175	108	7,389	1,317	646	1,669	147	2,019	436	428	9,961
Other Countries	—	—	192	—	1,407	71	466	335	147	1,490	35	3,030
Imports volume	5,955	8,274	17,810	16,801	12,599	9,050	30,453	6,912	9,667	7,792	7,510	22,462
Imports as a percentage of domestic markets	15	20	40	8	3	5	40	33	8	11	12	7

Note: All figures include specialized components, parts, and subassemblies.

Source: National Export Expansion Council, U.S. Department of Commerce, Washington, D.C., 1973.

large importers (Denmark and the Netherlands) and Germany being
a large exporter, as shown in Table 4.10.

One of the consequences of the shift to electronic technology was
the opening of many new markets to the electronic switching suppliers.
Low telephone densities in many countries created massive needs for
new equipment. At the same time, suppliers who were converting to
electronic switching were also adopting large-scale expansion plans.
Except in countries that had a clear national champion, these two interests were to come together, leaving the door open for international
suppliers to challenge competitors' positions acquired in the Crossbar era.

The relative size of telecommunications geographic market
areas was also changing, reflecting different growth rates. Table
3.1 showed that whereas the North American market was expected to
grow slowly, the European market would grow moderately (10 percent
per annum), the Asian market markedly (15 percent) and the Latin
American rapidly (26 percent). Table 4.11 portrays the market shift
between 1975 and 1985.

CONCLUSION

The technological evolutions described above, and their economic and industrial consequences, were clearly conflicting with the
patterns of customer-supplier relationships and the means and con-

TABLE 4.11

Relative Importance of Market Areas

Market Area	1975 (Percent)	Number of lines	1985 (Percent)	Number of lines
Europe	54	6,000	37	15,000
Japan	28	3,150	20	8,200
United States	25	2,770	10	3,900
Latin America	10	1,000	20	8,090
Asia	9	1,000	10	3,850
Africa	1	150	3	1,300
Oceania	2	220	1	350

Source: Estimates from various industry sources.

sequences of government interventions that prevailed in both industries. The technological stability provided by long-lasting Strowger and Crossbar technologies and the easy increase in turbogenerator unit power through the addition of compressor stages was ending abruptly. Changes were creating tremendous pressures for integration in power equipment manufacture, and also rather strong pressures in telecommunication equipment. Yet, there was no sign that governments would take a more accommodating attitude and relinquish some of the control they exercised on the industries.

The terms of the conflict were about the same for MNCs and governments alike: political security versus economic performance. Pressures were growing for MNCs to integrate and specialize their operations on a true multinational basis. For governments the trade-off was between supporting "national champions" often too small to compete internationally with much success, and allowing more freedom to MNCs. Various companies and different governments responded differently to the terms of this trade-off. Their responses are analyzed in the following chapter.

NOTES

1. Electronics, December 11, 1975, p. 90.
2. Commission of the European Communities, Situation et perspectives des industries des gros equipements electromécaniques et nucleaires liés à la production d'energie de la communauté, SEC(75)2770 (Brussels: Commission of the European Communities, 1975).
3. Barbara Epstein, Politics of Trade in Power Plants (London: The Atlantic Trade Study, 1971); and company interviews.

5

SUPPLIERS' STRATEGIES:
POLITICAL OR ECONOMIC?

Both the telecommunication equipment and the heavy electrical equipment industries are rather concentrated. In main-exchange switching, four firms supplied 42 percent of the worldwide market. If one leaves aside the U.S. and Japanese markets, 1974 concentration ratios reach 65 percent for four firms in Europe, 83 percent in Latin America, and 49 percent in the Far East (excluding Japan). Similarly (though yearly market shares were not very meaningful), the international power equipment industry was led by a handful of firms: Brown Boveri, ASEA, General Electric (GE), Westinghouse, Siemens (through its subsidiary Kraft Werke Union), and Hitachi. Only General Electric & Company (GEC) and Parsons in the United Kingdom, and Compagnie Generale d'Electronique (through its Alsthom subsidiary) in France also competed internationally with a wide range of electrical products. Both industries thus were clearly oligopolies.

Competitive behavior under oligopolistic conditions has been researched extensively. For instance, Ralph Sultan examined the domestic behavior of U.S. domestic suppliers of heavy electrical equipment. Internationally, in a large sample study of investment patterns by MNCs, Frederick T. Knickerbocker analyzed the competitive behavior of multinationals and the forces leading to investment decisions. Numerous other empirical and theoretical works have dealt with oligopolistic behavior.[1]

The central query in this chapter will be how and why is the behavior observed in this research different from both the studies of domestic oligopolies in the same industry (Sultan) and that of other multinational industries (Knickerbocker). This will also lead to the question of oligopolistic behavior under conditions of government control over markets.

Factual foundations have been laid in Chapter 3 (relationships between customers and suppliers) and Chapter 4 (economics and technology of the products). This chapter will build upon the foregoing to develop an analysis of competition in the two industries.

First, the differences between oligopolistic behaviors described by other researchers and competition in the two industries are reviewed. The French example will be described in some detail. Then, competition in the international telecommunication equipment and electrical power system industries will be analyzed from the perspective of the firms' management: what strategies can be followed, what are their limitations, and enabling conditions.

A FRAGMENTED WORLDWIDE OLIGOPOLY

Market Entry and International Expansion

The most exhaustive study of international oligopolistic competitive behavior is that by Knickerbocker. In simple terms, Knickerbocker links the product life-cycle model developed by Vernon[2] with the observed foreign entry behavior of U.S. firms. In summary, U.S. manufacturing firms devoted much of their energies, starting in the 1850s, to the development, mass manufacture, and mass marketing of goods suited to the U.S. market. As the U.S. mass market was the first to develop, these firms developed capabilities that foreign firms did not have. With some notable exceptions (Siemens in Germany, in particular) this pattern held largely true for the first decades following the invention of the telephone.[3] As supply and demand characteristics in other developed countries began to parallel those in the United States, products designed to satisfy these characteristics became suited for foreign markets. The initial response to this opportunity by U.S. manufacturing enterprises was exporting; they developed large markets abroad. As their products matured, they faced increasing competition. With their exports in jeopardy U.S. companies could, according to Knickerbocker:

1. Abandon the exports of old products in anticipation that the next generation of products would furnish them with a new export base.

2. Rent to foreign producers, by way of licensing agreements that part of their technological expertise not yet widely disseminated. . . and earn some return on their knowledge even if they could no longer exploit their knowledge through exports.

3. Invest in overseas manufacturing plants from which they could supply the threatened markets.[4]

Direct investment abroad also circumvented the obstacles to trade, tariff and nontariff barriers and enabled close relationships between suppliers and customers. Early innovators in both industries thus invested abroad very quickly. Brown Boveri's first foreign sale of a power station to the city of Mannheim, Germany, in 1903 involved a direct investment, first into after-sales service activities, then into manufacturing. Similarly, Siemens rapidly set up its own operations in Russia, and LM Ericsson (created in 1876) immediately started to create subsidiaries. Before World War I, Westinghouse had expanded throughout Europe. National independent companies too were rapidly created in European countries. In some cases patterns of licensing, complemented by minority ownership, developed. For instance, GE, beyond participation in Canada and France (Thomson-Houston Company), entered into agreements with Allgemeine Elektrizitäts Gesellschaft (AEG) in Germany and took a minority equity position in the company in 1904. In a similar vein GE also acquired a minority interest in a Japanese heavy electrical equipment firm, Shibaura, in 1910. Shibaura was controlled by the Mitsui group. GE also had wholly owned subsidiaries in the developing countries (Australia, Mexico, South Africa.)[5]

Knickerbocker has identified a pervasive pattern of "bundling" of investments by firms in a given oligopolistic industry into individual countries. He explains that risk-minimizing strategies of industrial rivals lead them to match their moves. Similar conclusions were reached by Robinson and Aharoni. [6] In both industries studied here, nontariff barriers to trade, and the very nature of the products involved, led to very early investments by product-pioneering firms and the closure of the various national markets to imports by other firms. The type of behavior analyzed by Knickerbocker thus does not apply to market entry and foreign investments in the industries studied here. After the very first foreign entries during the emergence of both industries, a pattern developed: acquisitions in mature markets, direct investments in newer markets.

With the exception of LM Ericsson and Siemens, early entries into the telecommunication industry in developed countries were by way of acquisition. For instance, almost all the European telecommunication equipment subsidiaries of ITT had been independent national companies prior to their acquisition by International Western Electric, which subsequently was sold to ITT. Similarly, Philips entered the industry by acquisitions. Siemens's Dutch subsidiary was seized and nationalized at the end of World War II. After a few years the government asked Philips to operate it, and finally sold it to Philips. Philips then acquired majority control of a smaller German telecommunication equipment firm, Felter & Guillaume. Philips also took control of Pye in the United Kingdom in the 1960s. The acquisition of a going company, already enjoying good and close relationships with its PTT administration, provided about the only means to penetrate mature national markets in a major way. Of course, nothing prevented a company from starting on its own, but its chances of breaking into the main-exchange switching market were slim. For instance, Philips set up a plant in Brazil, but could not get government contracts despite continuous efforts. Conversely, IBM, followed by others, was highly successful in the private switching market in Europe (in particular with its 3750 electronic PABX), but was careful not to try to extend its entry to public switching systems. As was seen in Chapter 3, LM Ericsson managed to enter the British market in the 1970s, but only because of the poor performance of existing local suppliers, and it ultimately had to ally itself with Thorn Electric, a local British firm, and manufacture equipment in the United Kingdom. LM Ericsson also managed to enter Spain, at the invitation of the government, to break the monopoly enjoyed by ITT in that country.

In the power system industry the same acquisition-only entry route dominated as early as the immediate post-World War I years with the participation of Brown Boveri in Compagnie Electro Mécanique in France. In 1929 GE acquired Metropolitan Vickers (which had acquired Westinghouse's U.K. plants after World War I) and merged it into a new GE-controlled group, Associated Electrical Industries (AEI). GE also increased its stakes in AEG in Germany but pledged to the government not to take majority control.

By the 1960s opportunities for acquisitions were drying up. One of the last major acquisitions was that of Ateliers de Constructions Electriques de Charleroi (ACEC) in Belgium by Westinghouse. What could be seen were transfers of ownership of already multinationally owned operations, for instance, LM Ericsson replacing GTE as Thorn Electric's joint venture partner in the United Kingdom. Only marginal operations could be acquired, and only by smaller MNCs not yet well implanted.

Entry was still possible in newer markets, provided the initial imports were accompanied by a commitment to local manufacture. One notable exception was Saudi Arabia, short on manpower but rich in foreign exchange, which bought more than a billion dollars worth of equipment and services from a trinational consortium (made up of Philips, LM Ericsson, and the Canadian Bell) without requesting local production. Rivalry between multinational companies often played a key role in precipitating entries into smaller markets in the hope that future developments would justify the investment ultimately. Few companies went to the extreme of Philips in Brazil (setting up a plant without any guarantee that it would not remain idle), but most were willing to carry the cost of early, scattered overcapacity. In some cases, when things did not work out, such facilities were closed (an LM Ericsson subsidiary's assembly plant in Singapore); in some others, rapid development permitted companies to recoup early losses (GTE and ITT in Korea); and in many cases the operation led to longer-term indifferent results.

In the initial contracts in new markets, worldwide oligopolistic behavior is clearly displayed. Competition takes place head-on among a few multinational suppliers. Price and product advantages are important mostly at that early stage, and this is where the behavior of companies can most closely approximate that in a domestic competitive oligopoly. Beyond that first entry stage, industry structure and firms' behaviors are more constrained.

Industry Structure Within Individual Countries

At the national market level in a developed country a typical oligopoly structure usually prevails, with up to four firms covering all segments of the industry. Often two of these firms are subsidiaries of international groups and two are independent domestic firms. The market share mix varies between countries, but usually a leading firm controls about 50 percent of the market for switching equipment, the others competing for the remaining 50 percent. Table 5.1 shows the distribution of main-exchange switching market shares in selected countries.

Market shares are allocated by the PTTs according to contracts. Price is usually not a competitive tool within a country, as prices are usually decided by the PTT and applied equally to all suppliers. Some price variation is possible, but only through indirect means such as quantity discounts. Price pressures or opportunistic pricing are not possible, at least not directly.[7] All companies are treated equally.

Yet the structure of each national market is such that the international companies have major advantages. In Western Europe, with the exception of Germany, national leaders such as CIT-Alcatel or SIT are relatively inefficient companies, lacking the experience necessary to achieve low-cost production and lacking international activities to spread the costs of product development. Public ownership in the case of SIT (through IRI), and dependence upon government policies in all cases, usually means that prices are set at levels that enable these weak national competitors to prosper. For instance, the respective labor productivity ratios of Italian suppliers are FATME (subsidiary of LME)—11; CTE—10.7; SIT—8.6. The market share of SIT, however, was larger than that of the other suppliers. Similarly, extraordinarily high prices in France had permitted CIT-Alcatel to be prosperous and ITT to make a fortune. By nurturing and protecting a local national supplier, some European countries provide the international companies with still higher earnings.

In developing countries and less mature markets, somewhat similar market structures have prevailed, with the dominant supplier usually being an MNC subsidiary. All suppliers are most often multinational subsidiaries.

TABLE 5.1

Main-Exchange Switching Market Shares in Selected Countries

	Company	Percent
Developed Countries		
Austria	ITT	25
	Siemens	25
	Sohne & Schrak[a]	50
Belgium	ITT	80
	GTE	20
Denmark	LME	70
	Siemens	22
	ITT	6
Finland	LME	76
	Siemens	17
	ITT	6
France	CIT-Alcatel[a]	43
	ITT[b]	41
	LME[b]	16
West Germany	Siemens[a]	55
	ITT	23
	TUN[a]	23
Italy	SIT[a]	54
	LME	18
	ITT	15
	GTE	13
Netherlands	Philips[a]	50
	LME	25
	ITT	25
Portugal	ITT	51
	Plessey	49
Spain	ITT	83
	LME	17
Sweden	STA[a]	50
	LME[a]	50
Switzerland	Hassler[a]	50
	ITT	30
	Plessey	20
United Kingdom	Plessey[a]	42
	GEC[a]	38
	ITT	20

(continued)

TABLE 5.1 (continued)

	Country	Percent
Developing Countries		
Latin America		
Argentina	ITT[b]	60
	Siemens	40
Brazil	LME	58
	ITT[b]	28
	Nippon	5
	Siemens	5
	Plessey	5
Colombia	LME	72
	GEC	13
	Siemens	10
	ITT	5
Mexico	LME	80
	ITT	20
Peru	ITT[b]	75
	Philips	25
Venezuela	LME	38
	ATE	30
	Siemens	24
	ITT	8
Others		
South Africa	Plessey	50
	GEC	31
	Siemens	18
Iran	GTE	87
	ITT	8
	Siemens	5

[a]Denotes locally independent companies.

[b]Denotes former subsidiaries of main international companies; these subsidiaries are in the process of becoming joint ventures in which national interests hold the majority of shares or complete control of some subsidiaries.

Note: Some market shares are estimates from various industry sources. Though the shares could vary from year to year in each country, the estimates above reflect representative values for the mid-1970s. Market shares below 10 percent usually reflect follow-up and expansion orders from previous suppliers, but not a strong position in the country. Measurement was made as a percentage of newly installed lines in main-exchange offices, irrespective of the technology.

Source: Compiled by the author.

TABLE 5.2

Some Significant Telecommunication Equipment Contracts

Firm	Country	Amount (in million dollars)	Equipment
Western Electric and Collins Radio	Saudi Arabia	408	Microwave network
Northern Telecom	Turkey	170	Components for 800,000 lines of switching capacity and 750,000 sets
Philips, LM Ericsson, Bell Canada	Saudi Arabia	3,000*	470,000 lines of switching capacity, and assembly and installation. Start-up assistance
Nippon Electric	Libya	105	Microwave system (5,000 km links between major cities)
ITT	Korea	100	Metaconta switches and setup of factory with 650,000 lines per year capacity in 1985
CIT-Alcatel	Ivory Coast	10	20,000 lines of time-divided switching capacity and installation

*Approximately.

Source: Compiled by the author from interviews and various issues of Electronic News.

TABLE 5.3

Typical Industry Structure Patterns

	Share (in percent)
Mature Markets	
Leading MNC subsidiary, operationally autonomous, highly efficient, highly profitable	+50
Following MNC subsidiary	+25
National supplier inefficient, low profits, licensee of MNC	+25
New Markets	
Leading MNC subsidiary (first in, originally), operationally dependent on MNC center, but local decision centers. Efficient and profitable if national market is large enough.	+60
Several marginal MNC subsidiaries used by the	+15
government to maintain pressure on leading	+15
MNC	+10

Source: Compiled by the author.

During the formative stages of a national industry, prices and financing conditions are extremely important. Whereas in mature markets contracts are mostly private and are allocated to existing suppliers on a routine basis, in new markets public tender offers are preferred most often. Few companies have the capacity to put together thorough proposals and to make firm commitments on price, delivery dates, and reliability. As we have seen, most contracts are conditional upon the establishment of a manufacturing subsidiary. Contracts are usually large in amounts as is evident in Table 5.2.

Once the local industry is established, competitive patterns become increasingly similar to those in mature markets, particularly as the national subsidiaries become more self-sufficient.

In summary, industry structure patterns at the national level can be sketched as in Table 5.3.

In some cases companies use various product lines to satisfy host country desires for local manufacture and balanced trade. For instance, GTE assembled PABXs in Latin American countries, both as a means to offset imports of main-exchange switching equipment into these countries and as a way to provide low-labor-cost sourcing for its equipment. As PABXs were often sold to commercial-end users, GTE could import them into the United States and Western Europe for sale there. In some cases only components were made at certain locations. LM Ericsson farmed out the assembly of all connectors (a very labor-intensive process) to its Ecuadorian subsidiary and was allowed to import switching equipment made in Sweden into Ecuador.

This pattern of compensation between product lines within smaller developing countries was even more prevalent in the heavy electrical equipment industry. There was no way for smaller countries to manufacture turbogenerators or other heavy equipment, but MNCs could farm out less scale-constrained activities. For instance, Brown Boveri had a light-to-medium transformer affiliate in Peru from which both the domestic Peruvian market and export sales were served. Similarly, Brown Boveri could set up small equipment (small motors, switches, contactors, and so forth) plants in developing countries to offset heavy equipment imports. Such actions were also carried out in smaller developed countries when necessary. For instance, Brown Boveri took over an ailing electrical motor company in Canada in order to help sales of large turbogenerators.

In summary, there was not always a direct correspondence between market structure and local manufacturing in smaller and developing countries. Yet, in almost all cases, offsetting manufacturing facilities were required. The only exceptions were a few oil-rich, population-scarce countries in the Middle East that were content with straight import contracts.

Market Exits and Nationalizations

There are few examples of voluntary market exits from the telecommunication industry. However, the delicate evolution of any given national market over time, from the initial imports to the maturing of an industry, created enough tensions for forced divestments to be frequent. The basic thrust is for individual countries to expropriate foreign companies once their subsidiaries are mature enough for self-sufficient operations. Table 5.4 presents some significant divestments.

In the long run, the trend is toward increasing pressures for national ownership and control in both industries. In that regard, the French example is instructive for both industries.

After decades of neglect the French government finally decided to improve the telephone system; telephones in France were a major public laughingstock. For a variety of political and administrative reasons whose origins dated back to the early twentieth century, the

TABLE 5.4

Significant Recent Divestitures by MNCs

Company	Country	Year	Divestiture
ITT	Brazil	1975	Majority ownership transferred to Brazilian interests.
ITT	Chile	1972	Nationalized.
ITT	France	1976	Majority ownership of one subsidiary transferred to Thomson CSF, a local French electronics company.
ITT	Argentina	1976	Majority ownership transferred to Argentinian interests.
ITT	Mexico	1974	Nationalized.
LM Ericsson	United Kingdom	1948	Sold to British group. Bought by Plessey in 1962.
Brown Boveri	India	1970s	Reduction of ownership to a minority interest (23 percent).
Brown Boveri-CEM	France	1977	Transfer of one division (turbogenerators) to French national company Alsthom-Atlantique.

Source: Nicolas Jequier, Les Telecommunications et l'Europe (Geneva, Switzerland: Centre d'Etudes Industrielles, 1976); and author's industry interviews.

TABLE 5.5

French Telephone Network Expansion Plan, 1974-78

Year	Number of New Lines	Approximate Budgetary Appropriations (in billions of dollars)
1974	580,000	2.0
1975	875,000	3.0
1976	1,300,000	4.0
1977	1,550,000	4.2
1978	1,550,000	4.2

Source: Ministry of Post and Telecommunications, Paris.

telephone system was hopelessly inefficient. [8] To remedy such a situation, drastic efforts were called for. Over a period of five years (1974-78) it was decided to reduce the average waiting period for telehpone installation from 15 months to 15 days. This required a major reequipment effort, as shown in Table 5.5

In the preliminaty analyses the problems were quickly defined in terms of: employment (to create 14,000 jobs in the telephone operating administration and 60,000 jobs in equipment manufacturing); new technology (electronic systems); export sales (after a series of failures to win major international contracts); and termination of the quota system (a priori allocation of market shares among the suppliers). A number of critics had accused the administration of collusion with the manufacturers in maintaining artificially high prices. The Centre National d'Etude des Telecommunications (CNET), a state-owned nonprofit research center, was entirely reorganized in 1974 following this allegation. Among other tasks, CNET had been in charge of price and cost control.

Aymar Achille-Fould, minister of posts and telecommunications (P&T), explained in an interview:

> We are trying to build for the P&T a new industrial policy
> to meet the challenge of the new demand. I am going to
> receive proposals for new groups [in answer to a request
> sent to all manufacturers for expansion proposals]. I am
> looking for industrial groups that have the following
> strengths: a technical competence, a satisfactory equity
> base, policy centers in France, a potential for design
> and manufacture of modern switching systems both for
> domestic and export markets, and the ability to com-
> pete successfully against other large international cor-
> porations. . . .
> The objective is to give the groups that constitute
> our national industry the opportunity to ally themselves,
> technically and financially, with foreign corporations
> that would be complementary. . . . I have mentioned
> the importance of decision centers previously. It is
> essential in order for our industries not to be prevented
> from competing internationally, that such decision cen-
> ters be located in France. . . . When the various in-
> dustrial schemes are proposed by the manufacturers,
> we shall judge which ones we find the best from the point
> of view of public service. [9]

Up to 1975, three companies had provided the bulk of P&T's needs: ITT, through several subsidiaries; LM Ericsson; and a subsidiary of the French Compagnie Générale d'Electricité (CGE) called CIT-Alcatel. ITT had been very successful in France and accounted for two-thirds of the French exports of telecommunication equipment. Its domestic market share was 43 percent, compared with 32 percent for CIT-Alcatel and 17 percent for Société Française des Téléphones Ericsson (SFTE).

During the summer of 1975 no less than six industrial group proposals surfaced. [10]

1. Thomson-CSF, in cooperation with Northern Telecom (Bell of Canada), wanted to make a comeback into that market after its ill-fated noncompetition agreements with CGE in 1969.

2. CGE complemented its agreements with Plessey by a flirtation with Nippon Electric Company.

3. TRT, the subsidiary of NV Philips, promised to transfer the headquarters of NV Philips telecommunication groups from Holland to France in exchange for a (large) piece of the action. Among other things, French insistence on a "francisation" of the management of all Philips companies in France led to the collapse of the offer. Moreover, some industry experts suggested that Philips's technology was not fully competitive with that of some other suppliers.

4. SFT proposed the nex AXE system developed in Sweden, and offered to cooperate further with CGE, with whom it already had a joint venture for a time-divided switching system, and with whom it jointly manufactured electronic components and relays.

5. SAT, a smaller French company offered to manufacture foreign equipment under license.

6. ITT, through its twin subsidiaries, Le Matériel Téléphonique (LMT) and Compagnie Générale de Constructions Téléphoniques (CGCT), offered an LMT-designed Metaconta electronic switching system with a French-made central processor (to be purchased from the French EDP industry).

Late in 1975, following a meeting chaired by President Valery Giscard d'Estaing, information leaked out: Three systems had been selected. First, the time-divided systems built by CGE's CIT-Alcatel would be continued and their use expanded. Second, ITT's LMT-Metaconta was selected, along with Ericsson's SFTE system (called AXE). It was very significant for these manufacturers to be selected, as their systems were almost untested and being selected in a major country such as France (among several competitors) was a key reference for further sales.

It then became obvious that the government had decided to reap as much advantage as possible from the power of allocating the orders. After protracted negotiations with the companies involved, the final arrangements were made known in June 1976.

FIGURE 5.1

Participation in the French Telephone Industry

Prior to 1976

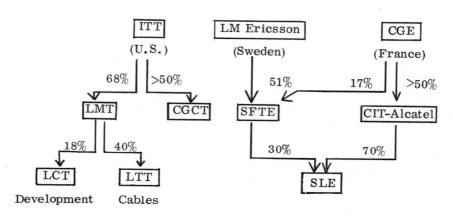

After 1976

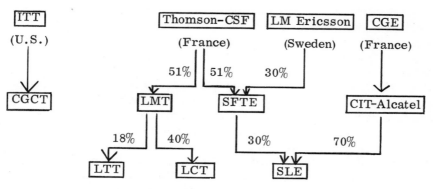

LMT: Le Matériel Téléphonique
CGE: Compagnie Générale d'Electricité
CGCT: Compagnie Générale de Constructions Téléphonique
SFTE: Société Française des Téléphones Ericsson
SLE: Société Laonnaise d'Electronique

Note: Figure may be slightly inaccurate as the situation has been evolving over time, but it depicts well the overall nature of the change; all percentage figures mean ownership of equity.

Source: Compiled by the author from published information.

Thomson-CSF was to buy (for $160 million) ITT's 68 percent share in the equity of LMT. The other ITT subsidiary in France (CGCT) was unaffected but would only receive orders for the older, less-advanced Crossbar systems. Thomson-CSF would also reduce the share of LM Ericsson in the equity of SFTE to a minority position by acquiring directly 16 percent of the equity from LM Ericsson, buying another 18 percent on the open market, and another 17 percent from CGE. Thus Thomson-CSF became the major telecommunications company in France. A clear leader corresponding to each switching technology emerged:

(1) conventional crossbar equipment—ITT;
(2) space-divided electronic equipment—Thomson-CSF and
(3) time-divided electronic equipment—CGE-CIT-Alcatel.

Both ITT and LM Ericsson would provide Thomson-CSF with the technology necessary to manufacture the Metaconta and the AXE, respectively.

Through this move the French government put the ownership of the national industry clearly in local hands as depicted in Figure 5.1.

Some difficulties later developed. In particular, SFTE had considerable losses and an argument developed between Thomson-CSF and LM Ericsson on the valuation of the company. SFTE's management was charged with excessively liberal accounting procedures, and LM Ericsson finally agreed to share SFTE's losses. The French group, Thomson-CSF, also faced tough export difficulties. After the initial surge in domestic demand, Thomson-CSF would be plagued by substantial excess capacity in the 1980s unless it found substantial export markets. As we have seen, export markets are quite limited and lead very quickly to local manufacturing commitments. Also, Thomson-CSF could hardly compete against LM Ericsson and ITT on export markets as it offered similar equipment at a higher price and without the long-term technological development guarantees and the far-reaching installation experience of the leading multinationals. These, however, had lost the very profitable French market.

Similarly, Brown Boveri and Westinghouse had to realign their activities in France. In 1968 Westinghouse wanted to buy from Baron Empain (through the holding company Electrorail in Belgium) a controlling interest in Jeumont Schneider. Jeumont Schneider was important, not only because of its experience in the heavy metallurgical field (it had been the major gun barrel and armor plates supplier to the French army) but also because it held the Westinghouse license for pressurized water reactors. This was done through a subsidiary, Framatome, 30 percent of whose equity was owned by Jeumont Schneider directly, and another 22 percent indirectly through a holding

company called Schneider S. A. The remainder of Framatome's
equity was owned by Creusot Loire, itself a merger from two old,
respectable, French metallurgy firms, Forges et Ateliers du Creusot
and Chantiers et Forges de la Loire. Creusot Loire was itself 50 percent owned by Schneider S. A. , and thus by Empain. The French government first delayed the acquisition of Jeumont Schneider by Westinghouse. In the meantime, Westinghouse bought from Empain the
Ateliers de Constructions Electriques de Charleroi in Belgium.

In 1969 Westinghouse appointed Louis Armand to head its European operations. Louis Armand was the honorary president of the
French national railroad (SNCF), a former chairman of Euratom,*
and a French academician. After negotiations between Louis Armand
and top French government officials (Valery Giscard d'Estaing and
Francois Xavier Ortoli, then minister of finance and minister of industry, respectively), Westinghouse let it be known that it would be
content with a minority interest in Jeumont Schneider, and hence
would not acquire the full 60 percent of equity Empain was willing to
sell. The issue was further complicated as the French government
simultaneously dropped the all-French graphite-gas natural uranium
reactor technology in favor of enriched uranium light-water reactors
of the types engineered by Westinghouse and General Electric.

EdF, the French national electrical utility, also let it be known
that the French heavy electrical equipment was too fragmented.
"Prices are too high and production inefficient, " argued EdF. EdF
thus would have preferred to have only two suppliers: (1) a French
group built around Alsthom that would have acquired Jeumont Schneider and Merlin-Gerin (a producer of breakers and transformers) to
compete across the board; Jeumont Schneider making nuclear reactors and steam supply systems under Westinghouse licenses, Alsthom
making primarily turbogenerators and Merlin-Gerin distribution
equipment and (2) Compagnie Electro Mecanique, affiliated with
Brown Boveri and taking full advantage of Brown Boveri's technology.

In December 1969 a majority of government members decided
not to authorize Westinghouse's planned purchase of a minority interest in Jeumont Schneider. In early 1970 a Westinghouse attempt at
resuming negotiations failed, and for two years Empain remained the
holder of Jeumont Schneider. In early 1972, F. X. Ortoli reopened

---

*Euratom was an EEC institution setup in 1958 to coordinate
the nuclear energy research and production programs of the EEC
member countries. Its early years had been very successful. When
the industrial stakes of nuclear energy became high, national policies
diverged and Euratom lost its key role in pioneering civilian nuclear
research in Europe.

"peace" negotiations with Westinghouse. A bargaining round took place, in which the following points emerged:

1. Framatome was confirmed as the main contractor for French pressurized-water reactors, but orders were to be split between Framatome and a Compagnie Générale d'Electricité subsidiary licensed by the U.S. General Electric to use the rival boiling water technology.
2. Framatome became an industrial company, with Creusot Loire transferring its heavy metallurgy works to Framatome. A new reactor assembly yard was to be established. Westinghouse ordered one reactor vessel from Framatome (for installation in Puerto Rico) and hinted at further orders.
3. Westinghouse subscribed to an equity issue by Framatome. As a result the ownership of Framatome became: Creusot Loire—51 percent (after transferal of the metallurgy works); Westinghouse—45 percent (after renewal of the license until 1982); and Schneider—4 percent.

In 1973 orders were placed by EdF with both Framatome and CGE (which had set up a subsidiary, called SOGERCA, to handle nuclear reactor work that was completely subcontracted to other companies, SOGERGA acting as an engineering firm only). In late 1973 Empain bought substantial blocks of shares of Marine Firminy, another shareholder of Jeumont Schneider. [11]

In the meantime it became clear that Westinghouse would not be able to honor the fixed-priced enriched uranium contracts it had entered into with U.S. utilities. In early 1974, following the oil crisis, the French government embarked upon a crash nuclear energy program and ordered 12 reactors from Framatome, with another 4 on option. In April 1974 Framatome began constructing a new assembly yard and proposed building nuclear reactors for exports to Iran, Korea, South Africa, and Brazil. In the spring of 1975, 4 more reactors were ordered by EdF. By then, the state nuclear research institute (CEA) had developed its own very successful small-scale pressurized-water reactor and demonstrated its performance by using it as the power unit of the new ballistic-missile-carrying submarines introduced by the French navy as a component of the nuclear deterrence force. All through the 1973-75 period, Westinghouse evinced great interest in French nuclear enrichment plans and declared itself willing to buy enriched uranium from the proposed "Eurodif" plant. *

---

*Eurodif is a company set up to produce enriched uranium using the gaseous diffusion process. The plant is being built in Tricastin

Finally, in 1975 the government launched a new round of restructuring. First, with growing opposition by environmental groups and local authorities, and with the height of the oil crisis receding into memories, the nuclear reactor construction program was slowed down to four or five units per year instead of the seven targeted in 1974. Given this rollback, the slow progress of SOGERCA on boiling-water reactors, and the high prices demanded by CGE, it was decided to concentrate all orders on Framatome and the Westinghouse technology. However, as a compensation, CGE was given all orders for turbogenerators, thus depriving Jeumont Schneider of its natural market. Empain was thus gaining through his 50 percent direct interest in Creusot Loire and his interest in Marine Firminy (about 30 percent), which in turn owned the other 50 percent of Creusot Loire. Jeumont Schneider, however, was losing its turbogenerator business.

Westinghouse's share in the equity of Framatome was reduced to 15 percent, the CEA buying 30 percent of the equity from Westinghouse. The CEA and Westinghouse agreed to share the results of their research on light-water reactors. (The research budget of CEA is about three times larger than Westinghouse's, but is spread over more different technologies and research domains.) By 1982, a new technical agreement will replace the licenses. It can incorporate new license agreements or be a cooperation protocol, possibly covering fast-breeder reactors—where CEA is a leader. [12]

The last part of the restructuring scheme was to regroup the heavy equipment division of Compagnie Electro-Mécanique (CEM) with Alsthom to make a single large French group in the turbogenerator market. Early negotiations in 1975 failed and in early 1976 Alsthom merged with the Chantiers de l'Atlantique, a successful, cash-rich, shipbuilding firm willing to diversify into other heavy metallurgy businesses and away from the declining shipbuilding industry.

The leadership role was taken by the Ministry of Industry, concerned about the ability of the industry to reach the 1,800 MWe power level and maintain production efficiencies. The ministry prevented EdF from signing further orders before a commitment to a "rapprochement" was forthcoming from the companies. The CEM management and Brown Boveri were more in favor of a link with Creusot Loire and Jeumont Schneider. This would have created a foreign company stronger than Alsthom Atlantique on the French market, an unacceptable solution to the Ministry of Industry, particularly as Creusot

---

(France) and scheduled to go on stream in 1980. The plant will serve the needs of various national utilities. Eurodif's ownership is multinational: France—37.5 percent; Italy—22.5 percent; Iran—20 percent; Belgium—10 percent; and Spain—10 percent.

Loire (through Framatome) already enjoyed a monopoly for the nuclear vessel core and steam supply systems.

Finally, in late 1976, CEM agreed to the scheme and transferred its turbogenerator business to Alsthom Atlantique in exchange for a 6 percent equity interest in the company. Alsthom Atlantique also accepted all liabilities from the turbogenerator business of CEM, which carried heavy long-term debts. Financially, the operation was thus rather satisfactory for CEM and its major shareholder, BBC.

These French examples have been described at some length as they illustrate the limits to the strategic freedom of MNCs active in the telecommunication and power system industries. It is also clear that by dealing with MNCs when they were weak the French government could get substantial benefits. In 1976 both LM Ericsson and ITT needed electronic switchgear orders by a major PTT administration to use as further reference.* Westinghouse became increasingly accommodating as (1) the French market for nuclear reactors grew bigger; (2) CEA's own research made progress and CEA emerged as a leader for future commercial fast-breeder technology; (3) Westinghouse, embroiled in the legal and financial consequences of the fixed-price enriched uranium supply contracts made in the late 1960s, became more short of cash; and (4) as the French encouraged CGE and SOGERCA as alternate light-water reactor suppliers. In the dealings with CEM, the exercise of power was even more straightforward: the threat of cutting off all turbogenerator orders, whether or not CEM merged its turbogenerator division with that of Alsthom Atlantique.

These examples of forced market exit by MNCs in France could be complemented by many others. The experience of Westinghouse with Siemens and Kraft Werke Union (KWU) in Germany appears even less rewarding than the participation in Framatome. Since 1970 Siemens (and its subsidiary, KWU) has freed itself from the Westinghouse licenses by making modification to pressurized-light-water technologies. Siemens is now competing very successfully against the U.S. nuclear reactor suppliers. Similarly, the international telecommunication equipment suppliers are being ejected from Brazil. Other comparable examples could be drawn from a number of different countries.

----

*Airbus Industries found itself in a similar position in 1976-77, desperately wooing Eastern Airlines to get an order that could then be used as a reference (up to 1976, the only major airlines to have bought the Airbus A300 were Air France and Lufthansa, both heavily encouraged by their governments). Eastern could extol extremely favorable financing conditions from Airbus Industries.

The examples above also evidence why, in any given national market, the behavior of MNC subsidiaries (or, for that matter, domestic companies) cannot even approximate the conventional oligopoly models. Yet it remains that within the constraints that governments put on market entry and means of entry and competitive behavior within national markets, and taking into account the risks of forced market exit, a small group of large MNCs compete for the dominant share of the world market. The second half of this chapter deals with worldwide competition, given the rules prevalent and the specific difficulties faced in each national market.

WORLDWIDE COMPETITION

As was seen in the previous section, the competition for the market of any particular country has been shaped by the maturity of that market and the respective sources of bargaining strength available to MNC suppliers and host governments, particularly in terms of market size and technology.

Any MNC thus had to cope with wide diversity between national markets and with the changes in technology. Let us see how diversity among markets and technology changes constrained the strategies of companies. Concrete examples will be used again rather than abstract reasoning.

Market Maturity

With a few exceptions, it was impossible to penetrate mature, well-established markets (except for the United States for power equipment, and the subscriber equipment and private-exchange markets in European countries and the United States). Moreover, the economic imperative's growing pressures for integration and rationalization, and the resulting tendency for governments to foster national consolidations, would make the penetration of markets even more difficult. These same pressures also made it more difficult for MNCs to stay in their existing markets.

Leading, well-established MNCs (those with larger market shares in mature markets) could more easily withstand the rationalization pressures and also find such a route more rewarding. As long as their subsidiaries could maintain a leading role in their respective markets, provide a high degree of responsiveness to local policies, and remain more economically efficient than national companies, their position was relatively safe. Thus, maintaining one's position in existing markets requires a special behavior, guided by responsiveness to local policies and the constant mending of status quo-oriented coalitions with powerful local interests and government agencies. The maintenance of such coalitions and the ability to respond to local needs are enhanced by a lack of integration, that is, by making each national company a relatively autonomous unit.

The scale of the MNC could help the efficiency of its subsidiaries in terms of production in two ways (beyond the pooling of risks), assuming these subsidiaries were entirely autonomous and separate. First, if the company could maintain a sufficiently similar technology in its various operations and avoid duplications of development efforts, it could spread its total R&D costs over a larger base. Coordination and specialization of R&D was one requirement, and various practical arrangements were possible. ITT, in developing the Metaconta electronic switching system, had allocated two responsibilities to each national subsidiary: (1) the engineering leadership for one aspect of the project and (2) the adaptation of all aspects of the project to national specifications and interface characteristics in its own country. A less closely integrated way of allocating work was to make each subsidiary responsible for a particular product line, as was done by Philips Telecommunication Industries: one country would handle all relay work, another all mobile radio development, a third wholly electronic set development, and so on. The disadvantage of this system, as compared with ITT's, was that it did not easily offer the flexibility to involve several locations in the same project. For instance, in the mid-1970s all governments wanted to support the development of optical fibers and other optoelectronic devices, and were willing to grant development subsidies. But a company such as Philips could easily take advantage of such outside assistance in one country only— that wherein its optoelectronics lab happened to be located unless it accepted major reallocations of development and production responsibilities among its national subsidiaries.

The second important advantage that multinationality could bring was the availability of a larger export network than a single national company could maintain or exploit fully. First, the sheer size of the operations could justify the maintenance of sales subsidiaries, regional offices, experienced intermediaries, competent installation and service teams, and large project proposal preparation staffs. That alone could increase the overall "take" of the MNC on the world's new markets and hence, at least in the short run, the export volumes of its subsidiaries. Furthermore, the availability of several sources for rather similar equipment was often a tremendous "plus" for MNCs. This enabled the MNC to adjust better to shifting diplomatic or cultural affinities. For instance, in 1974-75 ITT was negotiating a large contract with Algeria. First it negotiated out of France because that was a logical place to start for reasons of language and experience, as the French subsidiaries of ITT had set up the telephone system in Algeria when it was still a French colony. In 1975 the relationships between France and Algeria had greatly deteriorated over issues of trade balance, immigration, and, above all, over the future of Spanish Sahara. On that issue, France sided with Morocco against Algeria. Spain, concerned by Morocco's expansion, sided with Algeria. ITT also wanted to demonstrate its goodwill to the Spanish government, which had recently invited LM Ericsson to compete against ITT. The center of negotiations thus shifted to Spain. After the contract had been concluded, and as relationships between France and Algeria improved somewhat, it was decided that some of the equipment as well as technical support would be provided from France. By then, ITT was negotiating with France over the future of its subsidiaries there.

In summary, established market leaders in large, mature, well-developed Western European countries had good reasons to let their subsidiaries behave as domestic companies in the eyes of their respective host governments, but to centrally coordinate both R&D and export sales. This was the policy followed by ITT in telecommunication equipment and Brown Boveri in power equipment. To some extent other companies followed similar policies. For instance, direction and control from Stockholm over LM Ericsson's subsidiaries in France and Italy were minimal, almost nonexistent.

In new markets very different rules prevail, as was seen in Chapter 3. There, overall economic efficiency, leading to low-cost dependable equipment, is critically important. Initial entry into a market is usually achieved on price-performance levels, other factors being equal. Expansion and development in a market as it matures is usually a result of local adaptation and responsiveness.

In short, as a market matures over time, the way in which a subsidiary in this market can be managed has to change. LM Ericsson's management had developed a classification for its foreign subsidiaries that recognized this evolution of the management of the subsidiary.* There were three categories of subsidiaries according to the assistance received from corporate headquarters:

1. Category I covered smaller plants built in response to government demands in order to sell equipment in a new market. These plants normally did final assembly and wiring jobs on kits imported

---

*Purists might want to make a distinction between market maturity and subsidiary maturity. Though this is a sound a priori distinction, it is not justified empirically. Given the early investment demands made by developing countries, market motivation and subsidiary motivation proceed together in all but a few cases.

from Sweden. These jobs were entirely manual and not subject to economies of scale. They were managed from Stockholm.

2. Plants in category II were generally of medium size (200 to 1,000 employees) and corresponded to a transfer-of-technology period. A plant moved into category II when it started manufacturing mechanical parts and assembling the bulk of the exchange. A number of technical experts were sent from Sweden in that phase, but the supply responsibility and the general management function were assumed locally. Whereas quality was stressed in category I, plants in category II put emphasis upon timely delivery and efficient scheduling.

3. Category III plants belonged to mature companies and usually had an almost complete manufacturing process, importing only a few components from Sweden. The emphasis was on cost reduction, but assistance from Sweden was minimal except when new products or processes were introduced.

4. Finally, plants in France and Italy operated entirely independently of Stockholm.

After LM Ericsson had used its perfection of the Crossbar technology to penetrate the rapidly growing Latin American markets in the post-World War II period, most of its subsidiaries had gone through the various stages up to category III. LM Ericsson thus found itself in the same position in Latin America as had ITT in Europe. Yet it differed from ITT in two key respects: (1) with one exception (relays from France), all LM Ericsson's exports came from Sweden, not from the affiliated companies and (2) almost all R&D efforts were carried out in Sweden, again with a few exceptions such as marine (shipboard) telephone systems in the Netherlands.

Companies active in well-developed mature markets tended to pursue political strategies maximizing sociopolitical responsiveness at the national level, and only achieving what economic performance was necessary not to tempt the government into calling other suppliers. When the government was attempting to support the development of its own national suppliers, high prices usually led to handsome MNC profits as in France or Italy. Political responsiveness strategies usually involved leaving much freedom to the various subsidiaries and controlling centrally only their sources of superiority over purely national firms: the access to a wider technology pool, the costs of which were shared over larger operations, and the export effectiveness and flexibility offered by a large network and alternate equipment sources, respectively. Companies active in new markets had to achieve much tighter price and quality competitiveness targets to compete in a public tender-offer market, and such economic efficiency could best be achieved by centralized and integrated activities. As a market matured there appeared a need to shift over time toward more autonomy locally and less central involvement.

Technological Level

Technology changes also played a key role. First, as was seen in Chapter 4 and in the CEM example, when economic pressures for rationalization become extremely strong, no amount of goodwilled responsiveness can suffice. In the French case, Alsthom Atlantique's annual turbogenerator capacity was 8,000 MWe, while CEM's was 4,000. Separately, each was inefficient; together (assuming their operations can be rationalized), they are above the minimum efficient size. Thus technology, by increasing the minimum efficient size of an operation, can defeat the national responsiveness strategy. Predictably, governments will first favor the development of a single national champion (for instance, KWU in Germany, or Aerospatiale in France for aerospace) and then, if scale further increases, enter into government-sponsored consortia to match the minimum efficient size both in terms of production volume and captive market (for instance, the joint German-French-Italian development of fast-breeder nuclear reactors or the Airbus Industries venture).

Technology can also play another role: that of reopening closed markets by suddenly decreasing their maturity. When a PTT decides to go electronic, it finds itself in a position it may not have known for decades: calling for tender offers on an unfamiliar equipment, the technology and economics of which it does not perfectly understand. Though the French move to electronic switching did not permit any new competition to move in, other cases are leading to a reshuffling of the cards internationally. [13]

With no supplier (except possibly Western Electric, but only in the United States) having a clear lead in technology or accrued production volume, the electronic-switching market remains open (see Table 5.6).

Yet the stakes were growing rapidly, as in the electrical power system industry. One industry expert commented:

In the 1960s PTTs used to buy exchanges one at a time, and sometimes would swap suppliers. Now when they go electronic it is an all-or-nothing game: they will select from two to four suppliers, and that's the end of it for those who are not in at the start. By driving the stakes up they make the business more risky for the suppliers. Moreover, such all-or-nothing bargaining creates the kind of tensions in which suppliers might cave in on almost everything. They are under constant fear that someone else will give more to the government; when a huge market is at stake it's hard to live with such tensions.

TABLE 5.6

Electronic Main-Exchange Switching Systems

Supplier	Since	Experience by 1976	Markets
Western Electric	1966[a] (ESS1)	6 million lines	United States
GTE	1972[b] (no. 1 EAX)	500,000 lines	United States, Iran
	1978[b] (no. 2 EAX)	none	target markets: Europe and Latin America
NEC + others	1971	400,000 lines	Japan
ITT	1973[b] (Metaconta)	field trials under way	France, Spain, United States, Taiwan, Denmark
LM Ericsson	1977[b] (AXE)	prototypes	Sweden, France
Siemens	1976[a] (EWS1)	field trials underway	Germany, South Africa

[a]Year during which field trials were started.
[b]Year of commercial availability.

Source: Compiled by the author from various industry interviews.

With large electromechanical switching facilities, and serious employment problems if they converted rapidly to electronic switching, LM Ericsson and ITT did not take a leading role in the early development of electronic switching. Electronic switching was developed by Western Electric and independently by Philips, but with a more conservative approach. It was only when large, technologically refined markets such as France, Brazil, or Australia moved toward electronic switching that LM Ericsson and ITT actively pursued electronic-switching sales. In any case they are assured of long-continuing sales of electromechanical equipment to expand existing networks they already supply. The AXE system scored some important successes in Australia and France and showed promising performance. By 1977 ITT was also meeting success with its Metaconta, with large sales to Korea and other Asian countries.

U.S. companies that had been conspicuously absent from the international market for decades* were counting upon their electronic systems to stage a comeback.[14] GTE, with its new system (EAX), had already scored some great successes including two large orders, one from Iran and the other from Korea (both accompanied by a commitment to local manufacture). Though the equipment was developed to U.S. standards it could be sold to PTTs whose standards were closer to those in the United States than to CCITT norms. GTE was also developing a set of systems for the European and Latin American markets built according to CCITT norms, and a smaller rural system for low-population-density countries. GTE's long operating experience in telecommunications was a major asset in international sales. The same was true of Western Electric, which had by far the most extensive experience with electronic switching and very low production costs. Western Electric was expected to move into international markets shortly.

Northern Telecom and the Japanese cartel were already attempting to gain a foothold in the international markets with little initial success. Though Japanese prices were very low (50 percent to 80 percent of the "usual" international level), it seemed that negotiations between PTTs and Japanese suppliers were difficult. Japanese companies had been very successful on the transmission equipment market, but had not yet broken into the switching export market in a significant way.

---

*AT&T had made a policy decision of serving the U.S. market only. GTE lacked the advanced or semielectronic switching systems needed to compete on the international markets in the 1950s and 1960s, so it concentrated on other communication products.

Whether new companies will indeed be able to penetrate the switching market and capture a significant share of the industry remains to be seen; but offering technologically superior products certainly provides the potential for a successful entry. Undoubtedly, GTE, Western Electric, and the Japanese suppliers were seeing their experience with electronic switching at home as a major competitive tool abroad.

Conversely, companies that had neither a new technology nor a portfolio of established market positions were in an increasingly difficult position. Most purely national companies were in this predicament, and the British Plessey and GEC, which had let themselves fall behind technologically, were joining the group. Conversely, the French government was putting great hopes in CIT-Alcatel's unique experience with time division for future export, investment, or license income. It was thought that CIT-Alcatel enjoyed a unique technological lead, and the company did score some early export deals.

The introduction of nuclear reactors as steam sources of heat for electrical power plants not only increased the minimum efficient scale in the industry, but also introduced a new technology. Some industry experts argued that most efficiency increases in electricity generation would come from better heat transfer, that is, improving the steam supply system. In turn, companies with in-house knowledge of both the nuclear reactor technology and the turbogenerator technology would be better able to improve the steam supply systems to lead to better overall energy utilization. Only a few companies spanned all three technologies: Westinghouse and GE in the United States; Siemens in Germany; and to a lesser extent the Alsthom Atlantique-Framatome partnership. Brown Boveri and other companies were in a more precarious position as they did not master nuclear technologies. Furthermore, multinational consortia often found it difficult to agree on common restraints and trade policies. For instance, the sale of power stations by Brown Boveri to South Africa was scuttled by the reluctance of the Dutch government to allow exports of steel parts for nuclear reactors' vessels. South Africa subsequently signed a contract with Framatome.

That the dominant companies would be slow to introduce new technology and would try to control the pace of its introduction fits with conventional oligopoly theory. On the other hand, that a key factor would be the shift from an economic to a political strategy over time as a market matures is a direct result of the intensity of government intervention and of the neutralization of other key competitive tools normally found in a oligopoly.

Dynamics of Competition

Competitive patterns in the two industries displayed quite varied characteristics in the specifics of the sources of power used in bargaining with governments. The two French cases are revealing in that respect. At a more abstract level, competitive patterns are somewhat dull as most of the variables normally used in oligopolistic competition are neutralized by government control. Pricing is not a significant element for competition within an established market. Quality service and other marketing variables are not relevant except in the early stages of a new market. Cost positions and technological leadership have been found to be important, as we have seen. But it remains that the key trade-off faced by a company was that between rationalization of activities on a worldwide basis and the maintenance of autonomous subsidiaries in different countries. Companies can pursue both aspects in different countries and different businesses.

Companies with large market shares in several developed, mature markets followed a political strategy of local responsiveness and slow technological evolution. The leader in each industry, ITT and BBC, cultivated that approach. Companies with no strong existing positions in developed markets were more integrated, more aggressive technologically, and pursued expansion strategies based on price-performance ratio and other economic characteristics.

Of course, such generalization is to some extent an oversimplification of reality. A given company could vary its approach between different markets. For instance, LM Ericsson was pursuing AXE sales in developed countries desiring to shift rapidly to electronic switching (Australia and France) and which the company could then use as references, while pursuing electromechanical equipment sales in other countries. It was also leaving great autonomy to its larger subsidiaries in most mature markets, while devoting much attention to controlling and assisting its operations in newer markets.

Despite these reservations it is still possible to sketch the competitive posture of major companies in both industries, as in Figure 5.2. It is useful here to think in terms of clusters of firms following essentially the same strategy, that is, "strategic groups."[15] Within a strategic group, strategies are similar in a structural sense as they have about the same implications in terms of the profit-determining factors. Here one strategic group is composed of companies that favor adaptation to existing mature markets and the defense of their positions in these markets (see Figure 5.3). Another group is composed of firms that favor the development of worldwide economic performance, to the detriment of specific adaptive capabilities. Leading firms often have large enough subsidiaries to be economically efficient to some extent and to be used to penetrate newer markets. Firms

FIGURE 5.2

Competitive Posture of the Major Equipment Suppliers

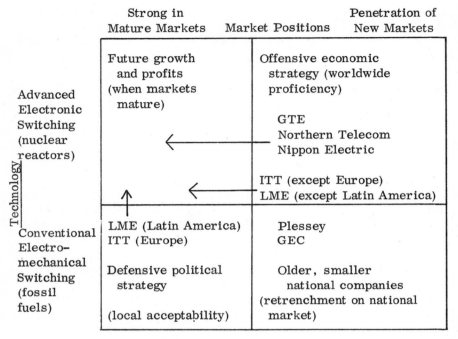

Note: This table applies to main-exchange switching and turbo-generators, not necessarily to other segments of either industry.

Source: Compiled by the author.

trying to penetrate new markets can grant enough autonomy to the few subsidiaries they have in mature markets to let them be responsive. Of course, the distinction is not black and white: the belonging to a strategic group is expressed largely in terms of more frequent preference and of structural form. In broad terms the differences between structural form in the two groups can be sketched as shown in Figure 5.3.

Some other companies were attempting to achieve the advantages of both strategic groups within a single structure. GTE, for instance, had both well-established subsidiaries in old mature markets (Belgium and Italy) and large orders in newer markets (Korea and Iran). The management was trying to provide for both national responsiveness and overall economic performance within a single structure.

FIGURE 5.3

Strategic Groups and Structural Forms

1. <u>Companies Privileging Sociopolitical Responsiveness</u>

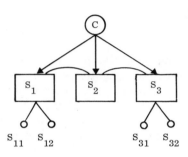

<u>Center</u>: Administrative tasks only—planning, budgeting, resource allocation, plus coordination of R&D and export marketing.

<u>Subsidiaries in mature markets</u>: Autonomous operations, full-fledged companies.

<u>Subsidiaries in new markets</u>: Administered by larger national subsidiaries.

2. <u>Companies Privileging Worldwide Economic Performance</u>

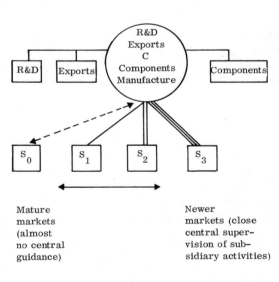

<u>Center</u>: Operational tasks, centralized R&D, and components manufacture; all exports take place from the center.

<u>Subsidiaries</u>: Catering to their domestic markets.

Amount of central guidance, control, and assistance varies according to market maturity.

<u>Source</u>: Compiled by the author.

131

It had adopted a matrix structure to develop such quality of orientation.

The strategic groups described above were most characteristic of the main-exchange switching business and of the transformer and heavy circuit-breaker segments of the heavy electrical equipment industry. In other segments of the two industries competition was freer. Despite tight controls for equipment artification, the trend in PABX and other station equipments was clearly toward more competition and market fragmentation. Many competitors, from IBM to small, very specialized firms, entered the private telephoning market with some success.

The transmission equipment market was also more competitive because interface problems were lesser, thus enabling wider supplier choices and more freedom in shifting suppliers. Yet, most domestic markets in developed countries were closed to competition. Developing countries often imported the bulk of the equipment (particularly as its quality improved rapidly with electronic componentry advances) rather than manufacture it.

In the heavy electrical industry, the large power-transformer and circuit-breaker markets evidenced close similarity with the main-exchange business in the telecommunication equipment field. Whereas the manufacture of turbogenerators and nuclear reactors was confined to a few developed countries, developing countries often requested local plants for transformers and circuit breakers. European suppliers were further plagued by overcapabity, tough price competition on export markets, and, in many cases, inefficient scattered production.

For a summary of the difference between the various segments of the two industries, see Figure 5.4.

SUMMARY

The direct intervention by monopsony customers and their governments into both industries neutralized most of the competitive rivalry dimensions usually found in oligopolies. The early requests by governments for local production, as well as the nature of the products, led to international expansion patterns and foreign-market entry routes substantially different from those in other international oligopolistic industries. [16]

Differences in government interests, competencies, and bargaining power as a market matures, lead to different demands made on suppliers: economic performance, quality equipment, low costs, timely delivery, attractive financing, and installation and start-up assistance when the market is new; general responsiveness, local

FIGURE 5.4

Characteristics of Industry Segments

Nuclear reactors and turbogenerators	Forbidding economies of scale. Extremely intense government involvement in industry structure, product technologies, ownership of suppliers, and the like. Industry confined to developed countries. Handful of competitors only. Large technological risks.
Transformers (high voltage)	Very high entry barriers, very high concentration. Closed markets in developed countries.
Main-exchange switching	Technological choices guided by governments. Intervention in industry structure and ownership.
Circuit breakers (high voltage)	Intense multinational rivalry for new developing-country markets. Initial sales generally followed by local investments.
Transmission equipment	Low barriers to entry, moderate scale effects. National dominant suppliers in most developed countries. Rapidly evolving technologies, incremental change. Relatively free competition, many competitors for developing-country markets; tender offers.
Industrial transformers and breakers	Corporate customers, but specifications and certification by PTT and utilities. Service and maintenance are important.
PABX and branch equipment	Price/performance competition in both developed and developing countries. Many competitors.
Industrial motors, contractors, power semiconductors, and other apparatus	Investments in developing countries for low-cost production and components sourcing.
Low-voltage residential electrical equipment	Private customers, but specifications by PTT and utilities. Relatively low entry barriers. Intense price competition, many competitors.
Customer attachments to telephone sets	Marketed as home-equipment good, advertising, product differentiation, service, maintenance.

Electrical Power Systems   Telecommunication Equipment

Source: Compiled by the author.

133

production, engineering cooperation with the customers, and maintenance of employment when the market matures. Advances in technology can transform a mature market into a new one with each generation of equipment, particularly when these generations represent quantum jumps in technology and are far apart (for example, mainexchange switching). According to the technology level and market mix they achieve, companies adopt different strategic orientations favoring either political responsiveness at the national level or economic performance at the worldwide level.

The different priorities given to each orientation by different firms, in turn, lead to different structural arrangements and different ways of dealing with research and development and exports. Some companies attempt to blend different orientations. Finally, companies have to reckon with very different industry-structure characteristics and competitive behavior patterns in various segments of the two industries. As one moves from large, salient, technologically advanced products manufactured by a handful of firms only, to products where competition is more dispersed, government interest and intervention lesser, and customers more dispersed, the nature of competition shifts from the patterns described in the two French examples presented in this chapter, to much more usual oligopolistic behavior.

In their management, multinational companies thus have to reckon with three basic dimensions of diversity in setting their strategies, structural forms, and administrative systems: differences between mature and new markets, differences between technologies, and differences between industry segments.

NOTES

1. Ralph G. M. Sultan, Pricing in the Electrical Oligopoly, 2 vol. (Boston: Harvard University, Division of Research, Graduate School of Business Administration, 1974); Frederick T. Knickerbocker, Oligopolistic Reaction and Multinational Enterprise (Boston: Harvard University, Division of Research, Graduate School of Business Administration, 1973). See, also, Martin Shubik, Strategy and Market Structure (New York: John Wiley, 1959); Michael E. Porter, The Evolution of Industry Structure (forthcoming).
2. Raymond Vernon, "International Investment and International Trade in the Product Cycle," Quarterly Journal of Economics 80(1966): 190-207.
3. George Siemens, History of the House of Siemans (Freeburg/ Munich: K. Alber, 1957); John Brooks, Telephone: The First Hundred Years (New York: Harper & Row, 1976).
4. Knickerbocker, Oligopolistic Reaction, p. 16.

5. Mira Wilkins, The Emergence of Multinational Enterprise (Cambridge, Mass.: Harvard University Press, 1970).

6. Harry J. Robinson, The Motivation and Flow of Private Foreign Investment (Menlo Park, Calif.: Stanford Research Institute, 1961); Yair Aharoni, The Foreign Investment Decision Process (Boston: Harvard University, Division of Research, Graduate School of Business Administration, 1966).

7. Sultan, Pricing in the Electrical Oligopoly, vol. 1, p. 332.

8. For a complete official critical description of the plight of French telephones, see Rapport Fait Au Nom de la Commission de Controle de la Gestion du Service Public du Téléphone (Paris: Assemblée Nationale, no. 1971, seconde session ordinaire de 1973-74, annexe au process verbal de la seance du 20 Juin 1974).

9. Translated from Entreprise 1945 (September 19, 1975): 52.

10. Les Informations 1566 (May 19, 1975): 50-53.

11. "A Belgian Baron Fights for His Corporate Domain in France," Fortune, August 1975; and "Empain, Jusqu ou?" Entreprise 959 (January 25, 1974).

12. Le Monde, weekly selection, July 17-23, 1975.

13. "The Common Market Rewires Its Phones," Business Week, April 13, 1974, p. 42.

14. A. B. Kamman, "Leader or Loser, the U.S. in the International Telecommunication Market," Telephone, October 13, 1975.

15. Michael E. Porter, "Note on the Structural Analysis of Industry" (Boston: Harvard University, Graduate School of Business Administration, ICCH no. 376-054, 1975); and idem, "Industry Structural Evolution," mimeographed (Boston: Harvard University, Graduate School of Business Administration, February 1978).

16. In particular, the small number of transactions and the high uncertainties characteristic of turbogenerator purchasing and main-exchange switching equipment selection created tremendous pressures for the customers (PTT or utilities) to internalize their transactions with suppliers. For a theoretical treatment of this question, see Oliver Williamson, Markets and Hierarchies (New York: The Free Press, 1975).

6

THE MANAGERIAL REQUIREMENTS
OF SUPPLIERS' STRATEGIES

As we saw in Chapter 5, the fragmentation of the world market for telecommunication equipment and electrical power systems into nationally closed and government-influenced oligopolies, added to the differences in production economics and technological evolution between individual product lines, resulted in considerable variety in the conditions the equipment suppliers had to face. Though different companies clearly pursued different strategies and had different ways to obtain their profits and maintain their long-term viability, their identification with a particular strategic group could be determined only in terms of overall preference for a given strategy. Thus, to the diversity of strategies followed by different firms in adapting to environmental variety was added an internal diversity, within individual firms, among different geographical markets, different product lines, and different technologies.

Such internal diversity makes the management of firms in both industries quite difficult. They have to develop a two-pronged management orientation: a variety of responses are needed to adapt to variety in the environment, yet a unity of response is required to remain more competent and more competitive than other suppliers, local or international.

Response flexibility and variety are needed because the multiple forms of government intervention, the various types of national administrations, and the differences in market size and maturity, technology level, and product characteristics added together result in a very diverse market. Moreover, the development of managerial uniformity is next to impossible because much information and many decisions are channeled through multilevel interactions between the company and the national administrations.

While a variety of response is needed at the local level, a unity of response is also necessary if MNCs are to bring to customers benefits that independent national companies and other international competitors cannot provide. A set of competencies that is more than the competence of each national subsidiary taken individually, therefore, is needed to maintain the MNC's market position and worldwide competitive posture.

The duality of focus required by the twin needs to be locally responsive and globally effective is needed to satisfy host governments. This duality lies at the crux of the difficulty of managing government businesses. The following sections explore this difficulty in further detail, describe administrative implications, and present a framework of different managerial modes used to administer such businesses.

STRATEGY AND STRUCTURE: THE INADEQUACY OF SIMPLE RESPONSES

It has become a general proposition that in large companies, the organizational structure responds to the demands of the strategy. Thus, in a broad sense, structure follows strategy. This proposition was first developed by Alfred D. Chandler in his landmark in-depth study of four large U.S. domestic corporations, supplemented by less intensive studies of another 100 corporations.[1] Building upon Chandler, other researchers have related classes of strategy to categories of structure. Following Bruce R. Scott's work on corporate development, a large research program at the Harvard Business School first identified various types of diversification strategies and diversified structures.[2] Then, the analysis related firms' performance level to the strategies they followed and the structure they adopted.[3] Though some aspects of this research have come under some criticism lately, it remains the main large-sample empirical study of the relationship between diversification strategies and corporate structure.[4] The analysis has been extended to Europe yielding comparable results.[5]

For U.S.-based multinational companies, similar research has been conducted by Stopford and Wells. Here, as for domestic companies, the relationship between strategic orientation and organizational structure is well recognized. In fact, it is so well accepted that Stopford and Wells characterize international companies by the type of structure they adopt. They identified four types of structural forms often used by international corporations.[6] These are:

1. Area Structure, where the organization is divided into area divisions, each responsible for one area of the world.
2. Product Structure, where product divisions are given worldwide responsibility for their products.

3. <u>Mixed Structure</u>, where some product lines are managed through worldwide product divisions whereas others are regrouped into area units.

4. <u>Grid (or Matrix) Structure</u>, where worldwide product divisions and local area divisions share jointly the responsibility over operations. Most managers operate with dual or multiple reporting relationships.

Stopford and Wells argue that the product structure is related to strategies of diversification in which the firm increases the number of its products sold and manufactured abroad, but with domestic sales remaining larger than foreign sales. Conversely, area structures follow strategies of foreign expansion with a narrow product line. Companies that have both many products and carry the bulk of their activities abroad resort to more complex organizational forms such as mixed or grid structures.

Franko extended the same type of research to multinationals based in continental Western Europe.[7] His central finding is that, though European firms became multinational early, the need for formal multinational structures was delayed by the fragmented and negotiated nature of the European environment. Till the 1970s most firms had kept simple mother-daughter structures with the subsidiaries reporting directly to corporate headquarters.

It is easy to see that the managerial requirements of the multinationals studied here do not fit very well in any of these structures. Stopford and Wells argue that area structures correspond to a desire to rationalize and integrate operations on a regional basis, à la IBM or Ford. Such rationalization is impossible in telecommunication equipment or power systems manufacture. Worldwide product divisions also favor integration, at least in high-technology industries such as those studied here.[8] In such worldwide product structures, where power to make decisions rests with worldwide product managers who often have only a scant understanding of the wide variety of national administrations, local diversity may be overlooked and conflicts with dissatisfied administrations are more likely to arise.

In an earlier study Franko showed that the move to area management structures was the main cause of joint venture instability between MNCs and local interests.[9] In a similar way, numerous studies suggest that high-technology companies that favor worldwide product-line management are very reluctant toward joint ventures.[10]

Conversely, in a mother-daughter pattern there is usually little central control or guidance and the power to make strategic decisions is allocated to country managers whose concern is mainly for local responsibilities. The focus is on the flexibility and diversity of response, to the possible neglect of overall capabilities. While this is

FIGURE 6.1

Comparison of Integration and Responsiveness

Worldwide Integration
MNC operating as a single
integrated unit that hap-
pens to have plants in
several countries

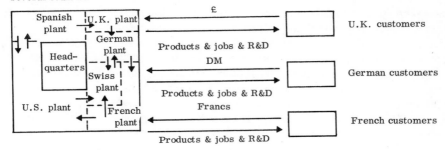

National Responsiveness
MNC operating as a col-
lection of nonintegrated
subsidiaries located in
different countries

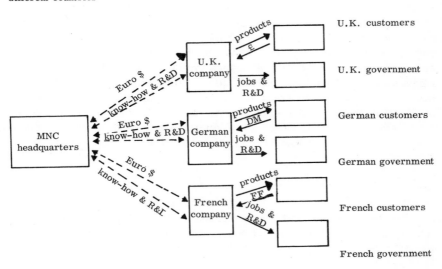

Source: Compiled by the author.

very successful in low-technology, low-scale economies industries, such as food, the disadvantages of national autonomy can be very serious in high technology industries. [11]

National subsidiaries run through a loose mother–daughter structure may often fail to maintain technological and economic competitiveness and may become very dependent upon the protection granted by local governments. In this situation the ability to penetrate new markets quickly disappears and, eventually, existing markets will be threatened by competitors offering better products or more efficient production methods. Thus it is unlikely that international competitiveness can be maintained in a structure that channels information decisions and competence on a local-for-local basis unless some specific organizational arrangements are made.

The mother–daughter flexible setting is contrasted with the regionally or worldwide integrated MNC in Figure 6.1.

If we consider industries such as contemporary telecommunication and power equipment, in which there is a broad diversity of markets in terms of maturity and size and in which the technology is far from stagnant, then a company adopting a pure area/product or mother–daughter structure faces considerable loss of opportunity by locking itself into a strategic posture that will effectively weaken its position vis-à-vis customers or competitors in the long run.

The mixed structure could be suitable if, in a diversified multinational, some businesses could be run with a clear worldwide (or regional) integration objective and a concern with the economic imperatives and some other businesses could be left primarily to the responsibility of various autonomous national subsidiaries. In Chapter 5, however, we saw that things are so complex for the telecommunication equipment and power system industries as to require both a concern for worldwide economic performance of the company and a responsiveness to national political imperatives.

MATRIX STRUCTURE

This leaves us with the matrix structure. One analyst of matrix organizational forms elaborated on some of Stopford and Wells' ideas in the following way:

> Organizations adopt a global matrix structure when the complexity of the businesses they are involved in is such that it becomes very difficult to decide whether being responsive to local markets (area structure) is more or less important than developing worldwide business coordination (product structure). [12]

The matrix structure had already been identified by Franko as a perceived solution to the difficulties of European multinationals.[13]
Though the formal recognition of the matrix structure by management
experts is recent, some significant evidence was accumulated about
it.

It is important to recognize that a matrix is much more than
just another formal structure; it is a way to manage ambiguity and
diversity. As a structure, because it criss-crosses products, functions, and geographical units in a grid, it is quite indeterminate in
terms of authority. Because it does not focus middle management's
attention in a single direction it can capture a large variety of perceptions. In a study of product-function matrix organizations in high
technology settings, Jay Galbraith explained that power considerations
had to be dealt with explicitly as the matrix no longer provided a clear
authority structure.[14] There is a range of possible balance positions
between product and functional forms. The locus of the balance (more
power to the product or to the function) depends on various elements,
principally what Galbraith calls coordination mechanisms and integrative roles. If ideally balanced, such mechanisms and integrative roles
would lead to equal power. Galbraith also explains how, in the case
of aerospace firms, shifting priorities in their environment led to
shifts in the internal balance between product program managers and
functional managers. In short, as long as technical performance was
the most critical dimension (during the 1950s) the functional managers,
who provided the needed technical competencies, dominated the joint
decisions. When government contracts shifted from a cost-plus-fee
basis to incentives and fixed-price contracts, the cost-conscious program managers became more influential (during the McNamara period at the Department of Defense). Finally, when publicity about
cost overruns (such as Senator Proxmire's hearings on the Lockheed
C5A Galaxy giant cargo plane), inflation, and shifting priorities all
combined to make cost reduction the top priority (as opposed to technological excellence), the project managers began to dominate the
joint decision processes within aerospace firms.[15] Harvey Kolodny
furthers Galbraith's argument by suggesting that a matrix organization is needed when an organization faces high information-process-
ing requirements (usually because of environmental uncertainty and
turbulence) in two different critical sectors of the environment.[16]
Companies in the telecommunication equipment and power system industries obviously fit such conditions. In Kolodny's argument each
component of the organization (for instance, program or function or,
in the MNC matrix, country management, worldwide product management, and functional management) corresponds to a critical sector of
the environment. The locus of the balance in the matrix will then be:

>A unique, situationally determined composite of the fol-
>lowing constraints: (1) the relative criticality of the en-
>vironmental sectors; (2) the basic strategy of the orga-
>nization; and (3) the top management determined value
>position about human collaboration in organizations.[17]

Kolodny then argues that in the case of an ongoing matrix structure
these constraints will be mediated by the political structure and accompanying power networks within the organization.

The arguments developed by Galbraith and Kolodny for domestic matrix management can be paralleled within the MNC setting.
Usually, the multinational matrix involves clear-cut product and country dimensions:

FIGURE 6.2

Simplified Multinational Matrix Structure

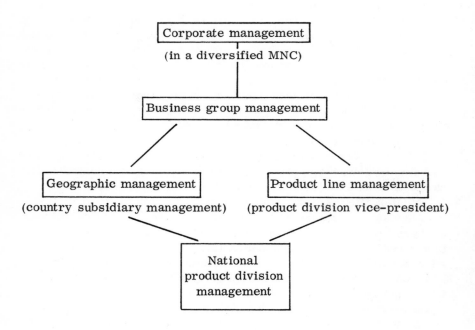

Source: Compiled by the author.

It is important to note that some companies adopt patterns of matrix management though they do not quite move to a formal matrix structure. Most matrix analysts have noted that point repeatedly.[18]

Yet, according to several authors, matrix structures are not a panacea for multinational management difficulties. Stanley M. Davis and Paul R. Lawrence, for instance, note:

> Experience so far with the worldwide matrix has indicated that firms have some trouble in maintaining a power balance between area and product divisions, more so than in the domestic product/function matrix we have primarily been examining.[19]

Davis and Lawrence contend that numerous difficulties face the matrix structure. In particular, they argue that nine pathologies threaten the matrix: tendencies toward anarchy, power struggles, severe groupitis, collapse during economic crunch, excessive overheads, sinking to lower levels, uncontrolled layering, navel gazing, and decision strangulation.[20]

Another multinational matrix researcher, C. K. Prahalad, started from different premises. Whereas Davis and Lawrence and most other matrix analysts argue for a balance of power between conflicting orientations where imbalances are checked and minimized, Prahalad, following Galbraith, argued for clear allocation of relative power, that is, for more power to product division or country managers. By raising the question of how strategy (a consistent pattern of resource allocation over time) could be formulated and implemented in a matrix, Prahalad concluded that unless there is an asymmetry in power between the components of the matrix, strategy cannot exist. Prahalad then explored the impact of the locus of relative power on the behavior of managers responsible for countries and product divisions. He concluded that:

1. The locus of relative power changes the concept of risk associated with projects as well as their content. A country responsive organization spreads risk over a portfolio of products. It may not see the need to achieve worldwide dominance in a particular product line since investments of this sort unbalance the portfolio. A shift in the locus of power toward emphasis on worldwide coordination by product group will change the concept of risk so that it is viewed in terms of a portfolio of countries. In the long run strategy is changed.

2. The locus of relative power influences the corporate capability to manage foreign exchange exposure risk. A

country predominant organization is likely to have very little interest in, and capability for, foreign exchange risk management. Only the cross-border flows of the sort managed by a worldwide product group can create real opportunities for foreign exchange gains or even avoid losses.

3. The locus of relative power determines the extent of stress in relationships with joint venture partners. A centrally led worldwide product organization has a very hard time coping with joint ventures.

4. The locus of relative power influences the development of managers in terms of their career progression and mobility. Country predominance leads to country generalists. Product dominance leads to product or functional specialists. In short, the locus of relative power influences strategic orientation and the process by which resources are allocated.[21]

Prahalad then concluded that the locus of relative power is to be assigned so as to match top management preference for diversity (responding to the variety between geographical markets) or interdependence (the desire to achieve global benefits of intercountry rationalization and integration within the multinational). A management seeking to achieve a high degree of managerial variety will seek to have relative power reside in the geographical components of the matrix. An effort to achieve a high degree of interdependence will result in an emphasis on the product divisions.

Prahalad then addressed the question of how the locus of relative power can be moved from one orientation to the other. Based on the clinical study of one multinational he suggested that several sources of top management influence are available:

1. People: Executives in an organization are seldom even in capability or temperament. By putting more capable or more aggressive managers in one part of the matrix the locus of power can be altered.

2. Technology: In most multinationals, the source of technology is laboratories in the parent country. Where standardization of technology is imposed (either to achieve benefits of scale or with proprietary knowledge) a considerable shift toward worldwide coordination can be effected.

3. Procedures: Where a common language system, a reporting format, a training process, or a common socialization is provided, it is possible to move the locus of power so as to achieve more interdependence.

4. Information Flows: Worldwide planning systems, change in reporting relationships, worldwide functional directors or coordinators, or other forms of organizational overlays can all be used to shift the locus of power.

Yet, Prahalad leaves largely unanswered the question of how to use the MNC matrix to manage such industries as telecommunication equipment or power systems. One can see from his argument how a matrix can provide for a smoother transition stage between a worldwide product-oriented organization and a nationally-oriented mother-daughter one (or the reverse transition), but not how it can be used to manage continuously contradictory demands of the political and economic imperatives. In short, it emerges from his analysis that a pattern of decision processes will crystallize over time in any organization. Once the pattern is set the main locus of decision making belongs to either the product or the area component, and follows a clear, unique focus accordingly. Information still flows from both components, but the emerging pattern of decisions results in a strategy with an overall orientation similar to that of either a pure mother-daughter or product division structure. Decisions can still benefit from the duality of perception, but unless relative power is more finely allocated than in the company studied by Prahalad, stable patterns of decision making will not be easily shifted to account for new information.

Using the analysis of the existing literature on the multinational matrix the following section will explore the issue of managing contradictory demands.

MANAGING DUALITY

The duality of economic and political imperatives in the telecommunication equipment and power system industries creates managerial demands not usually faced by other industries. For instance, whereas Prahalad studied a change in the allocation of relative power and strategic direction over several years, what is critical here is the ability to shift from one direction to the other—not globally over a period of years as Prahalad suggests, but locally, from country to country, and almost immediately from one decision to the next. For instance, the decision to submit a bid to a particular PTT administration, and the ensuing negotiation guidelines and limits, need to follow different processes according to which national administration is involved. For some bids relative power may lie with worldwide product management, for others with country management. It is the range of patterns—from one decision process to another, from one class of decisions to another, from one country to another—that is difficult to achieve. Not all decisions need to be made with a bifocal orientation, but they cannot all be made in an interdependent or a diverse mode. Changes in focus must be able to occur more easily than through the overall shifts analyzed by Prahalad. In other words, managing government-influenced businesses through a matrix organization requires avoiding a clearly set relative power and dominant decision pattern.

Combining this indeterminacy of decision making with consistent commitments of resources over time is an extremely difficult task. One needs to preserve the duality of perceptions and interests and to make sure the relevant variety of data and points of view is brought to bear on the analysis of strategic decisions. Deciding how to develop a new type of electronic exchange system—for instance, whether to design several variants each suited to a particular country, or a single, more flexible system with various interface control softwares—is the type of critical decision where both the point of view of the country managers and that of the worldwide product specialists need to be considered.

From a top management point of view, not only managers with strong commitments, and thought patterns consistent with their commitments, are needed, but also some neutral, uncommitted managers who can "oscillate between competing belief patterns put forward by sponsors."[23] The complexity of managing so that both the economic and the political imperatives receive adequate attention may thus be thought to derive from the difficulty of structuring the organization in such a way that different thought patterns based on conflicting, but necessary, perceptions will add up consistently in overall decision making processes.

Basically, three different elements contribute to making this complexity manageable. They are used by managers to simplify the management task and mediate between the worldwide product management and the national subsidiary management within an organization that is, formally or informally, run through a matrix management approach. First, as we saw in the last section of Chapter 5, firms within the same industry follow different strategies and use strategy to decide on structure. Second, not all strategic decisions need to be made with a duality of orientation, and functional managers (in a relatively uncommitted position) may be used to swing decisions one way or the other. Third, top management can purposively structure the premises on which lower-level managers perceive problems, look for solutions, and select one.

Strategy as a Guide to Decision

In our analysis of the industries it was concluded that companies with large market shares in several developed, mature markets usually followed a political strategy, giving the upper hand to national managers who saw it their duty to respond to political imperatives rather than to pursue economic rationalization strategies. The companies with large market shares in mature markets found themselves in a relatively weak bargaining position vis-à-vis host governments. They had a vested interest in avoiding sudden technological shifts that would prevent them from fully amortizing their plants and would challenge their existing market positions. Their plants were mostly noninte-grated ones located in developed countries where they could be na-tionalized and then operated easily by local interests.[23] As long as markets remained fragmented, these companies could be more prof-itable than their competitors, thanks to their larger market shares in large mature markets. In summary, these companies had a strong interest in preserving the status quo within their industry.

Given their external posture vis-à-vis host governments and competitors, these firms thus clearly favored political responsive-ness and consequently left relative power with the management of their national subsidiaries. The largest multinationals in both indus-tries, Brown Boveri & Cie and International Telephone and Telegraph, respectively, clearly followed this approach.[24].

Conversely, companies without a strong, existing position in mature markets could follow strategies based on price-effectiveness ratios of their equipment and other economic performance character-istics. These companies were also actively promoting new technol-ogies for more rapid expansion. Such economic strategies called for the allocation of relative power to worldwide product executives look-ing for opportunities to improve products and processes and push for higher overall efficiency and productivity in the company. Smaller, more technology-oriented firms in both industries, such as LM Erics-son in telecommunication equipment or ASEA in heavy electrical equip-ment, clearly followed such economic-technological strategies.

This allocation of relative power to the product or the geographic management, in line with the type of strategy being pursued and with the competitive posture of the firm within its industry, provided a preferred strategic direction to the business without losing the bene-fits of the matrix structure in dealing with a duality of demanding and contradictory environments. In some cases, individual operations were excluded from the matrix because they did not fit the preferred strategic direction. Such operations could be national subsidiaries or product lines, according to the preferred orientation. For instance, LM Ericsson's subsidiaries in France and Italy (mature markets, ma-ture technologies) were given a lot of autonomy from Stockholm and were managed locally. Correspondingly, ITT had its Business Sys-tem Group, not the telecommunication equipment subsidiaries, man-age its PABX product line in Europe. Since the early 1970s competitors using an economic strategy and considering Europe as a single market were competing to place PABX with large business customers, and ITT had to respond in kind. Its Business System Group was better prepared to compete in an openly competitive market against such companies as IBM than were its various national telecommunication equipment subsidiaries.

Yet, even if one strategic direction is generally preferred and deviant subsidiaries or product lines are managed separately on an ad hoc basis, there remain several problems. Not all decisions can be made within the framework of the preferred strategic direction and relative power needs to be checked and counterbalanced. If relative power were to become absolute power, the benefits of the matrix would be lost as it would degenerate into a mother-daughter relationship or an integrated area or product structure.

Functional Managers as Mediators

By influencing the alliances between functional managers and product or geography-related managers, top management can adjust the relative power of each side within particular functions. For instance, marketing within a national market can be left almost entirely to the existing subsidiary management that has developed expertise, understanding, and trust in dealing with national utilities or the PTT. Headquarters or the product division can provide technical support on specific questions. On the other hand, marketing to new markets may be handled by a proposal office at the corporate level or by the product divisions. When manufacturing is done primarily on a local-for-local basis, its operating management can be left to the individual subsidiaries, yet product divisions can play a key role in establishing quality control procedures or sharing production process knowledge and experience.

The same type of breakdown between tasks that are better managed by the national subsidiaries and tasks that are better managed at the worldwide product division level can be made for various functions. Because functional managers derive their power from expertise in their field, they are in a position to take a substantive, neutral view in the power conflict between product and geographic executives. They can genuinely ask the question of where each responsibility should be assigned and answer it based on the substantive merits of each solution. Functional managers are "uncommitted thinkers" who can provide balance in the conflict between product and geographic management.

Assuming the allocation of power for specific functional decisions to the geographic or to product management is done substantively, thanks to an in-depth knowledge of the industry and the expertise of functional managers, there still remain a few critical decisions that require the duality of focus to be present all along. The two major decision areas where local political considerations and global competitiveness concerns meet are the management of research and development and the coordination of export marketing. In order to make critical decisions in these areas the desire for integration and the need to respond to diversity between countries have to be managed simultaneously. Economic, political, and administrative considerations are so intertwined in these two decision areas that they deserve further exploration.

Product design and development is a function where the desire for uniformity and the need for diversity constantly conflict. There can be no set answer for how much diversity is enough. As was seen in Chapter 3, customers' requirements and demands may vary widely and the trade-offs between developing products (or variants) for each local market individually or aiming for a unique product sold to many markets are unclear. In both industries very high development costs make the choice critically important for all companies.[25] It is clear that a balance can only be reached by a decision in which both the local and the global focuses are represented.

Equally important in questions concerning product design and development is the fact that most governments (and customers) are insisting more and more on local development work to protect or increase national technical competence. Companies are increasingly required to carry out development work in multiple locations, but retain central management. Thus each local R&D laboratory is important both in defending the local political acceptability and in fostering the corporation's overall economic performance. Consequently, both managerial focuses have to be considered in managing the R&D function.

Export marketing is another key area where local acceptability and global proficiency meet. The penetration of new markets depends to some extent on exports, often as a first phase in telecommunications and, almost always, in heavy electrical equipment. Because of the trade and credit links between governments of exporting and importing countries and because of balance-of-payments pressures, exports are important to the local country managers. Because they are part of the overall worldwide expansion pattern of the business they are also important to corporate or product division management. Coordination of exports is part of the overall strategy. Judicious allocation of export orders between subsidiaries can improve their political acceptability as well as the corporate ability to get into new markets.

Certain other areas also require close cooperation between central and local management. This can be particularly true of manufacturing. Though large-scale cross-shipments seldom can take place for long, integration of production is possible for some parts, components, and subassemblies. How this integration develops affects both political acceptability and economic proficiency. Adopting common manufacturing methods and exchanging experience is another area where both local and global managements have interests and stakes. Since production methods, however, have no immediate, highly visible, external impact, priorities are often low when compared to product development or export marketing.

The Provision of Decision Premises

Beyond the overall allocation of relative power and the use of uncommitted, functional managers (whose power is based on expertise) to differentiate, check, and modulate this power allocation among functions and decision areas, top management can also use purposively a set of procedures and administrative tools to guide the behavior of lower-level managers.

Herbert Simon, followed by Richard M. Cyert and James G. March, explored the process of human decision making and concluded that human beings reach boundedly rational decisions, that is, decisions that are consistent with the information they have, however limited or distorted, and that achieve acceptable satisfaction levels in terms of the goal(s) they pursue, without attempting to maximize satisfaction, take into account all available information or possible choices.[26] But how, in a large complex organization such as an MNC, these various decisions taken by different members of the organization are made consistent, is left unanswered. Joseph L. Bower, in attempting to conceptualize the process of allocation of investment resources in a large diversified company, developed the concept of "context" to explain how various decisions distributed within the organization could be made into a consistent whole. He described context in the following way: "it shapes the purposive manager's definition of business problems by directing, delimiting and coloring the focus and perception, it determines the priorities which the various demands on him are given."[27]

Context goes beyond the lines of the hierarchical structure to encompass information flows and channels, control and measurement systems, and the rewards and punishments for managers. Because context shapes the perception of external events, and structures the priorities of managers, it strongly influences future choices. It also defines the rules by which managers will compete and what (or who) they will sponsor. Bower argues for the need to integrate phases in the strategic process in order to ensure "consistency along the multiple dimensions of strategy and structure of the initiating parts and the corporate whole."[28] The general validity of Bower's approach to managing large complex corporations was corroborated by a stream of research works that followed his research project.[29]

In the case of multinational companies the context within which the managers in product divisions and subsidiaries operate is basically made up of a set of administrative characteristics: organizational structure, information flows, planning and budgeting processes, and finally, policies for staffing, career paths, and rewards and punishments. The combination of these characteristics added to specific administrative procedures, will determine how the functions of production and research and development are managed within each national subsidiary, what links will exist at the national level with local partners, how joint ventures will be managed, and how the relationships inside the organization will evolve over time. Finally, the role of corporate managers in setting up the context, in developing standard operating procedures, and in selectively intervening in substantive decisions will tend to steer the organization in one direction or another.

Bower argues that consistency needs to be achieved in all these different characteristics in order to avoid contradictions and excessive ambiguity where thought processes could quickly become unstructured. It is quite unlikely, however, that complete consistency can be achieved, given the contradictory demand of economic and political imperatives. Consequently, ambiguity, lack of clarity, and a certain amount of self-protecting behavior are a way of life in complex international corporations. As some administrative processes deliberately create conflicts and channel power, politics are a usual side effect of complex administrative forms. The duality of focus also will necessarily involve conflicting perceptions of different needs, competing options with different sponsors, and breaking old procedures followed by the emergence of new ones.

In summary, context management provides a third way to manage the duality of political and economic imperatives, but it does not offer a clear-cut solution. Context management is rather a process of adjustment of individual administrative characteristics so that they maintain a tension between the fragmentation dangers inherent in a mother-daughter relationship and the lack of flexibility of a unidimensional product or area multinational structure. By acting upon the context, managers try to maintain a consistent pattern among decisions within the company, and yet to be responsive to specific competitive or host government demands.

CONCLUSION

This chapter has explored the managerial requirements of the strategies of companies active in the telecommunication equipment and power system industries. The central conclusion is that the relatively simple structures found among (1) companies operating in fragmented, national, oligopolistic environments or (2) companies operating in high-technology, worldwide industries do not fit the complexity of the managerial requirements found here. Despite their obvious weaknesses, matrix structures (or informal matrix management) seem to provide for the duality of economic and political imperatives characteristic of the telecommunication equipment and power system industries. The difficulty of providing strategic direction (an inherent problem in the matrix), and the strategic ambiguity created by the dual environments, can be overcome through several means. First, specific strategies usually favor one imperative over the other. Second, functional managers whose power is based on expertise can be used to differentiate the allocation of power to executives more responsive to one or the other imperative among functions and tasks. Third, various administrative characteristics (formal structure, information flows, planning and budgeting processes, and policies for staffing, career paths, and rewards and retribution) provide a context to decisions and can be used by top management to provide direction for particular decisions. Finally, it remains that top managers can directly intervene in the substance of decisions and swing them one way or another.

Before further analyzing these means for providing strategic direction while remaining responsive to the duality of imperatives, we will take a long pause to introduce clinical data from three selected companies. These data and the accompanying analyses will both illustrate and make clearer the argument developed in this chapter and provide the basis for further conceptualization. Each of the next three chapters consists of a short introduction placing the clinical descriptions within the overall framework of this book, a clinical description of one company (or product group within a diversified company), and an analysis of the clinical data.

NOTES

1. Alfred D. Chandler, Strategy and Structure (Cambridge, Mass.: The M.I.T. Press, 1962).

2. Bruce R. Scott, "Stages of Corporate Development," (Boston: Intercollegiate Case Clearing House, no. 9-371-294, 1971). On diversification, see Leonard Wrigley, "Divisional Autonomy and Di-

versification" (Ph.D. diss., Harvard Business School, 1970); and Norman Berg, "What's Different about Conglomerate Management," Harvard Business Review, November-December 1969, p. 112-20.

3. Richard P. Rumelt, Strategy, Structure and Economic Performance (Boston: Harvard Business School Division of Research, 1974).

4. See, for a critical view, Richard Bettis, William Hall, and C. K. Prahalad, "Diversity and Performance in the Multibusiness Firm" (Paper presented at the American Institute of Decision Sciences Meeting, St. Louis, Mo., October 1978).

5. See, Derek F. Channon, The Strategy and Structure of British Enterprise (Boston: Harvard Business School Division of Research, 1974); Gareth Pooley Dyas, "The Strategy and Structure of French Industrial Enterprise" (Ph.D. diss., Harvard Business School, 1972); Robert D. Pavan, "The Strategy and Structure of Italian Enterprise" (Ph.D. diss., Harvard Business School, 1972); and Heinz T. Tannheiser, "The Strategy and Structure of German Industrial Enterprise" (Ph.D. diss., Harvard Business School, 1972).

6. John Stopford and Louis T. Wells, Jr., Managing the Multinational Enterprise (New York: Basic Books, 1972), especially Chapter 2.

7. Lawrence G. Franko, The European Multinationals (Stamford, Conn.: Greylock, 1976).

8. See, Jack Behrman and Harvey W. Wallender, Transfer of Manufacturing Technology within Multinational Enterprises (Cambridge, Mass.: Ballinger, 1976); and Jack Baranson, Technology and the Multinationals (Lexington, Mass.: Lexington Books, 1978).

9. Lawrence G. Franko, Joint Venture Survival in International Business (New York: Praeger, 1971).

10. Joan P. Curhan, William H. Davidson, and Rajan Suri, Tracing the Multinationals: A Source Book on U.S. Based Enterprises (Cambridge, Mass.: Ballinger, 1971).

11. See, for instance, Ulrich Wiechmann, Marketing Management in Multinational Firms: The Consumer Packaged Goods Industry (New York: Praeger, 1976).

12. C. K. Prahalad, "The Strategic Process in a Multinational Corporation" (D.B.A. diss., Harvard Business School, 1975), p. 41.

13. Franko, The European Multinationals, pp. 208-10.

14. Jay R. Galbraith, "Designing Matrix Organizations," Business Horizons, February 1971.

15. For a full treatment see, Jay R. Galbraith and Daniel Nathanson, Strategy Implementation: The Role of Organization Structure and Process (Boulder, Colo.: The West, 1978).

16. Harvey F. Kolodny, "Matrix Organization Design, Implementation and Management" (D.B.A. diss., Harvard Business School, 1976).

17. Ibid., p. 156.

18. Michael S. Beer and Stanley M. Davis, "Creating a Global Organization: Failures Along the Way," Columbia Journal of World Business, Summer 1976, pp. 72-84.

19. Stanley M. Davis and Paul R. Lawrence, Matrix (Reading, Mass.: Addison Wesley, 1978), p. 206.

20. Stanley M. Davis and Paul R. Lawrence, "Matrix Organizations," Harvard Business Review, May-June 1978, pp. 131-42.

21. Prahalad, "The Strategic Process".

22. Adapted from Joseph L. Bower and Yves Doz, "Strategy Formulation: A Social and Political Process," in Strategic Management, ed. Charles Hofer and Dan Schendel (Boston: Little, Brown, 1979).

23. John D. Steinbruner, The Cybernetic Theory of Decision (Princeton, N.J.: Princeton University Press, 1974), p. 129.

24. See, David G. Bradley, "Managing Against Expropriation," Harvard Business Review, July-August 1977, p. 81; and Nathan Fagre and Louis T. Wells, Jr., "Bargaining Power of Multinationals and Host Governments," mimeographed (July 14, 1978).

25. Nicolas Jequier, Les Télécommunications et l'Europe (Geneva: Centre d'Etudes Industrielles, 1976) and A. Surrey, World Market for Electric Power Equipment: Rationalization and Technical Change (Brighton: University of Sussex, 1972).

26. Herbert Simon, Administrative Behavior (New York: The Free Press, 1945); and Richard M. Cyert and James G. March, A Behavioral Theory of the Firm (Englewood Cliffs, N.J.: Prentice Hall, 1963).

27. Joseph L. Bower, Managing the Resource Allocation Process (Boston: Harvard Business School Division of Research, 1970), p. 73.

28. Ibid., p. 289.

29. For a summary of these works, see Bower and Doz, "Strategy Formulation," pp. 12-22.

7

THE CENTRALIZED MODE

INTRODUCTION

In prior chapters the centralized management mode was suggested as a possible response to the conflict between the economic and the political imperatives. It was also suggested that it would apply particularly well to companies taking advantage of higher technology to follow an economic strategy. Such a technology-based economic strategy is most effective in penetrating newer markets or markets where the local suppliers have fallen behind technologically. In this chapter the example of LM Ericsson is used to illustrate the centralized mode. Within the concrete setting presented by an actual company the characteristics of the centralized mode are described and analyzed.

In the centralized mode the tasks of responding to national demands and adapting to the diversity among markets, on the one hand, and developing overall technological and cost competitiveness, on the other, are clearly separated. A strong central company, usually in the country of origin, carries out all international tasks, in particular, export marketing to new markets and research and development. This strong, and usually large, central company has a complete line and staff management, usually organized by product divisions and functions, respectively. The relative importance and strength of each usually corresponds not only to domestic diversity, but also to cultural characteristics and management behavior traits in the home country. A group of foreign subsidiaries catering exclusively to their own domestic markets provides responsiveness: each can adapt to the specific requirements of local administrations and customers. Yet, each subsidiary remains largely dependent upon the influx of technology and expertise from the central company.

The first section of this chapter describes the managerial tools outlined in Figure 1.1 in Chapter 1: the organizational structure; the information system; the planning, budgeting, and reporting systems; the patterns of staffing, career paths, and rewards and punishments; and finally, the pattern of top management intervention into the substance of business decisions and plans. The second section analyzes the impact of these managerial tools on the manufacturing policy, the location and management of R&D activities, and the relationships with local partners and customers in host countries. Finally, the third section of this chapter analyzes and comments on the clinical descriptions and draws some implications.

MANAGERIAL TOOLS

Organizational Structure

In 1976 the corporate domestic structure of LM Ericsson was functionally organized. There were "product divisions," but without their own functional support units and even without production facilities (all manufacturing was grouped in a single managerial entity). Hence the product divisions were more like product management units than full-fledged divisions. The first managerial echelon below the president was composed of functional managers and managers responsible for operations or divisions.

Functional managers at headquarters shared three orientations: overall international group management, management of the Swedish company, and control of the foreign subsidiaries. Integration between the first two roles was achieved easily because there was no separation between the corporate and the Swedish company management. Integration of the third orientation was achieved through directorship of the subsidiaries: nearly all functional vice-presidents and executive vice-presidents played active roles on the boards of several subsidiaries.

One executive vice-president explained the role of the subsidiary boards in the following way:

> The board is the policy maker of the foreign company. Of course, the directors representing the mother company have a strong position in elaborating that policy. Local boards play a major role in coordinating the activities with Stockholm. One would be tempted to say that, as our activities are similar, foreign companies should only be an arm of the Swedish operations, and that more continuous managerial contacts would be more natural. The local boards, however, have a different experience. There is a financial and controlling aspect, but not an operational integration.

All investment proposals were channeled through the local board, and
its members represented both the local subsidiary's point of view in
Stockholm and the Swedish point of view locally; but this was done very
informally, with no clear-cut allocation of responsibility.

The role of the local board varied according to several elements.
In some cases (France and Italy, in particular) older European subsidiaries operated very autonomously. In large and more recently
formed subsidiaries that had local participation in their equity, the
board was a real decision-making unit where the points of view of both
local shareholders sensitive to the subsidiary's responsiveness and
LME's central management were represented. Smaller companies
entirely owned by LME had boards whose main role was to relay information to corporate management in Stockholm. Finally, some
sizable operations were of an "off-shore" type because of restrictive
local legislation (in Egypt, for instance).

Product divisions and subsidiaries had little direct contact except for transfer of products to the subsidiaries. One marketing staff
manager commented:

> In a sense we want to be able to manage the relationship be-
> tween our domestic product divisions and our foreign sub-
> sidiaries; both are profit centers. We are not managing it
> from a position of authority, but as a group of consultants
> whose services are required. Transfer pricing is not too
> difficult usually; the two of them can come to agreement
> by starting from a fair price to customers. Delivery de-
> lays and faulty goods create more difficulties. When there
> is a conflict things come up to us.

In summary, integration of the subsidiaries was carried out on
two levels. Strategic integration was achieved through the interlocking directorships and corporate-Swedish management commonality.
Operating integration was carried out with the help of functional staffs
who coordinated the relationships between the Swedish product divisions and the local subsidiaries. Some subsidiaries had product divisions directly corresponding to the Swedish divisions.

Coordination could be kept relatively simple because each subsidiary was geared exclusively to its local market. Product transfers
usually went only from Stockholm to subsidiaries. Exports to markets
where LME had no production, as well as exports of parts or components to assembly plants, took place almost .entirely from Sweden.
Staff experts in such areas as production methods, proposal preparation, equipment purchasing, network design, installation, and marketing were continuously available in Sweden to be sent to assist subsidiary managements with customer negotiations, plant expansions,
investments, or productivity efforts. All international activities were
carried out from the Swedish headquarters. Because export sales

FIGURE 7.1

Simplified Structure of LM Ericsson

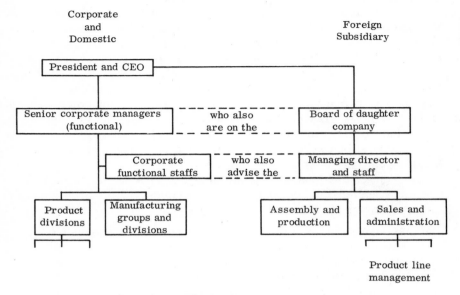

Source: Compiled by the author.

represented a sizable portion of its turnover, it had a strong international interest. The competencies needed to guide LME's penetration of new markets, as well as to provide superior assistance to its local companies, were centralized in Sweden. The organizational structure is diagrammed in Figure 7.1.

Information Systems

Almost all information circulated to or from the central functional managers and their staff services. Basically the subsidiaries filed reports on their activities and received advice and assistance from headquarters. The formal flow consisted of a set of exchanges between the subsidiaries and various functional managers in Stockholm. At LME, monthly marketing and financial reports were sent to headquarters. The former described the local situation in terms of new possibilities, political and economic evolutions, and relationships with the PTTs. The latter was a relatively detailed financial statement comparing performance with approved budgets and year-end targets. The complete set of reports was sent to the managers for marketing and finance and to the controller's office.

Twice a year a production report was also sent to the management office for overseas manufacturing (which reported to the executive vice-president for manufacturing). It stated the quantities of supplies, parts, subassemblies, components, and so forth needed from Sweden for the following six months. The report also described the production situation and included summary statistics on efficiency, local integration, productivity gains, training of workers, and so on. These production efficiency statistics were circulated internally among plant managers. Yet little use was made of the operating data collected from the subsidiaries. Routine comparisons and consolidations were made, but there was little evidence of substantive decisions or actions resulting from the analysis of such data.

Very little information circulated between subsidiaries. There were no formal channels, and meetings between their managing directors were rare. Specific meetings at a lower level were more frequent but they usually dealt with only one limited problem, for instance, how to launch production of a new type of switch.

Most communications, except for discussions in the quarterly board meeting, went along functional lines and covered a series of separate domains. One manager in the central staff commented:

> How coordination with foreign subsidiaries is carried out depends upon the subsidiary. If we deal with a well-established LME company, in a market where everything is strictly defined by the customer, we do not know of much. France and Italy, for instance, are companies which have a complete production process. Similarly, in Australia we have a highly integrated operation, with little direct involvement from Stockholm. A less self-sufficient unit would involve much more communication. For instance, some fellows would come from Stockholm to discuss new orders with the local customers. The intensity of communication grows naturally with the dependence of the company.

The intensity of communications varied not only among subsidiaries, but also according to functions, and tended to increase with perceived uniformity and decrease with perceived diversity for any given subsidiary. For instance, the rapid expansion of foreign manufacturing operations into new, less-industrialized countries resulted in a need to transfer competence easily to a new market, which usually involved an increase in manufacturing standardization. Thus communications had been stepped up in an effort to increase the uniformity of production methods. In marketing, on the other hand, diversity was well recognized and led to less intense communications.

Much exchange of information took place informally in face-to-face contacts. The corporate controller had a group of auditors who traveled extensively and the corporate marketing managers divided their time between Stockholm and the countries for which they were responsible. Some formal information exchange forums were set up. For instance, coordination with foreign subsidiaries' design offices was achieved through "development councils" (one for each major product line) where the central functional R&D staff was preeminent, though in Sweden divisions were in charge of product development. The same central staff role existed in manufacturing and marketing.

In contrast to the formal information flow, the informal communication network was rich and based on common training and personal knowledge of other managers in the organization. As one manager put it:

> We always have had a competitive advantage in the field: even at low levels in the hierarchy you are always able to speak freely, and you will be listened to with attention and respect. You can talk to Mr. Lundvall if you want to.* No manager will be embarrassed because a subordinate speaks differently.

Lundvall himself visited most subsidiaries from time to time. He had a direct understanding of their operations and a detailed knowledge of their financial posture. Thus, the rather narrowly channeled information flows in the formal system were compensated for by broader frank communications on an informal basis.

These informal, flexible information flows clearly dominated the formal systems. A lot of exchanges took place directly among old pals in the top management group. Some subsidiary managing directors spent much time directly communicating with Lundvall while others relied more on the various corporate staffs. There was no clear rule specifying who was to go to headquarters for any particular issue. But, informally, each subsidiary management had developed reliable channels.

Planning, Budgeting, and Reporting Systems

LME used a comprehensive planning process with a five-year time horizon. Yet, plans for the last two years of the five-year cycle were only broadly outlined, the two intermediate years were planned in some detail, and the first year underwent a detailed budgeting procedure. Thus, only the first year was really analyzed in detail. No corporate goals or corporate targets were issued. A corporate executive explained the major characteristics of the process:

---

*Lundvall was the president of LM Ericsson in 1976. Since 1977 he is chairman.

We evaluate market prospects and discount them; the initiator is the sales and marketing management in the subsidiaries. They develop scenarios of market size and growth for several years ahead. We then try to evaluate these broad figures in terms of investment, personnel, and financial return in the different countries. It is very important to get the local management deeply involved in budgeting if we want them to feel responsible for the subsidiary company. The budgets are discussed in Stockholm, company by company, and finally they are approved by the local boards. We do not want to be too closely involved. We like to delegate responsibility and only to control the main goals. We use the process for many important discussions, such as how to divide production between Sweden and the overseas companies.

When corporate marketing managers reviewed the market prospects of the subsidiaries, much groundwork had already been done. Product ranges and new development had been reviewed by the R&D staff and the product divisions, and the budget committee had held a special meeting to discuss and approve R&D projects and expense budgets. From the information provided by the subsidiaries on their market prospects, the domestic product divisions in Sweden were provided with sales forecasts for export markets, and the various countries were listed according to priority for deliveries by domestic divisions and allocation of corporate funds.

Following a meeting of the budget committee in June, a general report was made, summarizing all major aspects: financial situation, manufacturing capacity and utilization, market reports, licenses, administrative projects, personnel planning, and allocation of resources. In August the detailed budgeting process started once the budget committee had issued financial and operational guidelines based on the outcome of the five-year planning procedure. In September the plans of each subsidiary were reviewed and then approved by its board (see Figure 7.2).

Quarterly and monthly breakdowns were then produced to monitor the execution of the budgets and plans and to make projections for the end of the period. A team of internal auditors studied the accounts of each subsidiary at least once a year, and most subsidiaries were visited more than once. The efforts of the controller's office to maintain a constant understanding of the finances of each company were paralleled by those of the marketing and production departments in their own fields; both carried out substantial control activities and helped investigate serious financial discrepancies.

In summary, little overall guidance was exercised formally on the subsidiaries. They were largely free to determine their objec-

FIGURE 7.2

LM Ericsson, Simplified Diagram of the Planning and Budgeting Process

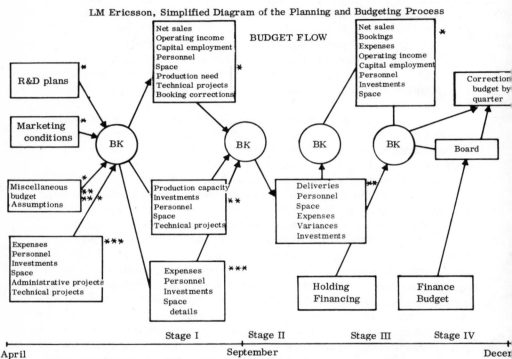

Note: Stage I encompasses five-year projections, Stages II, III, and IV only three-year projection

Source: Compiled by the author.

162

tives, and the corporate level was quite aware of performance differences due to differences between countries. Yet, once the subsidiaries had defined their prospects, a more tightly centralized control was exercised (partly informally) in order for the corporate level to gain detailed knowledge of the operations of each subsidiary and to measure its performance against its plans and budgets. In that process no specific measurement criteria or reporting highlights were singled out. There was a corporate willingness to go beyond aggregate measurements to understand the specifics of each subsidiary's situation and performance.

Staffing, Career Paths, Rewards and Punishments

The management of LME was quite inbred. Nearly all members of the top management group had spent their entire careers within the company. The training at LME created a very strong loyalty to the company after a few years. A manager, then close to 50, recalled the typical experience of a career at LME:

> People grow up in this company, as in few others. Very
> few leave us. In 25 years I passed from subject to sub-
> ject so actively I had no time to be bored. Characters are
> born in the company, and grow with it. I started in 1950
> as an engineer in proposal preparation. I was picked up
> to be sent abroad—most engineers in their twenties had ap-
> plied but only a few were selected. Instead of continuing
> in our jobs we got a very complete training and education
> about LME as a whole. In 1955 I was sent as a branch
> manager to one of our Latin American operations. Several
> times I was offered much better jobs, particularly by U.S.
> food companies, but they were wrong in firing people who
> merely disagreed with the top. One reason for the success
> of LME is the ability to develop people, to satisfy them, to
> find the right slot for them without letting someone go.
> This builds a very trusting climate among managers. Very
> few of our people go to the competition. There is so much
> education in the company, that it's like having an emblem
> tattooed on the forehead. Our people have so much loyalty
> that we can trust them easily, it creates a very good cli-
> mate.

Almost all LME managers had a similar telecommunication-engineering university background (most of them at the Stockholm School of Engineering) and nearly all had been with LME for a long time. Training abroad was acquired by working in bigger and bigger subsidiaries. Potential foreign managers usually worked in Sweden for some time, and in most subsidiaries there were at least a few Swedes in top management. In many cases the managing director was a Swede, and if not, the controller was usually a Swede. This allowed easier communications with Stockholm and a perfusion of the LME esprit de corps to the local manager.

In addition to managers who had an international career, Swedish specialists could be detached from the domestic product divisions, upon the local subsidiary management's request for someone to fill a vacancy. Contracts were usually for two years and the candidates were selected by the area marketing manager from a list provided by the division, subject to approval by the subsidiary management. After two years, expatriates could remain in the foreign country, come back to the division, or apply for a job in another subsidiary. This created some difficulties for local managing directors, as one of them explained:

> A division manager will be sent to me from the home switching division when I divisionalize my company. In the division, he was pretty close to the boss. This man will see his future in switching, not in my country. I tell him, "You no longer have any master in the switching head office, you do not serve the switching division in Sweden but the subsidiary here." The man is likely to think, "If I do my best he will help me, if he is influential in Stockholm." There is a reciprocal selection process, but unless someone develops a strong liking for the local country it is difficult to get a high degree of loyalty.

The fear of failure was not very strong. Managers were not compensated through individual incentive schemes, and instances of discharge from the company were very few. Top managers in subsidiaries almost had a lifetime position. Early in a person's association with LME great care was apparently exercised to assess his or her potential and to determine a suitable career orientation. The shift from a technical to a managerial job, and from middle to top management (for instance, from manager of a workshop to production manager) in local companies, were two critical changes that were carefully considered. LME had been, and still was to some extent, in a favorable position to attract outstanding people in Sweden: telecommunications remained a technically glamorous industry and the existence of both a strong domestic base and a worldwide set of activities enabled people to plan to return to Sweden in their forties after a career start abroad.

Top Management's Pattern of Intervention

At LM Ericsson Lundvall reserved the right to rule for himself when strong disagreements erupted. Disagreements would be brought to his attention through the corporate staff manager who managed the interface between product divisions and subsidiaries. One corporate marketing manager described the process in the following way:

> Trying to tilt the balance does not work. A managing director abroad might be tempted to try to relate to Mr. Lundvall alone, and cut off the relationship with the functional corporate managers. This would not work in the long run. First, I would go to the fellow and tell him not to push Mr. Lundvall too much. If the guy is tough he may well have made a very nice solid study and given it to Mr. Lundvall for approval and implementation. Mr. Lundvall in such a case, will send the study back to us and the division, to make sure it is ground through the normal decision process. It's a game where there can be no winner, but where some competition between managers is built into the system. A manager out in the field cannot pull all the strings himself, nor can a division have local "agents" within a subsidiary.

Direct top management attention was also directed to the boards of the subsidiaries. The president of LME, and in many cases the chairman of the company (Marcus Wallenberg, until Lundvall replaced him), approved the appointment of all directors of each subsidiary. Over the years, they had appointed outside directors taking a keen interest in the management of subsidiaries from a local point of view. Whenever a conflict between the board of a subsidiary and corporate managers in Stockholm could not be resolved easily, Lundvall would step in. One top manager commented:

> During Mr. Lundvall's era more emphasis has been put on the local board of directors as a managing body. We tend to represent the corporate perspective in these boards; however, we seldom confront a managing director on a key issue. You can limit the scope of what he rules, but on what he rules you can only work to convince him.

Lundvall's in-depth knowledge of the industry and of its customers also enabled him to intervene in the substance of business decisions. For instance, he personally approved all credit proposals for new businesses, and sometimes made decisions on pricing or on conditions to be set with a customer. Often, he himself negotiated with heads of state or government ministers for larger contracts or just to maintain good relationships with the authorities of important countries.

In the budget committee Lundvall frequently made resource allocation decisions between functional managers, all of whom hoped for a better share of total resources. He could decide upon the relative importance of functions and upon the balance between area and product managements in each function through the functional managers.

Lundvall also intervened on key managerial appointments in large subsidiaries and was routinely kept informed of key managerial and technical assignments.

The interplay between the various managerial tools described above will be analyzed in the last section of this chapter, but first, a review of the actual operating patterns of the company is needed.

OPERATING PATTERNS

Manufacturing

The pattern of manufacturing at LME was relatively simple: Swedish factories produced a complete product range in a whole production process, whereas subsidiary factories most often had neither a whole production process nor a complete product range. Concentrating some of the assembly and most of the components in Sweden brought large savings. More than 70 percent of the value added in Sweden was exported. Subsidiaries did not export. A very large part of the exports from Sweden were in the form of components and subassemblies going to subsidiaries. A corporate manager commented upon the manufacturing setup:

> So far the split of production into two stages has worked relatively well. Components are made in Sweden in highly automated plants at a low cost. We try to keep components production here, because it is not practical to make them abroad in smaller series. Assembly operations, provided we have some volume, may in most cases be cheaper abroad. By moving assembly and tests to the local markets we get some amount of national character. This scheme functions rather well profitwise: without having moved the assembly we would have lost the markets, by moving the components production we would have lost the profits.

In some cases, particularly in mature industrial countries, the company had had to start components manufacture; for instance, the French PTT had made this a condition. So, AB Rifa (the electronic component subsidiary of LME) had undertaken components manufacture in France, and also supplied from there the rest of the EEC. In 1975 the top management of LME had been somewhat upset by the decision of another joint-venture company to start manufacturing components, even though this made little sense economically. The alliance among the local managing director, unions, and local directors around national technical-autonomy arguments and the policy of "fait accompli" followed in their dealings with Stockholm were somewhat disquieting.

The overseas production department, reporting to the vice-president for manufacturing, was responsible for the establishment and development of foreign production plants. LME's successes in many developing countries, particularly in Latin America, had resulted in the rapid introduction of many new factories. Another task of the overseas production department was to provide constant advice to the local companies without interfering with their management. The need to develop many factories rapidly and to provide ready advice had resulted in a growing uniformity of production methods among the foreign subsidiaries. The manager of the overseas production department commented:

> We help the production function in subsidiaries but we are not in a position to tell a manager abroad what he is to do in his plant. We have power without authority. For all local circumstances, such as workers' compensation or union agreements, we do not interfere at all. At the other end of the spectrum of control, we do not allow a company to modify the product range it manufactures without our agreement. The policy regarding what each subsidiary is to manufacture is set here in cooperation with the marketing department. Because we have found ways to help them grow and be more profitable, we have really good relationships with the subsidiaries abroad. They do not see us as a nasty controlling body, but as a positive partner with whom few harsh words are exchanged.

As we saw in Chapter 5, there were three categories of subsidiaries according to the amount of assistance received from corporate headquarters. Category I covered smaller plants built in response to commercial conditions in order to sell equipment in a new market. Sometimes such plants were called for in the agreements with customers; sometimes they were started at LME's initiative to improve the relationships with customers (in Ireland, for instance). These plants normally did final assembly and wiring jobs on kits imported from Sweden. These jobs were almost entirely manual and not subject to strong economies of scale. Such plants were, by and large, managed from Stockholm.

Plants in category II were generally of medium size (200 to 1,000 employees) and corresponded to a transfer-of-technology period. A plant moved into category II when it started manufacturing mechanical parts and assembling the bulk of the exchange. A number of technical experts were sent from Sweden in that phase, but the supply responsibility and the general management function were assumed locally. Whereas quality was stressed in category I, plants in category II put emphasis upon timely delivery and efficient scheduling.

Category III plants belonged to mature companies, and usually had an almost complete manufacturing process, importing only a few components from Sweden. The emphasis was on cost reduction, but assistance from Sweden was minimal except when new products (or processes) were introduced. Finally, plants in France and Italy operated entirely independently of Stockholm. (See Figure 7.3 for a diagram of the production flow between Sweden and subsidiaries.)

There were certain tasks that were centrally controlled for all subsidiaries by several corporate units: an inventory-control unit to monitor use of parts supplied by the parent company; a central quality-control unit in Sweden to which quality-control specialists in each foreign plant reported; a training center providing uniform, systematic training packages; and advice concerning plant equipment from the overseas production department, with the monthly production-efficiency comparison reports described in a previous section.

The rapid penetration of new markets accompanied by local investments corresponded to much uniformity between new subsidiaries. Yet, much diversity remained because managers were selected and trained to blend into various types of customs and to achieve social acceptability in countries. To some extent, the uniformity of administrative procedures and the tight control were counterbalanced by the number of local executives and engineers appointed and by the rapid phasing out of Swedish expatriates.*

The policy of high quality and low cost used by LME to penetrate new markets also required tight control and the rapid achievement of a high degree of economic efficiency locally, in order to keep the promises made in the contracts. In many developing countries

---

*For instance, LME had started large-scale manufacturing in Spain in 1970. The number of Swedes in the production function followed this evolution: 1970—5; 1972—25; 1974—15; 1976—6; 1980 (plan)—1.

FIGURE 7.3

LM Ericsson, Product Flows between Parent Company and Foreign Subsidiaries

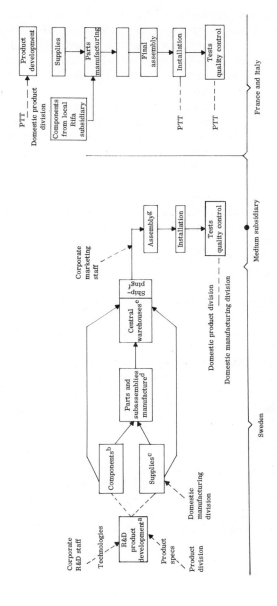

[a] Product development is carried out in divisional laboratories in Sweden.
[b] Components are developed and manufactured by AB Rifa, a subsidiary in Sweden.
[c] Supplies are determined by the domestic manufacturing division.
[d] Subcontracted to the domestic manufacturing division by the domestic production division.
[e] Foreign assembly supply centers in Sweden.
[f] Components, parts, subassemblies are sold, mostly as "kits" to the foreign subsidiaries by the domestic product division.
[g] Foreign subsidiary.

Source: Compiled by the author.

169

LME's ability to start up plants smoothly and to increase local integration had provided a strong competitive advantage. LME had also been willing to incur losses for a few years to absorb start-up costs wherever the market size justified rapid installation of a large-scale operation (for instance, operations in Brazil and Spain had not been breaking even until after several years).

At LME, the differentiation of plants by categories and the institutionalization of different objectives and degrees of central intervention were used to achieve a custom-designed balance between political acceptability and overall efficiency. Where the political imperatives were strong and where strong international and weak local competitors were present (as in France and Italy), LME did not intervene at all; the local management was entirely free to run the company. Moreover, some balanced trade was achieved: imports from Sweden were compensated for by exports to third countries from the French and Italian subsidiaries.

In newer markets, where economic considerations still mattered most, LME was freer to make local production more dependent upon inputs and imports from Sweden. In some mature developed countries similar moves were possible. For instance, the market share allocated to LME in the Netherlands became too small to warrant a whole production cycle when the switching technology shifted to Reed relays from rotary contacts. The local factory reverted to assembly tasks only, with components imported from Sweden. According to LME's Dutch subsidiary managers, the presence of Philips as a mighty "national champion" allowed LME to have very straightforward commercial dealings with the Dutch PTT. The degree of local integration, or the production of components locally, was not an issue for the Dutch PTT. In countries where it was, such as Brazil, LME tried to replace Swedish-made components by local ones, but the lack of custom design of components raised serious technical problems. In countries where providing jobs and avoiding foreign exchange drain were priorities it was possible to start the labor-intensive assembly process quickly and to carry it to almost full integration efficiently, provided that components were still imported from Sweden.

Location and Management of
Research and Development

Research and development (R&D) activities were heavily concentrated in Sweden when compared with sales (85 percent outside of Sweden) or even production (45 percent of total value added outside of Sweden). Of all development work, 80 percent was done in Sweden. The executive vice-president for R&D explained this concentration:

So far we have not gone to the point where any of the subsidiaries would develop a system of its own somewhere in
the world, under contract from Stockholm. For complex
systems the technical knowledge required is only to be
found in Stockholm. France, technically the strongest of
all subsidiaries, could not develop electronic switching
on its own. The 20 percent of development work moved
to subsidiaries involves applications to local markets
mostly. Yet, there is a strong tendency to move more
development work abroad to be closer to customer's
needs.

The central laboratories of LME and ELLEMTEL, a joint venture with the Swedish PTT, carried out most R&D work in an integrated
way. Product development was the responsibility of the product divisions, but it was monitored and guided by the corporate staff, which
took into account the needs of the foreign markets. However, up to
1975, the products of LME had been remarkably similar and the company had been able to avoid product diversity by adapting its products
to a multitude of possible interface situations. The new AXE electronic switching system was also being designed with the aim of solving most interface problems through software adaptation, with little
or no modification to the hardware.
     The manager of main-exchange development was keenly aware
of the difficulties involved in developing rigidly uniform products for
a variety of markets. He pointed out that the increase of R&D activities in subsidiaries, sometimes involving large parts of new systems,
would require a more elaborate scheme for coordination of the technical activities. In some cases subsystems or small systems would
be developed and optimized to fit the need of a given market. One
reason for such a change would be the increased use of electronic
components in telecommunication products. Customers were expected
to demand the use of domestically produced components in their systems.
     Technical coordination normally took place through a series of
meetings. Product needs in the various markets were typically explored at sales coordination meetings, in which the corporate area
marketing managers and development managers met with representatives of the subsidiaries. These meetings were used by the corporate
staff to keep abreast of the evolution of local markets and to try to formulate global product concepts to answer local needs. Development
councils made up of representatives from the corporation and from
individual subsidiaries met separately to organize new projects, to
allocate work between labs, and to keep all technical managers informed of activities. Ongoing research projects involving several

countries were run through lower-level project management groups where both the corporation and all involved subsidiaries were represented.

There was no general rule for funding R&D activities. Smaller projects, which were not a priority for subsidiaries but were to be carried out abroad, were entirely subcontracted from Sweden. Larger projects of strong interest to specific local subsidiaries were jointly financed according to shares determined on an ad hoc basis. Problem projects were rescued by high-caliber specialists sent from Stockholm on a short-term basis. Projects were seldom killed unless they were deemed absolutely beyond recovery. Control of projects was informal.

So whereas in the production function a rather complex organization had been built to provide flexibility and diversity of response, in the management of R&D, diversity had been almost ignored. Requirements for diversity were met by designing versatile products. As long as foreign countries looked for the control of end products only (and not of technical development processes themselves), the absence of a managerial answer provided an efficient response. The technical superiority of LME's Crossbar exchange system and of its long-distance exchanges had made acceptance of a standard type by customers easier.

Links with Local Entities in Host Countries

The Swedish origin of LME was an asset to the development of links in newer markets. The absence of a recent Swedish colonial past and the Swedish government's stance in favor of the third world in international forums were facilitating factors in places strongly marked by colonialism, such as Black Africa or Latin America. On the other hand, Sweden's lack of international clout did not help political sales, and the blunt comments sometimes made by Swedish officials about the domestic policies of foreign states generated some reluctance in certain countries, such as Chile and Spain.

According to its managers, LME's tradition of straightforward commercial dealings, without political undertones, and LME's dedication to long-term penetration and maintenance of a market, had permitted the development of strong local links in Latin America and in some Middle Eastern countries. Furthermore, a specialized company coming from a small, neutral, socialistic country did not raise the same fears as did large, multifaceted, diversified multinational groups headquartered in more powerful nations.

Yet as subsidiaries matured in various countries, and when the market size and the local technical capabilities permitted it, customers requested LME to transform its operations into a joint venture or to sell part of the equity to the public. As of 1975 LME's operations in the following countries were not wholly owned:

	Percent of LME Ownership
Norway	43
France	51
(to decrease to 25-30 percent)*	
Spain	51
Italy	51
Mexico	60†
Brazil	75†

All these companies were fairly large operations, often producing their own components, in contrast to LME's fully owned subsidiaries.

The centralized management of LME was quite effective in penetrating new markets, but its compatibility with the maturing of markets and the aging of its subsidiaries were questionable.

COMMENTARY

Analysis

LM Ericsson was using all three means outlined in Chapter 6 (strategy, functional managers, and administrative systems) to provide central guidance toward (and pressures for) integration while making central influence little visible and leaving it informal.

First, in the operating patterns, the dependencies were clearly from the center to the subsidiaries. All subsidiaries were dependent on the center for components and for product and process technology. Yet, with very few exceptions (relays in France, connectors in Ecuador), the subsidiaries did not supply components or finished products to each other or to the center. Subsidiaries were responsible only for some special product lines that did not impact the main businesses (for instance, the Dutch subsidiary had specialized in shipboard telephone and intercom systems). In terms of product flows, interdependencies were sequential; thus they limited the vulnerability of the center and decreased the need for coordination of the subsidiaries.[1] Henri de Bodinat, in an empirical study of influence in the multina-

---

*After the acquisition of the AXE system by the PTT.
† Slowly decreasing to follow progressive "localization" plans.

tional enterprise, found that sequential interdependencies often led to less central influence than reciprocal interdependencies (that is, a system where subsidiaries would be dependent on one another).

The very nature of the products also made central informal coordination easier. It was only at comparatively long intervals that new technologies were introduced in the subsidiaries. In main-exchange switching, telephone sets and PABX technology, as we have seen, evolved little between the emergence of major new generations of equipment. Technology transfer management could be made rather informally without too much permanent control from Stockholm. The spread over several years of the adoption of any new technology by the various countries where LME had subsidiaries also made the management of transfer easier, as the attention could shift from subsidiary to subsidiary over time. The management of technology was also made easier as only the parent company in Sweden was heavily involved in exports. What small export volume issued from subsidiaries was subcontracted by Stockholm, except for very specialized product lines. The parent company maintained a complete production capability and usually had a first pick on export orders.

Thus in both key areas, management of technology and of export coordination, the strategy reflected by the operating patterns of the firm was clearly one of integration and rationalization. Yet, strong product divisions did not match centralization. The corporate level was managing the interface between subsidiaries and domestic divisions quite closely. Strong corporate functional managers were used to manage this interface. These functional managers could effectively determine the balance between area and product management, not only because the structure favored the central functional managers but also because the intensity of information flow was controlled from headquarters. In functions that required much sensitivity to diversity, such as marketing, considerable autonomy was left to local managers. In functions that called for much interdependence (or centralization), such as product development, they favored product managers.

The flavor of the key balancing role is well rendered by the description an area marketing manager (responsible for coordination between the product divisions in Sweden and a series of subsidiaries in one area) gave of his job:

> For us, the number one requirement is to know one area
> well; the type of knowledge you develop when you have
> worked and lived there for many years. You need to have
> known the people well, the PTT officials and the LME lo-
> cal executives, since all were junior engineers. You ba-
> sically help the local managing directors; they can call on
> you whenever they get into a matter about which they are

not too sure themselves. You get into a whole spectrum of questions, from late deliveries to the overall LME strategic coordination for one continent. To the division, you represent the fellow in the field, and vice versa. You have to lead them to compromise, to make decisions come out in a way we think best for the whole LME, and acceptable for both of them. There is also some arbitration between divisions.

Our competitors often behave in identifiable ways. The fellow from the transmissions division may wish to do nothing against, say, ICO [a disguised name] in selling switching equipment somewhere, for fear of a reaction in transmissions where ICO is strong. That sets up a conflict where the local manager is caught between different inputs from two domestic divisions. When I have trouble convincing either side (or both), I go to Mr. Stein (marketing executive vice-president) with my advice on what to do. He talks to the fellows himself; or if it is a serious disagreement, he goes to Mr. Lundvall. Mr. Lundvall then makes the coordination between the vice-presidents. I would set that in motion only as a last recourse. Normally I have to show restraint, and intervene upward only when I feel it is really necessary and when I think I can convince Mr. Lundvall. In addition I do not like the idea of asking him to clobber someone. People know that if they disagree with me, they may have to present a strong argument to convince Mr. Lundvall. In a sense it is power without formal authority. Of course, if I start being wrong too often my power will decrease, so I move only when I am sure of myself. Sometimes you have to give more support to the local weak company than to the big tough division, but the key to success is to remain neutral, to behave as a broker. The situation is balanced enough for that. Everybody implicitly understands the need to be well behaved, and seldom do I have to use a show of power to resolve a conflict.

In other words, whenever a local or division manager tried to shift the power balance to his own advantage, the top management would give more power to the involved corporate functional managers. These would then thrust their weight on the weaker side to protect the balance and their own preeminence. The manager quoted above illustrates the powerful integrative role played by functional managers. The fact that they could decide "what we think best for the whole of LME" assumes an overall substantive strategy defined from the top.

The whole arrangement permitted the functional managers to act as "uncommitted thinkers" and to perform an integrating role in the management process. Their understanding of the overall strategy of the company, combined with their role in sorting out operating problems and allocating decisions between national subsidiary and product division managers, left them uncommitted to either, but with a strong overall framework within which to assess decisions and actions. So the overlap between corporate management and the local boards, as well as the relatively low status of domestic divisions, made the power structure congruent with the key role assigned to functional managers.

In turn, such informal balancing and mediating could work, thanks to three conditions. First, both the area functional manager and the top management of the company had a deep enough understanding of the substance of its businesses in various countries to intervene directly and show expertise and authority in dealing with controversial issues. Second, the formal system was quite loose and offered great flexibility in choosing how to deal with particular issues. Informal information channels were more important than formal information systems. Third, there were deep links uniting all LME's managers. These links were a guarantee that the outcomes of individual decisions could be decoupled from career and compensation issues. The homogeneous recruiting base, the lifetime employment policy, the thorough training program, the short-term foreign detachment system, and the leniency of formal reward and punishment systems all contributed to foster a common climate in which cooperation developed easily.

So, within the overall preference for integration and uniformity, great liberty was left for deviant solutions. The informal management process, combined with the key mediating and balancing role of the area marketing managers, left a variety of solutions possible according to the development of particular alliances. Yet, the dangers of politicization and power play usually presented by the opportunity for coalitional decision making could be checked by the in-depth knowledge of the industry shared by the management group, their common past, and the leniency of individual reward and punishment schemes. Thus, the integration of subsidiaries to the parent was managed through a common sense of loyalty and belonging more than through formal procedures.

This conclusion is consistent with the findings of other researchers. In a study of the international food industry Ulrich Wiechmann found four types of "integrative mechanisms" used in multinational marketing coordination by the international firms he studied.[2] Besides pure centralization, he found corporate acculturation (training to indoctrinate managers), systems transfer (uniform framework for planning and budgeting), and people transfer (meetings, short assignments abroad). He concluded:

It seems that the choice of integrative devices has to be
linked to the nature of the firm's products. For companies selling products that . . . do not require extensive
local adaptation, high centralization as a primary integrative device may be an effective way of integrating
multinational operations. . . . Conversely, for multinational enterprises selling highly culture-bound products that require local custom-tailoring of marketing
programs, high autonomy of subsidiary managers seems
to be indicated. Many food companies fall into this group.
Since in these firms headquarters' control over marketing
decisions has to be limited, integration must be achieved
primarily through corporate acculturation, system transfer and people transfer.[3]

De Bodinat, in a study of manufacturing policies of some international corporations in Western Europe, developed an argument
closely akin to Wiechmann's.[4] He studied the influence patterns in
the manufacturing function, and differentiated between direct influence
(control systems) and indirect influence (socialization), and between
styles of influence (authoritarian and collaborative). These categories
are not essentially different from Wiechmann's. For instance, Wiechmann's centralization mechanism closely corresponds to de Bodinat's
direct authoritarian influence. Similarly, other categories used by
Wiechmann and de Bodinat approximately correspond to the same
reality though they apply to two different functions. De Bodinat developed an argument on influence and the host governments:

Nation states will want to reduce influence. Multinationals
could attempt to reduce influence to the strict minimum required by the internal variables. In order to minimize the
visibility of this influence, multinational firms could attempt to progressively drift from direct influence to indirect influence through control systems or even through
acculturation.[5]

In summary, it seems that given the demands of the political
imperative, LME was able to reach some centrally managed integration, thanks to the quality of its technology and the informality of its
management processes. The informal centralization of all information
pertinent to the interface between product divisions and subsidiaries
with corporate functional staffs close to the president of the company
permitted a balance to be found between political and economic imperatives in a flexible way for each situation.

Implications

LME had found a relatively simple way to organize itself to achieve a measure of integration in scale-sensitive activities (component production, R&D activities) and, yet, to manage its operations with little visible formal management centralization. The informality of centralization, however, was skillfully managed through the corporate functional staffs (and in particular the area marketing managers), through the imprecision of information systems and planning systems, and through a pattern of career paths, management mobility, and composition of the top management group that fostered long-term loyalty to the corporation as a whole. In summary, central control was maintained through:

1. The dependence of subsidiaries upon the center for key inputs such as components and technology.
2. Extensive informal control through long-term socialization within the company and the internalization of rules of behavior that led the local subsidiary managements to do what the corporation would expect without being narrowly controlled from Stockholm.

Within that overall orientation toward centralization and uniformity, the absence of formal control and the imprecision of subsidiary reporting into the corporate level permitted much differentiation to be achieved among subsidiaries. First, the relatively formal categorization of plants according to the level and type of assistance needed from Stockholm provided an easy means to differentiate operations. Second, the composition of the subsidiary boards could also be used to modulate the central guidance provided to any particular subsidiary. Third, the fact that area marketing managers could act flexibly to influence individual decisions toward national responsiveness and flexibility by siding with subsidiary managers, or toward uniformity and integration by siding with the product divisions, provided another way to regulate the differentiation among subsidiaries.

The overall orientation toward centralization and uniformity could be maintained because of the strategy followed by LME. The most notable features of this strategy were the reliance on superior technology and the orientation toward new market penetration. Technological excellence had for long been a cornerstone of LME's strategy. It had developed and perfected the Crossbar switch and introduced it widely right after World War II. In the 1960s it was the first to use Bell Labs' invention of stored program control (SPC) commercially. First, through the 412L project for the U.S. Air Force, awarded to its Northern Electric affiliate, it perfected the SPC technology. In 1968 it introduced at Tumba, Sweden the first operational electronic main-exchange office in the public telephone system. The flexibility inherent in the SPC technology was exploited to provide for interface flexibility. Such flexibility was first put to use in international "gateway" exchanges. Finally, in the mid-1970s, LME successfully developed the AXE system, a flexible local main-exchange switching system using space division.

Technological excellence permitted the penetration of numerous new markets. First, LME was in a position to penetrate mature markets where existing suppliers did not fulfill all PTT expectations. The superior gateway-exchange technology had been the initial wedge in opening the British market for LM Ericsson. Its overall competence had been a key factor in the Spanish government's invitation in the early 1970s. After a slow start, the AXE system met with considerable success. It was first selected in France, and then by such discriminating PTTs as the Australian and the Dutch. Many developing countries were quite satisfied with follow-up orders for Crossbar equipment. For instance, LME won, with Philips and Bell of Canada, the huge Saudi order in 1977 and also sizable follow-up orders from Venezuela, Nigeria, and several other countries. As we have seen, a strategy oriented toward new market penetration permitted, and required, more centralization than a strategy based on maintenance in existing mature markets. Yet, in Europe, LME left almost complete autonomy to its most mature, largest subsidiaries in France and Italy.

Still, as more markets matured, this strategic orientation toward centralization, technological excellence, and new market penetration was put to question. First, the centralization of R&D was straining relationships with host governments. A corporate manager commented on this aspect:

> Long ago we had but a few manufacturing locations abroad and most were only assembling. This was ideal for profitability since we had very large, efficient plants in Sweden. Then we had to move more and more of the production abroad to enhance the national character of our subsidiary companies. All countries have been trying to get production.
>
> Every country now wants a basic investment to combine manufacturing with the use of local skilled engineers and technicians. When the country develops it also gets the ambition to form a joint venture so it can have a strong say in the management of the company. After a while we have to accept. We now have to decrease our ownership at least in large rich countries.

Then, the various countries where LME had invested wanted a growing share of the R&D activities. LME had very little experience in managing R&D activities in many locations simultaneously, and it was not clear how a single switching system could result from development work done in many distant locations. It was feared that a loss of efficiency would result from dispersed R&D activities. Another difficulty of dispersed R&D was the greater risk of technological leakage to competitors. Whereas all electromechanical switching systems, including the Crossbar, had well-known and readily available technology, the new AXE system as well as most other electronic systems had distinctive features to be protected. Similarly, spreading the production of key components between many locations increased the risk of key manufacturing secrets being divulged.

The amount of exports from subsidiaries also raised tensions with governments. More and more countries insisted upon the development of exports, though the available export market was fairly limited. So far LME had been able to maintain the employment level in Sweden and make Sweden the only export base, except for a few special cases of limited importance. It was feared that growing insistence of host countries upon exports would raise serious labor and employment problems in Sweden. Moreover, the coordination of exports from many sources would create complex management issues at LME. A manager commented:

> We shall have to make local companies more autonomous, and follow patterns of international cooperation if they develop. To decentralize product development will be necessary as well. We shall no longer have a majority in the equity of our companies either. The only means left to control such operations is to be very good at managing conflicting areas. International management had to be developed inside LME. Our stage of internationalization is intermediate, we need to go further.

LME, unlike some other multinationals, was not in a position to strike a hard bargain with governments demanding a larger say in the management of national subsidiaries. A top manager explained why:

> We are entering a new period where you find that you must follow a set of conditions dictated by the local authorities, and you can only choose the most profitable alternative among very constrained ones. One alternative would be to decrease the sales volume and move out of countries which impose too many constraints. With the technological evolution we already spend 7 percent of our turnover

on R&D. To remain technically competitive we need to
increase the volume over which to spread R&D expenses
by at least 10 percent a year, in real terms. If we were
to reduce our turnover we would rapidly face a dead end:
our sales would be too small to provide for R&D expenses,
or our profits would shrink. In addition, with the move
into electronic technology chances of a stable technology
enabling us to spend less on R&D become slimmer than
ever before.*

LME was not very well equipped to respond to these changes.
It was clear that as LME's activities in various countries grew in
size and maturity, so did the pressures for local responsiveness and
greater autonomy. But this was awkward for the corporate management because the precedents in France and Italy showed that once a
company was no longer part of the centrally influenced, informally
managed system, headquarters encountered much difficulty in assert-
ing influence over it. LME was ill equipped to deal with joint ventures because it did not have a very well-developed system for exer-
cising formal control. When the managing director of a joint venture
decided to make components (against the advice of Stockholm) by gaining in advance the commitment of workers and local shareholding interests, the move was perceived in Stockholm as next to betrayal.
Similarly, the decision of a large company to choose its own computer
supplier without conferring with Stockholm came as a surprise.
    Even more seriously, the indirect integrative mechanisms used
to indoctrinate LME managers were under the threat of being disman-
tled. National authorities more and more insisted upon local managers in the LME subsidiaries. Up to 1976 the issue of local managers had not been directly addressed. A key part of LME's system
was the reliance upon Swedes (who saw the corporation as key to their
future careers) to manage local companies. As the proportion of local nationals increased among managers, some centrifugal tendencies
were bound to develop. After describing the family communal spirit
at LME, one manager stressed:

This system is going to be submitted to much stress very
soon. It was designed for Swedish expatriates committed

---

*It was generally believed in the industry that the shift to elec-
tronic switching and digital coding technologies would link the telecommunication industry to the regular innovation streams in the
semiconductor and computer industries.[6]

to the domestic LME in the long run. When local integration increases and when many host country nationals reach a high level in our companies, they are likely to get more control. As long as we keep a step ahead of them technologically we keep a means of control. They will understand they need the inputs from us. Then . . .

The advantages and difficulties described above, using the example of LME, are inherent in the centralized mode. As markets mature, and as the host governments demand more responsiveness, a stronger voice in the management of the national subsidiaries, and their participation in exports, the centralized mode is submitted to more stress. By choosing a technology-based strategy, LME had been able to delay the emergence of such stress by the 1970s. However, the question of adapting the centralized mode was clearly raised.

NOTES

1. For a treatment of interdependencies and their effect on management coordination needs, see James D. Thompson, Organizations in Action (New York: McGraw Hill, 1967). For an application to the MNC, see Henri de Bodinat, "Influence in the Multinational Enterprise," (D.B.A. diss., Harvard Business School, 1976).

2. See Ulrich Wiechmann, Marketing Management in Multinational Firms: The Consumer Packaged Goods Industry (New York: Praeger, 1976).

3. Ulrich Wiechmann, "Integrating Multinational Marketing Activities," Columbia Journal of World Business, Winter 1974, pp. 7-16.

4. De Bodinat, "Influence in the Multinational Enterprise."

5. Ibid., chapter 9, p. 8.

6. See, for instance, James Martin, Future Development in Telecommunications, 2nd ed. (Englewood Cliffs, N.J.: Prentice Hall, 1977).

8

THE DECENTRALIZED MODE

In the decentralized mode, the MNC maintains a number of full-fledged national companies of relatively equal status in various countries. For instance, Brown Boveri & Cie (BBC) has three major national companies: the parent company in Switzerland, a company in France (Compagnie Electro-Mécanique), and one in Germany (BBC-Mannheim). In the decentralized mode, each affiliate of the multinational can behave in its domestic market as if it were an independent national company and yet derive many advantages from its affiliation to the multinational network. Because of the flexibility gained by having a choice of responses on a local level, and the choice among full-fledged companies on an international level, a decentralized network of companies seems at first glance to be a very effective way of managing salient businesses.

Each national company retains almost complete operational independence and much managerial autonomy. The managements of these various companies cooperate in carrying out tasks that require pooling of resources or making choices between companies. Prominent among such tasks are product development and export marketing. Top managers of each company attempt to integrate the activities into a coherent whole through intense coordination.

To illustrate the decentralized mode, this chapter draws on a description of BBC. The outline is essentially similar to that of Chapter 7: a description of managerial tools and operating patterns, followed by a commentary.

MANAGERIAL TOOLS

Organizational Structure

In a decentralized network, several major companies or groups of companies of comparable weight cooperate in undertaking critical tasks. Usually, the structure of the corporate management reflects the leading role of national affiliates that cooperate only when their managements, as a group, find it helpful. For instance, the corporate top management team at BBC was comprised of six executives: the heads of five geographical groups and the president of the Swiss corporation.* They formed the Konzern (corporate) managing committee. The makeup of the top management team corresponded directly to the power of the local companies.

Major foreign-based BBC companies were also not wholly owned by the Swiss company. For example, in its French affiliate, Compagnie Electro-Mécanique, BBC had only a minority interest but remained by far the largest stockholder. Though the large national companies clearly dominated the organization, the two other managerial dimensions were not entirely absent; some form of worldwide product management and corporate functional management coexisted with the geographical structure. These three managerial dimensions as they were found in BBC are briefly reviewed.

The geographical groups (significantly, referred to as the "primary structure" in all BBC documents) included the three major national companies (Germany with 40 percent of the total sales volume, France and Switzerland with around 15 percent and 20 percent, respectively) and two composite groups. The first composite group was made up of seven medium manufacturing subsidiaries, located in other European countries (including Austria, Italy, and Norway) and in developing countries (Brazil and India). These medium manufacturing subsidiaries were not essentially different from the three major national compnies. However, they were too numerous to be reporting directly to the top and too small to warrant much individual top management attention. The second composite group, called Brown Boveri International (BBI), included a number of smaller companies, whose major activities were selling and installing imported products.† This

---

*There was no legal split between the Swiss national company and the whole corporation. However, administratively the corporate services (Konzern) were clearly distinct from the Swiss BBC company. The president and chief executive officer (CEO) of the corporation was not the CEO of the Swiss company (see Figure 8.1). ("BBC" always refers to the whole group managed by the Konzern.)

†At least this was the case in 1969 when the international group was created. With mounting pressures for local integration in many developing countries, a number of smaller subsidiaries had to develop larger-scale manufacturing activities, both for salient products sold on the local markets (transformers, for instance) and for less salient ones (low-voltage equipment) to be reexported. Consequently, the dis-

group also coordinated a worldwide network of BBC agents and technical offices. BBI was basically the international marketing arm providing required services for penetrating new markets. Both composite groups were based in Baden, at corporate headquarters.

The structure of each major national company closely followed a divisional pattern, with a series of product divisions (see Figure 8.2). In addition, in France and Germany there was a series of business aggregate managers.* With some variations each product division had been allocated to one of three business aggregates: heavy equipment, systems and engineering, and series products.

These business aggregates differed in many managerial requirements, and each of them was to follow a "company within the company" approach. Each business aggregate was different in nature, though the range of systems and engineering work was so broad that each aggregate was a hodgepodge that might get involved in everything from railroad equipment to steel mill gears or turbosuperchargers. At the divisional level great diversity existed, as the lines between businesses were not drawn similarly in the three major national companies. For instance, a particular product line could be in the transformers division in Germany and in the industrial installation division in France. These differences were partly due to the physical plants' layouts and also to different diversification axes followed by individual companies over time.

Corporate services were organized on a functional basis. A small research staff was maintained in a central laboratory, doing basic research in physics in close contact with universities. Except for the research staff (and a technical coordination group working on manufacturing methods), most other corporate services provided support for the general management function at the corporate level. The Konzern (corporate) marketing staff had a somewhat broader function: it was responsible for the coordination of worldwide export orders between the various companies. For heavy equipment this was done on a case-by-case basis. Other Konzern services dealt mostly with planning, organization, and control. Their roles will be detailed in further sections. Altogether, excluding the research scientists, the corporate services did not number more than 200 managers or analysts. Most

---

tinction between medium manufacturing subsidiaries and BBI companies was becoming increasingly blurred.

*The U.S. terminology would normally be group vice-presidents. Because in BBC the term group always designated the five major geographical entities, the term business aggregate is used throughout as an equivalent to product group, and business aggregate manager as an equivalent to group vice-president.

FIGURE 8.1

Brown Boveri & Cie

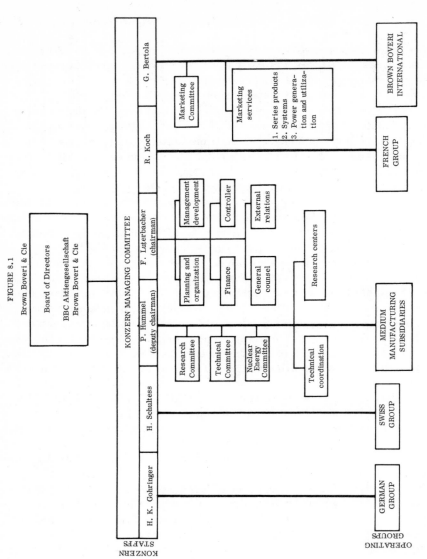

Source: Compiled by the author.

186

FIGURE 8.2

Simplified Structure of a Major National Subsidiary

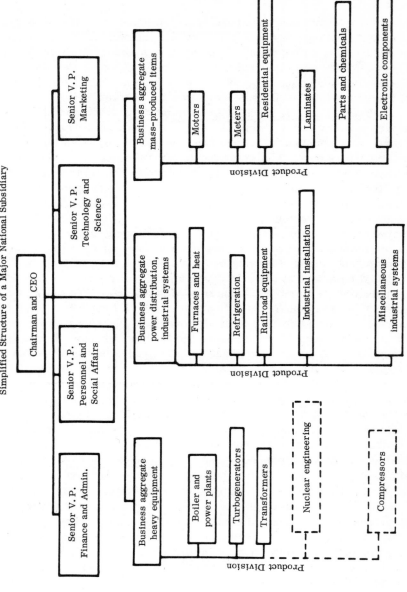

Source: Compiled by the author.

187

corporate department heads had been promoted from line management positions, with Swiss nations somewhat predominant.* As can be seen in Figure 8.1, management-oriented corporate services reported to the president or to his deputy, P. Hummel, who was also the CEO of the medium manufacturing subsidiaries group. Only the marketing services reported to Bertola, who was the head of BBI.

International product line coordination at BBC took place in a series of committees, forming a "secondary organization." No managers were assigned full time to the secondary organization, so it had no staff of its own. The whole range of BBC's activities was split into 16 major businesses, with each subdivided into from two to ten product lines (in all, about 100 product lines). For each product line a "Konzern product team" (KPT) grouped department (or division) managers from the various producing companies within BBC. For each major business, there was a "Konzern assortment team" (KST) grouping division managers. The corporate marketing staff also had a delegate on each team. For single-source products the KPT or KST only included members of the manufacturing company (group) along with corporate staff members. The task of KSTs and KPTs was to evaluate product lines and businesses from an economic, technical, and commercial standpoint. This included formulating corporatewide objectives and business plans to ensure the best exploitation of opportunities for rationalization and coordination of activities between the various groups.

The secondary structure clearly was not very prominent. One major reason was that it was difficult to coordinate managers at divisional or departmental levels who possessed limited power to commit their national companies and who were judged primarily on shorter run results obtained for their national company. Thus, both the national business aggregate management (or top management) and the corporate staff enjoyed a higher status than the secondary organization. The real role of the KST-KPT system depended largely upon the kind of coordination that had developed at higher levels. In summary, the structure of the integrated mode can be sketched in Figure 8.3.

Such a structure offered the possibility of communications in many directions. How these possibilities were used determined to a large extent the flexibility or rigidity of the structure. The following section will examine these communication flows.

---

*Stringent Swiss federal regulations on residence by foreigners and the location of Baden in central Switzerland made the appointment of non-Swiss to Baden more difficult.

FIGURE 8.3

Schematic Structure of the Decentralized Mode

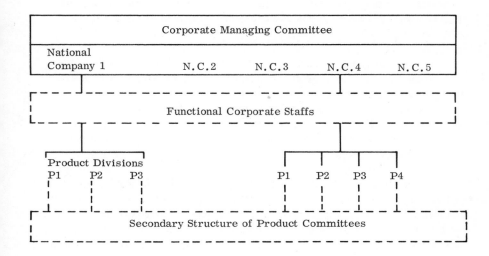

Source: Compiled by the author.

Information Systems

Information flows were informal, multilevel, and multidirectional wherever a tradition of cooperation had developed. Indeed, efficient functioning of the decentralized mode assumed many informal communications. Information had always circulated freely in BBC's turbogenerator business, but less so for the other heavy equipment products. Low diversity and the clear technical leadership of the Swiss company in turbogenerators made the circulation of information both simple and necessary. In energy distribution the diversity among customers' requirements made communications more difficult. Complementing the informal channels, the formal information systems revolved around several committees. Foremost among these was the secondary structure and a set of functional coordinating committees.

The agenda of secondary structure meetings would typically involve product specifications, development budgets, capacity increases, rationalization of production, licenses, and subcontracting among BBC companies. The general consensus was that the secondary organization provided a useful observation and information system. It was an arena to identify problems, to analyze them, to propose solutions, and

to explore their acceptability in light of the interests of the various
national companies. It was felt, however, that the quality of the information circulating in the secondary organization was negatively affected by the lack of integration of the secondary organization meetings into normal day-to-day management in the national companies
and by the lack of scope of some discussions. One manager commented:

> Most members of the KPTs adopt a narrowly defined inter-
> est. . . . One cannot force decisions upon the companies:
> they immediately retreat behind their national interests or
> particular customer requirements to reject whatever is pro-
> posed. KPT members do not want to see problems; when
> confronted with them they react purely as members of their
> national company.

A series of formal meetings was also held among the functional
managers of the various groups, with the participation of corporate
services managers. For instance, the export coordination activities
of the corporate marketing services were the object of a marketing
steering committee. Technical developments and production methods
and processes were discussed in technical coordination meetings.
Similarly, meetings were held to compare accounting methods and to
make them more compatible.

As important as the substance of the discussions was the fact
that multiple meetings and exchanges of information were used to develop and maintain a common group spirit. Managers used these
meetings to convince each other that they were working in the best interests of the corporation as a whole. In a decentralized organization,
where decisions affecting the whole company were reached by consensus, and where many had veto power, it was not clear where exchanging information gave way to decision making. So the multiplicity of
the informal information channels greatly facilitated the development
of well-balanced decisions. Multiple information channels were also
used in building commitments once decisions were made. Finally,
the central corporate services needed to rely on the many channels in
order to gain acceptance by the national companies that could go their
own way.

Planning, Budgeting, and Reporting Systems

Planning and budgeting were carried out along the lines of the
formal profit-center organizations, that is, by national companies.
Most of them followed similar procedures set up by the corporate

planning staff. Planning was carried out in each national division on
an annual revolving basis for a period of five years. Each year the
plans were made and reviewed in the companies between January and
June. In June the top management of each company developed its overall five-year plan, studying how the company was to grow and operate, according to its own top management's objectives and strategies.
The only corporate input was a set of Konzern guidelines, which targeted return on equity, return on sales, cash flow, and a balance between long- and short-term liabilities and capital expenditures as a
percentage of cash flow. The guidelines were established separately
for each company by the Konzern managing committee, but they were
indicative only, not binding.

By early July the five-year plans of the divisions had been finalized in the various companies and approved at the national level. Over
the summer the corporate staffs reviewed the plans submitted by each
company to prepare them for approval by the managing committee.
During the summer the export allocation budgets were finalized in ses-
sions of the marketing steering committee. In the meantime the assumptions and scenarios made in the plans provided the basis for
drafting investment proposals and development projects. By October
all elements required to work out detailed budgets had been gathered.
Capital expenditure and development projects were discussed in the
secondary structure meetings. Final budget proposals of the national
companies were then submitted to the corporate staffs for review and
recommendation to the managing committee. In December the overall budgets were discussed by the managing committee and commitments made. The fact that the managing committee was made up of
the managing directors of the groups and of the president of the Konzern sped up the review and approval processes considerably.

The formal planning and budgeting process described above emphasized the critical importance of acceptance within the national companies. Seldom were plans and budgets seriously challenged in the
secondary organization, and by the time they reached the managing
committee they were usually in almost final form. Up to 1975 the
primacy of the national companies in the planning and budgeting process had not been challenged. No worldwide product strategies were
developed, though since 1976 some moves have been made, as corporate planning manager Fischer commented:

> Product planning is only on a voluntary basis. KSTs should
> do it but there is a lack of agreement on how to carry for-
> mal planning for product groups. The operational company
> plans should, however, add up to consistent horizontal world-
> wide product plans. KSTs and KPTs have begun to review
> worldwide competition and to study product strategies. But

this is very limited. This year we are standardizing the
first phase of strategic planning (study of product markets)
between Switzerland, France, and Germany. We are doing that at the level of business aggregate managers. Their
interests are focused more on the global long-run success
of their company than on single advantages to be gained for
individual divisions. We are moving, over time and slowly,
to a more centralized system where plans will be standardized and coordinated to allow a product strategy to be developed. There must be a way for the corporation to develop
policies in terms of product portfolios, worldwide.

Among line managers in the heavy equipment business a widespread view was that worldwide product strategy had been informally
developed for the turbogenerators for a long time and that market diversity for transformers and breakers (for which each national utility
had its own standards and specifications) would defeat any attempt at
a meaningful worldwide strategy. In other businesses the development
of worldwide strategies raised difficult managerial questions.[1]

Reporting from the national companies to the corporate controller involved a monthly report, comparing results to the budgets.
More detailed reports were also submitted quarterly. The formats
and methods used by the different companies to present these reports
were standardized. No consolidation of accounts (or translation into
Swiss francs) was undertaken. The information from each company
was evaluated in its own currency. As the accounting practices differed in various countries, however, the overall accounting was not
fully standardized between countries, so only approximate comparisons
of product line accounting was possible. Similarly, it was very difficult to reach a common understanding on what was to be charged to
specific projects (development budgets, for instance) and what to allocate to general overhead. Transfer prices were another source of
bias in the formal information flows. Divisions were not entirely free
to buy and sell outside the company on their own; some prices were
determined by standard formulas, others in arm's-length bargaining.
Each unit inside BBC was considered a profit center. This sometimes
created difficulties in circulating information among companies.

Staffing, Career Paths, Rewards and Punishments

These mechanisms were all nationally oriented and clearly reflected the dominance of national companies and groups. Very few
exchanges of managers took place between countries, except for supporting missions in developing countries. Each of the major companies

was staffed by local nationals at all levels. The ties with national administrations required by the local responsiveness strategy made the reliance upon local nationals important. Managers with the same educational and social background as high civil servants could more easily develop good relationships with them. Companies were very reluctant to accept foreigners, even in series products where negotiations with governments were not an issue. Altogether there were only 120 expatriates, most of them in medium-size and BBI companies.

Such predominant long-term attachment to a national company, and the concomitant lack of international exposure, encouraged strong local loyalties and hindered any worldwide integration effort. Though some managers had been sent to medium subsidiaries abroad for short periods of time, their loyalty remained with their national company.

Only in a few large companies at BBC was there a system of compensation in which a large proportion of a manager's income was tied to measured performance. In some instances a certain percentage of a manager's annual salary would be based on a bonus system. However, throughout the corporation much weight was attached to meeting annual budgets and a strict profit-center approach was implemented. The corporate controller commented on this:

> Every single product, plant, division, and company must stand on its own feet and be profitable on its own merits. Subsidizing a factory because it helps exports to the country where it is located is not an acceptable justification for a poorly run operation. The career of any individual is directly influenced by how well he has been doing profitwise. Each division has its own technical, production, and marketing people and can function effectively as a profit center. Each plant is also a profit center.
>
> In some cases, when problems develop and the company head is failing to get them under control, we may terminate his association with BBC. Below the level of company managers, promotions, salaries, and career paths are left pretty much to the local management.

Management turnover varied with results; in some subsidiaries it had been high, but this was not always a consequence of unsatisfactory performance. In fact, only when a failure was the sole responsibility of a manager was he held accountable. As the corporate controller explained:

> Before we put someone on the grill we always ask ourselves who is responsible for the mess. For instance, a manager

was promoted against his will because he was the only one
available who also knew the local language. He felt someone else would be better for the job. When troubles developed after that appointment the Konzern was at least as responsible as the individual.

In summary, there was very little intersubsidiary mobility
among managers; staffing and career paths were almost exclusively
national. Among the national companies stringency of reward and
punishment systems could vary substantially, yet in general the
profit-center and management-by-objective approach was tight and
meeting budgets was a key evaluation criteria.

Patterns of Top Management Intervention

The managing committee, meeting every other week, was responsible for many critical substantive decisions. Because of the
lesser status of the secondary organization and the lack of an inter-
mediary level of international coordination, many key decisions came
up to the managing committee. In fact, through the KST-KPT system
the members of one group had complete veto power over all critical
decisions affecting its interests. For any common rule to be established, unanimity of the groups concerned was required. Again, this
mechanism reinforced the power of the geographical groups. At the
same time the lack of long-term or international perspective by the
division or department managers in the KST-KPT structure, often
combined with the tight incentive system under which they operated,
tended to push all critical decisions upward to the business-aggregate
manager level. Critical decisions then often reached the managing
committee level, where they might cause overload in a structure that
only consisted of temporary meetings. The burden of horizontal integration fell very much on the managing committee, particularly for
decisions concerning the heavy equipment. A manager commented on
the problems created by that set-up:

When an important or complex decision reaches the managing committee, the corporate staff which has an overall view
of the situation usually prepares a carefully balanced recommendation. However, each managing director also relies
heavily upon his business-aggregate manager for advice re-
garding particular issues, especially when not personally
familiar with the situation himself. Naturally, a local manager is interested in looking out for the best interest of his
company (or division) above all, and managing directors are
often reluctant to let their subordinate down.

Generally speaking, the degree of effective integration varied among businesses at BBC. In turbogenerators, where Baden had long held the technological lead, and where Hummel (Konzern deputy CEO) had been recognized as the informal "boss" of the business, worldwide integration was high and efficient. There were relatively few export orders so that the production planning and coordination could be done carefully on an individual order basis. Moreover, the lead time was usually long enough for planning adjustments to be made. Because turbogenerators had been BBC's top business, the whole managing committee had a thorough knowledge of and a keen interest in them. That business, as a result, was substantively managed by the managing committee, and a great mutual trust developed. The low product diversity among markets made it easier.[2]

The gap between levels was more serious in businesses that required more formal integration, particularly in those with which top management was not so familiar. In those the managing role of the top was far less clear. For instance, equipment such as low-voltage apparatus was integrated at the business-aggregate level between France and Germany, thanks to the personal understanding that developed between the two business aggregate managers; but there was no formal way to develop such integration. The managing committee would not get involved in running the integration between the groups for all businesses.

Up until 1972 the various groups had, altogether, remained very autonomous, each national company being able to behave as if it were locally owned and fully responsive to the needs of the host government.

It was only with some difficulty that management coordination could be developed among the various groups after 1972. In fact, the decentralization of the national groups was anchored in the operating patterns of BBC and it was mainly in the management of research and development activities and in the coordination of export sales that more centralization was visible.

OPERATING PATTERNS

Manufacturing Policy

BBC maintained a complete range of factories in each of the three major countries: France, Germany, and Switzerland. Some products, such as turbogenerators, were essentially similar between countries; others, such as circuit breakers, were produced according to a variety of standards. The medium manufacturing subsidiaries had a narrower product range and they did not produce turbogenerators, except in Italy and on a small scale in Spain.

Until the 1970s this setup had been quite effective in permitting each national company to adapt to the demands of the host country and of the national utility. Yet, the rapid increase of minimal efficient size in the turbogenerator industry through the 1970s worried BBC managers. One made the following comments:

> If we look at the international market as a whole we have a much bigger share than that of our competitors, but spread over a number of national markets, with an average 20 percent of each. In all cases we face a purely national competitor which is bigger in its home market. With the shift to higher unit power we have to build new plants and acquire heavier equipment. The trouble is that if we make three pieces a year in each market, Siemens or Alsthom make twice as many for their national market alone. So their utilization rates should be better. Our market shares being small, our profitability is not sufficient.

Over the last few years there have been many talks at BBC about overcoming these problems. At one point a trinational heavy equipment yard had even been contemplated on the upper Rhine, between Basle, Mulhouse, and Schaffhouse, where the three countries' borders (Switzerland, France, and Germany) meet. Some of the workshops would have been in each country. The complexity of the proposal, the anticipated moving costs, and the lack of suitable financial arrangements caused the idea to be abandoned. Instead, heavy equipment workshops were built separately in each of the three countries.

Schemes to develop cross-shipments had not progressed past the discussion stage. Sizable economies could be achieved by producing such items as turbine blades in one location only and then shipping them for assembly in various countries. It was felt, however, that such arrangements would weaken BBC's competitive posture in several countries. Moreover, since division managers were evaluated on their financial results, and since each division usually made higher profits on manufacturing than on resale activities, there was no short-term incentive for rationalization of production.

Rationalization of production methods, however, had gone much further, and the coordinating committees were deemed very useful in transferring manufacturing know-how from one company to another. Production engineers from the various companies had many sustained contacts, which enabled each plant to benefit from technical improvements made throughout the Konzern.

Though production specialization (where factories manufacture specific types of products only) was not carried out, factory loading and production programs were coordinated between countries. Each year an export budget was made, taking into account the available capacity in each plant. Whenever possible, some subcontracting was un-

dertaken between BBC companies. In the end, however, factory loading and production scheduling remained entirely under national control
in each country and all export contracts were made directly between
the exporting factory and the customer. Thus, there was no corporate
responsibility for scheduling production. Investments in production
capacity also remained the responsibility of the local company. Each
company was expected to stand on its own financially, and to self-
finance its investment programs. Only when growth was extremely
rapid (as in Iran and Brazil) did the Konzern provide funds from the
corporate accounts.

Still, despite the local origin of funding, all investments had to
be approved by BBC in a series of stages before they could be made
by the local company. The first step consisted of a review of the initial proposal by the KST meeting. The KST usually approved the
project after simply evaluating economic and technical criteria.
(Many managers deplored the fact that the KST did not consider how
well the investment "fit" into an overall business strategy because
members typically wished to avoid getting into power struggles.)
The second step involved the technical justification of the proposal by
the technical director of the local company so that it could be approved
by Walther, the technical director of the Konzern, who would then
recommend it to the managing committee. The managing committee
and the national board would then approve the investment, which would
be added to the content of the following planning and budgeting cycle.

Location and Management
of Research and Development

The success of BBC had been, and to some extent remained,
based on technical excellence. BBC's national companies had usually
been successful because they had provided their countries with new
technologies. Since the early days of Charles Brown, BBC had always
been a leader in the industry, regularly building the largest and most
reliable steam generators in the world and inventing new products
(turbosuperchargers, air blast breakers, and others). Though BBC
had long been dominated by Baden technically, a more balanced system
had evolved over the years. Basic research was done mostly in the
Dattwil laboratory near Baden. There were, however, basic research
labs in Heidelberg, Germany, and in Lyon and Le Bourget, France,
which carried more limited research programs.

In areas of applied research there was one technology leader
among the companies. For instance, Mannheim was the technological
lead house for all nuclear energy-related questions, Switzerland for
all turbine alternator and turbosupercharger developments, and so

forth. In fact, the Swiss group remained the leader for many major technologies. Modifications of specific technologies or products for local application were made in national development centers. Though the core competence for each technology was clearly assigned to one company only, others could also gain some depth of knowledge through the adaptations they made. Final adaptations for industrialization of new products or processes were usually carried out simultaneously in several national companies.

The decentralized principles according to which the R&D activities were managed closely paralleled those used in manufacturing. All development costs were paid by the company using the technology, process, design, or product being developed. When several companies were involved, costs were shared among them according to agreed-upon estimates made and negotiated by the research committee. In all cases the responsibility for appropriating and using funds lay with the company that undertook the project, not with the Konzern nor with other beneficiary companies. Similarly, the Brown Boveri Konzern as a whole did not issue licneses and did not receive royalties. Licensing to companies not members of the BBC group was carried out largely through the Swiss national company and was an important source of revenue for it (4.9 percent of sales in 1974).

A company could not proceed on its own with a new development project, however. It had to describe a set of specifications outlining the expected results and explain the needs that the project was expected to fulfill. These data were presented in a secondary organization meeting, together with a schedule and an expense target. Approval by the concerned KST was required before the company could go ahead. A top manager commented:

> Members of the KST are experienced line managers who usually know the business very well. We want to make sure that the line management of the various manufacturing companies is convinced of the need for a development before money is spent on it. We also want them to review and appraise the capabilities of the leaders in the domain.

This negotiation, approval, and review process by the KST was also important to provide some support and consensus for the sharing of costs not geared to short-term profits. At the corporate level there was a general desire to avoid "creeping diversification" by controlling new product development or new technologies, as well as a desire to limit the duplication of development work by the BBC companies. One manager described the difficulties:

> In some businesses development coordination works well, in others not so well. There are some systems in which

the specifications are rather obscure, and a KST has a
hard time judging the development and understanding the
motivation behind it. Unless the companies get directly
into negotiations and agree not to oppose each other, it
may be difficult to disentangle conflicts on who should develop what. Conflicts are moved upstairs, where they become still more difficult to resolve. In rapidly evolving domains the KST response is too slow. Five or six months
may elapse before a decision and you are not going to hold
off a research team for that long, so development just goes
on.

How can we build procedures for work in domains we do
not understand yet? There is too much domain delineation
going on too early; maybe we should leave more elbow room
to the companies. When we speak of development we consider the action and rule on the process. We then judge developments on how well they are administered. Without a
commitment in terms of markets and businesses, we cannot get anywhere. But an approach which considers development as part of product group activities, defined in terms
of market, technological, and competitive evolutions, has
not come into being at the Konzern level.

Most criticism was focused upon series products and electronic
systems where the characteristics and market potential were difficult
to comprehend. Integration around heavy equipment, on the other
hand, was very good. For instance, when EdF ordered the first 600
MWe turbogenerators from CEM, the development group in Baden was
not ready to go ahead since it had not expected to reach that power
level for several years. However, Baden readily agreed that leadership be taken by CEM and crack engineers from Baden were hurriedly
dispatched to France to work for CEM and the project was very successful. The joint designs were then used by other BBC companies.

Links with Local Entities

At BBC the exclusive responsibility of the national companies
for dealing with all local matters was clearly established and well accepted inside the Konzern and out. At the same time, the international affiliation of the national companies was well known to the local
administrations, and even publicized. In fact, the influence of each
national company on the whole potential of BBC and their ability to
tap into it was sometimes developed as a negotiation argument with
government officials, at least in France and Germany.

The heads of each national company were responsible for preserving the local coalitions upon which their acceptability was based, and this preoccupation took clear precedence over managerial requirements of the Konzern. Because of that precedence, BBC appeared to be a "group of companies," not a unified corporation. Their autonomy enabled the national companies to have a broader range of relationships with local authorities, thus decreasing their dependence upon any particular government agency or political group and allowing them to build a much broader-based coalition. For instance, Koch, the chairman and CEO of CEM, was sufficiently recognized in the French environment to be named chairman of the Syndicate of Electrical Equipment suppliers.

Because decision making at the corporate level was almost on a voluntary basis, BBC could easily accommodate itself to joint ventures. In fact, BBC's major European companies were only partly BBC-owned. BBC willingly accepted the creation of joint ventures in developing countries. An executive of BBI described BBC's attitude toward such investments:

> When an investment need emerges, we send people to study it. When we invest, we talk with the customers, get a real understanding of what they are after. We cannot fool them. In Peru we have had a 40-year relationship; you cannot tinker with that. We do not give away our patents, but provide descriptions of the manufacturing process only. When the license expires the government generally wants to "nationalize" the technology. By then it is often obsolete and they have to come back to a major company again. We like to have them come again to us and develop a trusting relationship. We can put some funds into the venture and take over responsibility for the projects we do together. We are not interested in short-term shadow factories to be used for political propaganda.

Export Marketing

Since purely political factors of international relations between nation-states played an important role in the choice of suppliers for heavy electrical equipment, BBC could use to its advantage the multiplicity of its available sources for any particular equipment. Multiplicity of manufacturing sources for similar products enabled BBC to respond to export policies dictated by political affinities between governments, as it could choose the appropriate national company to fill the order. However, when BBC had to call upon several national companies to create an international consortium to satisfy the needs of a customer, it had to clear the sale with several governments, which put BBC at a disadvantage compared with purely national companies. This was particularly true when very salient products and technologies were involved. For instance, in May 1976, an international consortium headed by BBC lost nuclear power plant sales in South Africa to Framatome, because of Dutch reservations about supplying nuclear technologies to South Africa.[3]

One of the major roles of the marketing staff in Baden was to coordinate the export efforts of the various national companies. Every year a tentative export budget was drafted, which tried to reconcile incoming orders forecasts received from local BBI companies and agents, with the expectations for export business presented by the national companies as a result of their own internal capacity and production planning. The Konzern marketing staff, in cooperation with BBI managers, evaluated the realism of market forecasts and of export expectations in order to draft a coordinated tendering program as a basis for the companies' export budgets. These proposals were circulated among the companies and discussed in a marketing steering committee until agreement was reached. This agreement, then, was the basis for designating the tendering company for incoming customer inquiries, which was done by the central marketing staff, either individually or on a market-by-market basis during the year. The growing share of exports in the turnover of all BBC companies was a tribute to the success of this coordination process. One marketing manager commented on the success of his service:

> First, we avoid duplications. We do not want to prepare
> several bids for each potential order, it would not be rea-
> sonable, nor economical. We consider available capacity,
> if any choice is left by external conditions. We seldom,
> almost never, have complaints made about individual allo-
> cations of inquiries. This reflects the fact that each com-
> pany is well aware of the importance and complexity of our
> task. Our key role has been recognized largely because we
> are able to promote the overall business very successfully.
> We always try to improve, find what should be done, look
> for information, work closely with everyone.
>
> We do not normally get involved in capacity decision. If
> we get into a tender inquiry we ask a company to lead the
> tender; this company will subcontract some work to others.
> Once this has been fixed we let them continue autonomously,
> without a Konzern man breathing down their necks.

The ability to coordinate export orders gave some power to the Konzern marketing managers, particularly when domestic markets were stagnant. One marketing manager commented on these aspects:

> Because we coordinate export orders, we have some control. For instance, we want to prevent a company from looking for export orders on its own and messing up the BBI network. Now companies will not do it. They know how important it is to be on good terms with us. It is not that we are higher than any profit center in the organization or that we run the show all by ourselves. We are at the crossroads, a policeman of business traffic, and it is only the authority given to us by the managing committee that enables us to do the job.

Once an order or an inquiry had been allocated to a national company, it was the responsibility of the chosen company to tender for the contract. It was free to subcontract part of the order to other BBC companies, but was under no obligation to subcontract to BBC companies rather than to third parties. Decentralization was complete once the responsibility for the contract had been allocated.

In summary, with the exception of the allocation of R&D projects, the sharing of their costs, and the allocation of responsibilities for export orders, no operating tasks were carried centrally. Little product strategy coordination or production integration or rationalization had been achieved, even for businesses where the political imperatives were not so strong as for heavy equipment. Almost complete operating decentralization continued to prevail.

COMMENTARY

Analysis

Whereas LM Ericsson favored centralization, leaving much autonomy only to mature subsidiaries in mature markets and centralizing all R&D and international marketing tasks at headquarters in Sweden, BBC favored decentralization of all activities, developing only some form of central coordination of R&D, export orders allocations, and some attempts at centralized product-line strategies. Of the companies studied, BBC was clearly the one that had most clearly chosen to be nationally responsive. Fundamentally, each BBC affiliate was identified as a national company in its domestic market.

Until 1970 very little coordination had been exerted. A study carried out by McKinsey and a change of top management (Luterbacher formerly head of Oerlikon, a company that merged with Brown Boveri-Baden, acceded to the chairmanship of BBC) provided the impetus for the development of stronger corporate-level coordination.

Until then, because there was no mandatory set of administrative policies and procedures imposed from the top on national companies, they were free to respond to local demands in whatever way they saw fit. This allowed local companies to integrate their activities only when they felt cooperation and interdependence would be helpful. Local links were so clearly privileged that some medium manufacturing subsidiaries of BBC had little to do with the Konzern, and the Konzern paid little attention to them.

Following the McKinsey study a whole range of coordination mechanisms were established (Figure 8.4). First, the role of the managing committee was reinforced and formalized. As we have seen, coordination worked well, and informally, for heavy equipment, the orders for which were few enough and sufficiently far between to be studied individually and allocated by the managing committee in its fortnightly meetings. For other products, the whole range of corporate staffs developed after 1970 was to assist the managing committee.

For individual businesses, among these staffs, the marketing managers came the closest to central business managers. As was seen, the secondary structure was a relatively good information forum among national company managers involved in the same business, but not a very effective decision-making body. Thus, most critical decisions had to come up before the managing committee. Members of the committee relied on the advice of business aggregate or division managers in the national companies, but also on the advice of the marketing staff. One of the tasks of that staff was defined in the following way: "To assist the managing committee and the Operating Groups in the evaluation of market potential of products, systems, and service competitiveness, and in the formulation of corresponding product and marketing policies."[4] Marketing managers also took part in all meetings of the secondary organization, both at the KPT and KST levels.

Because they monitored a wide range of information channels and because they played an important role in enhancing the national companies' export business through BBI, the corporate marketing managers could provide the nucleus of a more assertive, central product-oriented management function. In fact, the growing importance of exports to third countries, and the need to avoid wasteful competition for export orders between BBC companies, increased the need for a higher degree of interdependence between companies.

The role of the central marketing staff varied between businesses. Since large turbogenerator contracts were often determined by political conditions and were few and far apart, they were looked at on an individual basis with the market needs of particular national companies

FIGURE 8.4

Brown Boveri & Cie, Intercompany Coordination Structure

Typical Organization
of a Major National
Company*   Coordinating Body

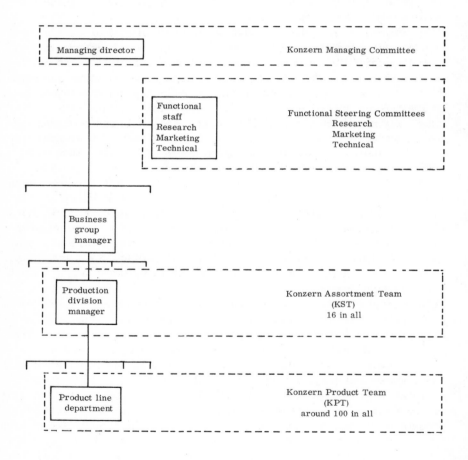

*For example, Switzerland, Germany, and France.

Source: Compiled by the author.

taken into consideration. For series products, individual export markets tended to rely on a given national company to fill most of their needs. The power of corporate marketing managers varied accordingly. In some series product businesses, where a permanent network of distributors and dealers had to be maintained, the allocation of export markets to national companies was done on a stable, once-and-for-all geographical basis. Thus, once that allocation was made, the corporate marketing managers had little influence on the markets allocated to a given national company.

The other corporate staffs found it more difficult to gain influence, partly because they had no operational responsibility. The managing committee, and Luterbacher in particular, had signaled the importance of staffs by relying on them for advice and making sure they were staffed by extremely competent specialists. Their expertise could provide them with some influence, but they did not have the kind of leverage that control of export sales provided to the corporate marketing managers.

One key problem was that the coordination teams were not as effective as expected in developing product and business strategies among national companies. Rationalization efforts had not gone very far, as one manager described:

> We could at least try to manufacture all export products of one category in one location; but there again we depend on customers. The customers are often consultants to foreign countries; moreover, all sales of heavy equipment are political and several sources are an invaluable asset. Chauvinism exists, even among private customers. Selling German-made low-voltage transformers in France is already difficult. If we decided to rationalize we would have to make wild guesses on what market shares would be lost, on future exchange rates, et cetera. This does not mean that nothing can be done. Once the difficulties are recognized there still is ample room for improvements, particularly for exports. We could not go all the way because, Turkey for instance, only buys German-made equipment and Greece only buys French equipment, but we could have common types and interchange parts. In that respect the KST-KPT is not efficient. The Konzern is functionally organized and geographically split. In this set-up, any effort for rationalization will be stopped by someone who fears his company (or division) will be hurt.

The coordination teams did not provide an effective counterbalance to the weight of the national companies and left their autonomy unchallenged. Yet they offered a strong review and evaluation process for the decisions and investments of the national companies. They widened the group that had to clear key decisions in national companies. A line manager in one of the national companies commented:

> To successfully get a project going you need to prepare well, to get informal reactions to your ideas, to see what elements would be accepted easily, to collect the opinions of many people. You need to play along with the Konzern, to behave responsibly toward the Konzern. You make unofficial contacts, secure alliances, gain neutralities, take each person individually. So long as you do not have unanimous approval in the KST, your plans are delayed. You need to enlist the support of the corporate staffs. You also make sure that your managing director will not find himself caught in a discussion where negative judgments will come up from key managers who are opposed to the project. A project which has been stalled once hardly has more than a one-out-of-ten chance of getting through the second time; a well-prepared project for which the informal groundwork has been done will get through easily.

A corporate staff manager made similar comments:

> National companies are self-protective and do their best to cover themselves. Konzern staffs have only limited consultative powers. Since power is diffuse, things can only happen by agreement. One can work only informally with the persons directly concerned by the problem. In the end, of course, everything has to fall in line with the hierarchical structure, but in the meantime decisions have to be sold. There is no general rule. I follow rules only when I want no responsibility for a failure. To kill an idea the easiest way is to play by official procedures. For success you get the key persons to agree with you before you go along the formal lines. Before you even start you need to weigh your chances of success, study the climate, and decide whether you will be able to get the right people committed. Once you have located the persons with the interest in what you want and with the power to implement it, you try to convince them. After that you can start the formal phases of your project, whatever it is.

In summary, the BBC structure and management tools left responsibility and authority for strategic decisions and their implemen-

tation to the national companies but provided for the corporate level
to be informed and for the other national companies to check on one
another's decisions. The effectiveness with which the secondary
structure performed such checking varied between product divisions;
there were personality differences, and some activities were more
difficult to understand in depth.

Only some key strategic issues were pulled out of the structure.
First, the whole nuclear energy question was closely followed at the
corporate level. Another key issue handled at the corporate level was
that of acquisitions. Most interesting to BBC was penetration into the
U.S. market. Serious consideration was given to a partnership with
a U.S. manufacturer (not involved in the industry, because of antitrust reasons). Rockwell had been the most serious candidate, but
talks did not succeed.

Implications

Among the three managerial modes identified in the course of
this research, the decentralized mode was probably the most efficient
in terms of successful response to the difficulties of government intervention. It provided for both full-fledged national companies that
could be very responsive locally and for the efficient global pooling of
resources and competencies for some critical tasks.

Decentralization enabled companies to respond successfully to
various types of national pressures. First, by leaving much autonomy
to each national company, it met the desire of most governments for
"national decision centers." The managers of the French EdF only
had to deal with CEM, not with BBC-Baden, and for all practical purposes they could ignore BBC altogether.

Second, by involving the national companies in complex technologies, it diffused and circulated knowledge and spread the creation of
it between various countries. So decentralization substantially satisfied the desire shared by the governments and public opinion in most
countries for national technological upgrading and for participation
in genuine discovery of advanced technologies.

Third, export sales from each national company could rely on
the services of a particularly strong worldwide sales network. For
products such as main-exchange switching or turbogenerators, this
was an invaluable advantage. Negotiations, project engineering, installation, and maintenance were all critical, long, and costly activities that usually could make or break the profits of any particular contract. No national supplier could have the export volume necessary to
pay for the expenses of a global sales and service network. Thus, it
was easier for national companies in a multinational group to develop

exports and create new jobs than for purely national companies; and most governments were highly sensitive to balance-of-payment surpluses and employment-creation potential.

Furthermore, sourcing flexibility between various countries enabled the decentralized MNC to follow closely the political and diplomatic evolution of markets. For instance, BBC would be able to shift suppliers in response to considerations dictated by foreign policies and financial conditions. Thus, to some extent, each national company's export activities could fit squarely into the foreign policies of its government.

In summary, the ability to be responsive to national sensitivities in a number of key areas was strongly enhanced by the decentralized mode. Yet it also helped to maintain the overall leadership position of companies using it. Because of this responsiveness, national companies of MNCs using the integrated mode were often favored over other MNCs, which often helped them to strengthen their grip on domestic markets. Moreover, since development costs could be spread over a number of companies, each of them could usually maintain a competitive edge in terms of technical excellence and prices over purely domestic suppliers in each national market. The flexibility of choice of supply also tended to increase the "take" of the decentralized group as a whole on the international export market, thus further improving the position of each of its national companies. So, both domestically in the various countries where national companies were located and internationally on the export market, the decentralized mode provided very strong advantages. While the managers of some multinational companies saw the unfeasibility of high managerial interdependence and physical integration and rationalization as terrific constraints, BBC was able to capitalize on the diversity between countries, on the fragmented nature of markets, and on the very sources of government intervention to exploit the potentials of multinationality to their full advantage and preserve their well-established positions.

NOTES

1. See Brown Boveri & Cie (Boston: Intercollegiate Case Clearing House, 1977).
2. Ibid.
3. Le Monde, June 20, 1976. A Dutch firm was a pressure vessel subcontractor to BBC.
4. BBC: Organization du Konzern (Baden: Brown Boveri & Cie, July 1973), p. 3.

9

THE POWER-BALANCE MODE

Of the three managerial modes identified during the research, the power–balance mode most explicitly recognizes the matrix organization as a solution to the duality of the economic and the political environments. Concretely, instead of separating the responsibilities for overall proficiency and local responsiveness as in the centralized mode, or incorporating them into each major national affiliate as in the decentralized mode, the matrix organization attempts to encompass both responsibilities within a single organization. A matrix organization has both a country (or geographic) management component and a product management component. The product management component has worldwide responsibility for a given product line. The country management component is responsible for all product lines nationally. Because the responsibilities overlap at the national product-market level, both are brought into play for major decisions. A national subsidiary product division manager must relate to both in order to operate adequately. The duality of reporting lines creates some ambiguity.

In the matrix organization it is expected that geographic managers will defend positions favoring local responsiveness, and product managers will defend positions favoring integration, rationalization, and overall economic competitiveness. Because their past experiences and their interests do not coincide, geographic and product managers tend to behave differently in a given situation. By making sure that both orientations receive adequate attention in decision making, managers who use that mode hope to create a duality of focus. They also develop methods to avoid the difficulties analyzed by Stanley M. Davis and Paul R. Lawrence and the clear allocation or seizure of relative power described by C. K. Prahalad.

This chapter follows the outline used in the previous two chapters: first, descriptions of managerial tools and operating patterns; second, analysis and assessment of the power–balance mode. The case of GTE is used here to concretely describe the power-balance mode and as a springboard for conceptualization. As GTE is a widely diversified company with little interaction and few interdependencies among its product groups, the description and analysis deal only with the International Telecommunication Equipment Product Group, which was organized as a geography-product matrix.

MANAGERIAL TOOLS

Organizational Structure

The structure of the power-balance mode is characterized by two clearly distinct components of equal hierarchical status, but different by nature. The first component is the geographically organized line management with members in a number of different locations. The second component is the product-oriented management, located mostly at headquarters. At GTE the line responsibility ran along geographic areas. The reporting relationships were thus quite clear: the product division managers in each country did not report to corresponding product managers at headquarters but to the head of the local company.

Central product-oriented managers had been introduced recently by Wilson [disguised name], GTE's International Telecommunication Equipment Group vice-president. This corresponded to a desire to improve businesses that had been left to the local management. Wilson commented on the development of product management in the main-exchange switching equipment product line:

> In our European subsidiaries, problems appeared. The switching equipment developed there had a small domestic market and little profitable international potential. We could not go on like that, particularly since we had a new system developed in the U.S.* We had a personality available: Bob Dole.† He is now responsible for the general product line policy, internationally, of all our equipment falling within his specialty, regardless of source. In addition, I look to him for guidance in development, rationalization, component sourcing, et cetera.

---

*The location of the major U.S. domestic telecommunication switching equipment factory and research centers of GTE was Northlake, Michigan.

†Dole had been area vice-president for the Far East and manager for European Marketing of GTE (Telecom) prior to 1972. He then became main-exchange switching product vice-president.

Dole made similar comments:

> For the last decade our international sales of sw
> equipment had been very low. The problem wai
> competitive product. There were several attem
> velop a system which would be well compatible i
> ally, but the expenses involved were too large for us. Fi-
> nally, in the late '60s our domestic labs came out with a
> new system, the no. 1 EAX, which was very competitive
> among SPC systems. We found it was quite usable in for-
> eign countries which did not follow the CCITT standards
> too closely. Moreover, costs had increased so much in Eu-
> rope that exports from the U.S. were made price competi-
> tive. At that time (1973) there was little experience or com-
> petence in switching inside the division, and we needed to
> rebuild a marketing organization. We were then competing
> against ITT, and we got an order. We needed one man to
> head the drive and develop a product line strategy to get
> into the switching market. The area management could not
> do it because of local view. Somebody "above" the area
> managers was needed, "above" in the sense of having a
> global view instead of a regional one.

In communication products other than switching equipment, the
need for overall product management had not appeared so quickly.
Over the years national leadership positions had crystallized and European companies had maintained strong technical competence. For
instance, they had developed a strong position in microwave transmissions with products following the CCIR (Comité Consultatif International de la Radio) standards.* In some other products, such as PABX,
the situation was more closely akin to that in main-exchange switching. Still, following Dole's appointment, two other product vice-presidents were appointed at the group headquarters. The role of the transmission equipment vice-president was not fully clear. Some commonality could probably be achieved between the United States and Europe,
but the need for a product management function, distinct from the major European company, was not very clear—at least not so clear as
for main-exchange switching or PABXs. Certain central functions
in transmissions, however, had been developed for a long time. For
instance, there was a Telecom proposal office (TPO) operating in Eu-

---

*The CCIR standards were closely followed internationally out-
side North America. These were very different from standards used
in the United States and Canada.

rope since 1963 to prepare transmissions networks proposals. This office continued to report directly to Wilson in New York.

Formally speaking, the area vice-presidents retained complete veto power over what took place in their areas. The product vice-president, however, carried the authority of the group vice-president's office in a whole series of critical management decisions. Some amount of conflict and ambiguity resulted from such overlap. How these responsibilities were to be shared was not indicated by the formal structure nor by the broad definition of authority. In order to monitor sources of conflict and avoid negative reactions other managerial tools had to be carefully used.

The matrix structure is sketched in Figure 9.1.

Information Systems

A major advantage of the matrix structure, already noted by previous researchers, was the provision for two channels of information from the local product divisions managers, one along area management, the other along product management. Informal multiple-direction information flows were characteristic at GTE. The head of the largest European subsidiary commented on these:

> The organization is very informal, all doors are open. Mr. Ferrario* is not upset when I go to Mr. Wilson. The product vice-president for PABX was here last week. I did not even know of his visit and did not devote any time to it. My division manager had explained his approach to me and I agreed. Everybody can go to whatever level needed for discussion. I can go to Mr. Fitzgerald† and spend a day with him in his home talking over what is on my mind. Most Europeans have some problems with this way of operating. They are used to more formal hierarchal relations.

Yet, formal information flows at GTE remained principally structured along regional lines. In fact, up until the early 1970s, each national company had remained very autonomous.

In some areas, the exact flow of information was well codified. Proposal preparation was one example. Drafts of all proposals had to be widely circulated and approved at a high level (Fitzgerald, for

---

*Ferrario was the area vice-president for Europe.

†Fitzgerald was the executive vice-president for all communication products, worldwide; Wilson reported to him.

FIGURE 9.1

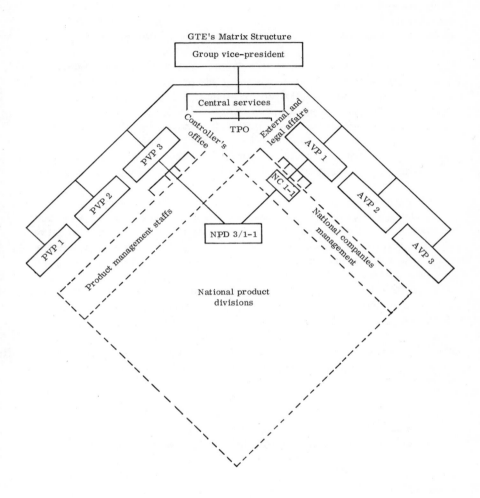

AVP: area vice-president
PVP: product vice-president
 NC: national company
NPD: national product division

Source: Compiled by the author.

all contracts of more than $5 million; Wilson for contracts of more
than $1 million). All proposals for large offers were drawn up through
a combination of efforts by the local area management and the product
management (or TPO).

A member of the product management group commented:

> We need a pooling of information. The area management
> has two key roles in proposal preparation. First the man-
> agement overview and the introduction to the proposal are
> usually worked out by area people with specific members
> of the customers' organization in mind. The whole of the
> proposal is reviewed with them. Second there is a period
> for questions with the customer. These are put forward by
> the area management and time is left to massage the cus-
> tomers.

The overall GTE-International Telecom organization was small
enough, with only three major product lines and five areas, to allow
for multiple informal communications. Top management inside the
Telecom group was closely knit by a common experience, and much
of their communication was done on an informal basis.

Some of the informality had been lost, however, when the headquarters of the product group was transferred from Europe to New
York and when central services began to assume a more important
role. In Europe centralization had already been relatively high, at
least for some decisions such as bidding or quotations. After the re-
location, control procedures became more formal. A manager commented on these aspects:

> TPO has been very meticulous about not taking power for
> itself. It has developed an information system to make
> sure that everybody knows the bids. The information sys-
> tem allows TPO to make an appraisal and a recommenda-
> tion of potential sources inside GTE and to determine which
> approval level is required. This information goes up and
> down, but the factories are not well into the picture. We
> have a very narrow structure of people and it is difficult
> to keep everyone informed when people travel a lot. Some-
> times you cannot wait for two weeks, so you just go ahead.
> At the same time it is possible to bypass someone, then
> find an excuse! Bidding activities are too centralized. De-
> cision making should be pressed down closer to where the
> action is. The data for decisions is better at a lower level.
> In fact, much more critical decisions are made at much

lower levels: what to tell the unions or how to supply the domestic markets.

Because a certain amount of centralization was needed so that top management could influence the balance of power and avoid the development of an overall stable pattern, much information had to rise to a high level. Instead of using functional managers as mediators, as at LME, GTE's Telecommunications' information flows were used to tilt the balance of power differently according to the administrative process. This was achieved by letting individual managers favor either a product or an area orientation, and develop in-depth knowledge of different aspects. This often resulted in some conflict. By ensuring enough centralization of key information, top management was able to throw its weight either to the product or area side whenever a conflict surfaced. By retaining some flexibility and not being all-encompassing (the formal information channels called for a large amount of informal flows) Wilson could gain influence by acting through informal channels.

Planning, Budgeting, and Measurement Systems

Planning and budgeting were interactive processes across levels of the geographic structure. The planning horizon at GTE was five years. Each year, past achievements were reviewed and a general telecommunication equipment target established by Wilson, who took into consideration general trends (state of the economy, market growth and market shares, new products, cost factors, and so on) and the expected role of telecommunications in the whole of GTE. The proposed volume was then split up between the area vice-presidents and discussed up and down at meetings they held with the national company managers, product coordinators, and area marketing services.* After these discussions, the area vice-presidents would come up with a target that was acceptable to both their subordinates and to Wilson. Plans would then be drawn, taking that target as a basis.

Later in the cycle, projections for the first year would be submitted to a detailed budgetary exercise. At all steps the product management groups would be involved, but their influence would be indirect: helping the local managers with targeting costs, export sales, investment, and so on. Once each national company management had

---

*For instance, Ferrario, area vice-president for Europe, had a marketing service for export sales in countries in Europe, Africa, and the Middle East where GTE-Telecom had no subsidiaries.

drafted the local budget, a presentation was made to the area vice-president who, after approval, consolidated the various national budgets into an area budget. This, in turn, was presented to Wilson and to his product vice-presidents (broken down by product line).

Provisions for investments and research budgets were then made and discussed by the area and product vice-presidents. Managing directors of the national companies also were very involved. One of them commented on the process:

> The product managers in the U.S. have only staff responsibility. Mr. Dole will be talking to the switching division manager here for operating problems. If he talks of major developments to be incorporated into our plans, he will talk to me. Thus here there are only two people involved. I develop a company budget. A product vice-president may go to my division manager; however, any investment or change in the budget, if it involves a large amount, needs to be part of an overall strategic plan discussed with me. If I decide to invest, it's a sound business from my point of view, otherwise the operation vice-president here will not be funded. If he thinks differently, the product vice-president will come here to try to convince me. Later I shall discuss my budget with Mr. Wilson. I make the allocations and decide who gets how much. I generally follow, but voice my reservations. I must say that they try to convince me. I do not recall something ever having been imposed on me.

The planning and budgeting systems provided another instance of the formal preeminence of the geographic management, but with an intensity of communications that gave much indirect influence to product management. Unless he successfully appealed to Wilson, a product vice-president could not make a subsidiary manager change his budget or planned investments. The informal influence of product vice-presidents on the overall process was considerable, however. First, the general planning guidelines were largely determined by them, at least in terms of market shares and new products. Second, in a staff advisory role they could also influence the content of the whole process. Finally, because they were part of the staff reviewing the plans and budgets of each area, they could influence the commitments made by line managers.

The budgeting process was very different from the proposal preparation process. In all cases, the proposals were prepared centrally, whether it was by the TPO or by the product management staff. The factory engineering temas did the groundwork, but the product management group retained the overall responsibility. Penetration of new markets was thus managed centrally, whereas a considerable degree of independence was left to the company managers in well-established markets in Europe.

Accounting and measurement practices reflected the formal role of the geographic structure. Accounting remained along geographic lines, and it was only in 1976 that product line results began to be computed. Up to 1976 there was no common accounting format and no common definitions. Moreover, overhead was allocated differently in each country. So the computation of meaningful accounts by product line was not possible.

Though they were not directly comparable, the various subsidiaries produced detailed monthly reports on their activities. These reports were carefully scrutinized by the group's controller's office. The relatively small number of large subsidiaries with complex manufacturing operations allowed much attention to be devoted to each of them without resorting to very tight procedures. Performance was monitored against budgets, and variances closely analyzed, yet evaluation remained very sensitive to local factors and uncertainties that could affect the performance of subsidiaries.

Staffing, Career Paths, Rewards and Punishments

The managerial staff of the International Telecommunication Group was not large enough for clear formalized patterns to have developed. Still, some general staffing characteristics could be identified.

In Europe the companies were staffed almost entirely by local nationals. In other areas the proportion of U.S. managers was higher, particularly in Asia where it had been more difficult to find qualified telecommunication specialists. In both cases, however, staffing and promotion decisions inside the national companies were left to their managing directors, as one of them explained:

> We have very few Americans here. Mr. Coleman is one
> of my assistants, not a line manager. We want the Amer-
> icans to perform one function: teach new skills to our peo-
> ple . . . and leave. Mr. Gavin* is the only person in the
> top management group who is not European. Promotions
> are decided here. Appointments to the first level† in this

---

*Gavin, a Canadian, was a manager of the Italian station equipment and PABX division.

†For instance, the selection of a successor as managing director.

company are followed by Mr. Wilson and Mr. Fitzgerald.
Mr. Johnston, vice-president for personnel of GTE, keeps
records of the various careers and openings. On the second level I can assign anybody I want. However, I look to
Mr. Ferrario and sometimes to Mr. Fitzgerald for personal advice. Both know all the people in my company.
The vice-president for administration is the only person
I would not appoint on my own against New York's advice,
because he has a functional responsibility to the international controller.

There had been no general pattern in the appointment of product
vice-presidents. The transmission vice-president was a former European marketing manager, Dole had been an area manager and a
marketing manager, Hurd* had come from domestic (U.S.) data
transmission companies. The staffs developed in New York were of
international experience. A member of Dole's staff commented:

Historically we all have had an emotional involvement with
areas. All of us here are ex-area people, and we have not
forgotten what running an area is all about. There is a mutual respect and a clear understanding between area and
product people. Our difficulties derive from too few people in the areas who could get into the technical heart of
switching.

The difficulties of spreading out technical competence in electronic switching into the areas were tackled by Dole. It was decided
to station product specialists in the areas. Nationals from countries
of each area were hired (or taken from the existing local staffs),
sent for a few months to the United States, where Dole's group trained
them, and then sent them back to the area. Dole commented on this:

Product specialists are going to report to the area vice-
presidents, with only a functional reporting relationship
to us in New York. The area vice-presidents always
agree before someone is assigned. Conversely, I make
a point of interviewing all future product specialists. The
normal basis for deciding on pay level and promotions for
these people will rest with the area managers, without our
influence. It is only if I feel someone is doing a bad job

---

*Hurd is the product vice-president for station equipment and
PABX.

and is promoted that I will talk about it to the area managers.

The functioning of the organization, with the high degree of co-operation it implied, was made easier by the relative leniency of the reward and punishment systems. A remarkable degree of cooperation had developed in the matrix. No one had a sizable proportion of his income tied to measurement of short-term performance against budget. The close involvement of Wilson in the targeting and budgeting process made the budget system more a planning tool than a performance yardstick.

Two other elements made the development of cooperation easier. First, the company management took good care of its employees: not only did it provide generous insurance plans, but its top managers also showed genuine personal concern. Second, the International Telecommunication Equipment Group was one of the most successful units in the whole of GTE. Not only did it grow rapidly, but it contributed more than its share to the income of overall GTE activities. A combination of rapid growth and good profits provided employment security and boosted the morale of employees.

Top Management's Role

Wilson could directly intervene in the balance between the area management and the product management. However, he seldom did so because most often the two could reach an agreement on specific decisions without referring the matter to him. The balance settled relatively smoothly, largely because both sides perceived the importance and the need for the other. Wilson commented on this:

> We have a unique advantage. Until three years ago we had no product managers, but there already was a drive to grow rapidly in the group. So, with no real exception, none of the area vice-presidents was an administrator, having carved out a domain for himself. Each of them was striving to build a strong market share, and they had started with almost nothing. Moreover, they had been chosen for their entrepreneurial spirit. Aggressive product managers then came into the scene, bringing a new technology. Area managers were so happy to have the products that they welcomed the product managers. In transmission I was urged by the area managers to appoint a product manager. In a multifactory setup they had

no central point where they could go for assistance in product competence.

Wilson did not formally establish authority in matters between the area and product managements. He commented on his role:

> The conflicts do not develop over what a company does with its internal market. That doesn't have much to do with product managers, and they only get into it on their tiptoes. Problems do come up between the product vice-president who feels direct responsibility for all international marketing, and the man who has the P&L of Europe, for instance. That's where conflicts sometimes come up and where they are irreconcilable. I have somewhat of a tendency to side with product managers when they present overall technical arguments. If they tell me that designing a part the way an area would like it would compromise our competitiveness for the next 20 years, I tend to lean on their side. Also, and very importantly, product managers are still new. There have been efforts to give them a measure of authority, so my instinct is to back them up. They have been around a lot, so they know by themselves what to do and do not go too far. For instance, we know that governments will not permit us to achieve economies by centralizing main-exchange manufacturing. Even in France, they want a locally designed PCM, and impose criteria which take it apart from the North Andover technology. Mr. Dole has been around long enough, and on the area side too, to fight his instinct to abandon that. He understands that our European companies need to go ahead with their own technology in cooperation with other European companies.
>
> I decide for people, based on notions of integrity and honesty. I know who tends to exaggerate local pressures, who understands difficulties, what they have done in the past. Both the area vice-presidents and the product vice-presidents call for clarity, but somehow this would destroy the spirit of what we do. I am not going to provide them with delineations of authority. My job is to make choices to the best of my judgment, to support people, to see what the interest of the product group is.

Wilson's role had been made somewhat simpler by the alignment of the interests of both product and area managers in the rapid expansion of the company and by the introduction of the new technology. He commented:

So far both sides have perceived that the other one is important. When product managers get assertive and shift from
advising to usurping (in the eyes of the area management),
I may need to stop them. Sometimes they already ignore
the area managers in some correspondence and documents.
I have to take care of who is attending which meetings, of
who gets what documents, and all such nonsense. I need
to bring back the balance when they go too far.

OPERATING PATTERNS

Manufacturing Policy

The basic manufacturing setup had been simple: main-exchange
switching plants were located in the United States, Canada, Italy, and
Belgium; equipment was manufactured in each country, for its domestic market only, and according to very different standards. Production methods, tools, and machines differed among the locations, except for some similarity between the United States and Canada. Transmission equipment was manufactured in Canada and the United States
for their respective domestic markets, and in Italy for the international market. To help market penetration in Latin America, small
transmission plants had been set up, but these were satellites of the
European plants. PABXs and telephone sets were manufactured in
several locations, but with little coordination and few similarities in
design and production methods.

Large export contracts, first to Taiwan and later to Iran, led
to more coordination and some rationalization. Their mere size and
tight delivery schedules required splitting the work up between several factories. The product management was quick to realize the potential this offered in terms of unification of the production function.
Leduc* commented on this:

No single company was able to carry the whole load. We
had to split. I tried to find out the special capabilities of
each organization. I learned about factory loading and manpower at each factory. From a practical standpoint I had
to take into account the cost of labor in our various factories.
I established a group here to standardize production methods
and standards. How to share the profits was a tough aspect.

---

*Leduc was in charge of managing the export contracts in Europe;
he reported to Dole.

The contract did not involve the same margins for all business. What we had to do was to establish a standard cost for each item, and allocate profits to all companies on a pro rata basis, independently from the jobs they handled. Variances were compared to agreed-upon costs and resulted in differences in profits.

Beyond the immediate contract implementation it meant establishing a common technology, common factory accounting methods, similar production processes and quality standards. Initially it was an accident; we were just responding to the pressures of the large deals. Then we decided to go ahead and break national barriers between our companies. We also concentrated low-level productions; for instance, one factory makes all connectors. National customers would never accept a completely foreign product, even if we engaged in careful reciprocal trade. The issue very much exists: up to what point can we integrate production between different countries? One must realize that we never tackled these questions until they were forced upon us by the magnitude of the export deals.

Cross-shipments had increased between factories and were expected to increase more. There were many difficulties, however. A switching division manager commented on these:

Now we have more coordination with the U.S. and other European companies. If there is some spare capacity somewhere we subcontract from one plant to another. The possibility of further cooperation exists between European plants, but there is not too much going. We have some cuts in production compared to previous forecasts, particularly with the stretch out of the big contracts. Integration could no doubt bring savings, but you cannot lay off your people, or even change their jobs. There are two arguments against rationalization: the standards of quality and control procedures vary between customers, and politically it may be impossible to specialize much.

The worries about unemployment, respect for customer's criteria, and fear of adverse political reactions were shared by the whole European management team to a greater or lesser extent. Dole had somewhat different views:

Now we are going to work with another rule. So far we have had all kinds of manufacturing methods, not an effi-

cient use of resources. The export contracts could not be
split easily because we had different methods. Our electronic switching system will have basically the same hardware everywhere, but the software will be different; 90 percent of the system will be physically identical. We can
produce the switches and test them similarly in any factory, so we can allocate jobs whichever way we want to.
We shall buy components centrally to get the advantages
of high volume purchasing. Because of these commonali-
ties, centralization will become very important. These developments call for a central point, particularly to decide
where to put up factories. An area vice-president could
want to have six small factories for himself, all very inefficient. We need a central point to decide, we shall probably need only a few bigger factories.

The export orders to Taiwan and Iran called for factories to be
built locally to serve the domestic markets in a second phase, and
later for exports to smaller developing countries. Production of
PABXs was started in Latin America to offset sales of other equipment to the local PTTs.
    It was unlikely that the drive to penetrate new markets in the
future could be successful without being accompanied by commitments
to set up local factories. One could expect that the PTT in any sizable market would want to gain some amount of control over the operations of the local GTE subsidiary. So it seemed that the ideal of a
network comprised of only a handful of highly efficient, integrated
plants was unlikely to be reached. It remained that the relative con-
formity brought by the first large export contracts was sufficient to
allow for a coordinated answer to export sales and to permit the orderly transfer of new technologies and products from the United States
to Europe. The fact that each national company remained a self-con-
tained unit with a complete production process, satisfied their respective national customers. The conflict in focus guaranteed that both
the overall proficiency advantages and the local responsiveness constraints would be duly considered in investment decisions. Differing
assessments of investment proposals would come up to Wilson. He
would then be able to throw his weight one way or the other.
    Significantly, the perceptions of product managers led to a re-
liance on technology and costs as a key competitive advantage (à la
LM Ericsson) whereas the area managers negated the relevance of
cost and technology as marketing tools, stressing instead local manufacture and compliance with the customer's sociopolitical criteria
(à la Brown Boveri). This divergence had, as we have seen, extensive implications in terms of manufacturing policy. In product development the dominance of the product orientation was much clearer.

Location and Management of
Research and Development

The International Telecommunication Group's European subsidiaries had learned the hard way that the resources needed for the
development of an electronic exchange system were beyond their
grasp. When their competitive position in the traditional markets
became threatened by crossbar and semielectronic systems, the
group's subsidiaries reacted by starting several development projects
locally. Though they provided ad hoc responses for domestic needs,
the semielectronic systems they developed lacked the potential for
export sales. It then became clear to everyone, and was well accepted, that the basic technology would come from Northlake and be
applied in the foreign companies. Only small staffs, working on specific software, were maintained in Europe.* This dependence upon
research efforts carried out in the United States and the role of the
product management groups in Stamford in transferring the results
to Europe, increased the power of Dole. Hurd, product manager for
station equipment, was also in a stronger position because the technology for station equipment was derived from main-exchange technology and because of a series of mishaps in Europe that led to increasing reliance upon Northlake.
Attlee, the product vice-president for transmission equipment,
faced a rather different situation: a large proportion of the 700 persons involved in R&D in Europe worked on transmission projects. By
industry standards the staff of the Telecommunication Group's European transmissions laboratory was strong and numerous. Consequently, technology did not provide a power base for Attlee and his
transmissions product management team.
Dominance of the development function by the product component
of the matrix, worried some managers, as an R&D executive in Europe explained:

We must not exaggerate and develop only one system. First
it would not comply with local requirements. Second, in the
relationships with national customers it is increasingly important to do engineering locally. There are several reasons. In the relationship with the customer you need to provide technical assistance easily and on short notice. You
need a great amount of expertise locally to solve particular
interface problems. Finally, from a political standpoint,

---

*About 1,000 persons were employed in Northlake, and only 10
in Europe for main-exchange electronic switching development.

the administration is under pressure for strategic independence, i.e., to produce, maintain, improve, and update
the system locally. They recognize that purely local development is impossible for a company like ours, but they nev-
ertheless require some local activities.

Wilson was quite aware that spreading the development programs
between several locations was becoming a critical element of political
acceptability. The extent to which foreign customers would consent
to rely on the Northlake technology was not clear.

Links with Local Entities

It was clearly established that the responsibility for dealing
with national customers in countries where the Telecommunications
Group had subsidiaries rested entirely with the local management.
Beyond that general orientation there was a lack of clear perspective:
the product management teams minimized the importance of local
links whereas the area component stressed their criticalness. So
far, difficulties did not really exist, partly because GTE did not have
dominant market positions in other countries. The management of
the Telecommunications Group was well aware of the possibility that,
in the future, national customers might insist on joint ventures and
new policies might then be required.

Export Marketing

Export marketing was the responsibility of the product management. The selection of markets as well as the drafting of proposals
was carried out by the product management team for main-exchange
switching and by the Telecom proposal office (TPO) in Geneva for
transmission equipment. So far, the European subsidiaries had not
been involved extensively in main-exchange switchgear exports. Recently, however, export orders were so big that a separate project
management team had been set up, and Leduc was appointed to coordinate the activities of European factories.
There was no precedent to determine how the relationship between product and area management groups would be structured around
export sales of main-exchange switching, though an indirect example
had been provided by the setup of the TPO. The manager of the TPO
described its operations:

All calls for bids received in the areas come to our office.
We analyze the specs and come up with a summary of the

call for bids. We make an evaluation and recommend what
to do. When it turns out one factory can do the job on its
own, we make it responsible for the rest of the job. When
the proposal is to be mixed, we coordinate its preparation.
We take advice from the area management, and it has to approve our activities before we go ahead. The final responsibility for price levels rests with the area vice-president.
The factories work on the basis of commission payments
to the division. They are eager to get jobs. Area managers lead the negotiations with customers, but we are able
to help them on some elements.

The training of switching specialists to be members of the area
teams suggested an outcome similar to TPO, in which the role of the
central staff of Dole would decrease somewhat. Price levels would
be the object of negotiations between the area managers and the supplying subsidiaries. At least so long as the operating profit and loss
responsibility remained with the area managers, it seemed unlikely
that the same extent of preeminence would be retained by the product
management as when exports from the United States were taking place.

Allocations of export orders had an immediate impact on the
profits of the various subsidiaries through their effect on factory loading. Up to 1975 factory loading was done locally in Europe, but already the impact of the new export contracts was such that there was
a need for central coordination. Such coordination was already taking
place for some products that could be supplied from several sources.
The area vice-president analyzed bids, and proposed an allocation, in
light of his own P&L account. Approval of that proposal, however,
involved Wilson and possibly Fitzgerald for the largest orders. They
had information on the overall situation and could convince the area
vice-president to shift the allocation. There was constant communication throughout the organization around these issues, and enough
different points of view were represented to blend the economic and
political considerations.

COMMENTARY

Analysis

Contrary to LM Ericsson and Brown Boveri, where a clear
strategic preference for international rationalization and integration
(LM Ericsson) or national autonomy and responsiveness (Brown Boveri) prevailed, strategic preference was left unclear at GTE-International Telecommunication Equipment Group.

The product vice-presidents were competing against the area vice-presidents to obtain power over resource commitments. There was no a priori, across-the-board determination of who, among the two, should have the power to commit resources to a particular project. The definition of the role of the product vice-presidents provided for considerable influence, but left them with little direct authority. The role of product management was defined somewhat vaguely:

> Product management is responsible for all matters relating to international planning, development, sourcing, manufacture, and marketing of transmission equipment. They will also participate in all significant matters affecting the domestic market of our manufacturing subsidiaries to ensure that the needs of the international market are given proper consideration by those primarily concerned with local requirements. It is a staff organization reporting to the group Vice-President-International Telecommunications.
> The Primary Goals are:
>
> 1. Formulate development plans and objectives as a framework for the realization of coordinated developments among GTE's manufacturing subsidiaries.
> 2. Extend the effectiveness of our product line.
> 3. Balance the overall design efforts to ensure economically controlled developments without duplication of efforts.
> 4. Support GTE manufacturing in product line improvement through planned controlled evolution.
> 5. Coordinate all planning and development activities.
> 6. Expand the GTE market share and strengthen our position in the market. [1]

This charter did not clearly assign responsibilities to product vice-presidents in any precise way. What, concretely, their responsibilities would be was left to their own decisions and abilities.

On the whole, then, power was left unclear, shared between the area vice-presidents and the product vice-presidents. Top management, in this case Wilson and occasionally Fitzgerald, remained close enough to the operations to rule on a case-by-case basis when the area and product managements conflicted.

In switching equipment the development of a successful new electronic technology by Northlake, combined with cost competitiveness, made an expansion strategy possible. This strategy, in turn, called for an organization able to muster resources on an international scale. No one in the area management, either individually or as a group, could develop a comprehensive and competitive international drive. The selection of markets to pursue had to be done centrally. This provided a justification and a leverage point for the product vice-president to gain some ascendency. Dole commented:

> We need to plan a strategy for our own long-term best inter-
> est. We choose which markets to pursue. The local mana-
> gers have only part of the whole picture; their perceptions
> are local; they would often like to pursue all opportunities,
> even the less likely ones. Here we have a fear of being too
> dispersed. We feel better controlling our destiny than
> leaving it to the areas. In essence we tell them: "We de-
> cide on specific markets, and you go there to sell."

Whereas area management retained full P&L responsibility, the product management drafted proposals and participated in nego-tiations with customers, thus playing an important role in area man-agement's results. The primary purpose for cooperation at the pro-posal/negotiation stage was to combine the in-depth knowledge of the national markets possessed by area managers, with the understanding of the new products possessed by product managers.

Technical coordination and development of main-exchange switch-ing became clearly assigned to the product management, following the technological lead of Northlake over the international subsidiaries. By building a link between the domestic operations and the interna-tional subsidiaries, Dole could take advantage of the technology of the former to further his influence on the latter.

Logging-in two large export contracts provided the basis for gaining influence, by making both the domestic and international man-ufacturing operations dependent upon him for significant export sales. Previously they had served their domestic markets almost exclusive-ly. As we have seen, these export contracts also provided a rationale and created a need for unifying accounting methods, quality, and stan-dards, and for coordination of production schedules. The uniformity brought about by these contracts, as well as the project management team headed by Leduc, was seen by many as a test run for the or-derly introduction of electronic switching systems into the European factories later in the decade. Indirectly, by decreasing the diversity between plants, the export contracts had thus created a basis for more influence from the main-exchange switching product management team.

In the private-exchange business, the situation developed along similar lines. A series of difficulties caused by poor coordination be-tween the various development labs and factories in Europe resulted in product-development lags and cost escalations. As a consequence, Wilson had decided that a full line of private exchanges of various sizes and configurations should be developed in Northlake as a by-product of the main-exchange switches. Again, instead of pursuing the various projects in Europe, it was decided to use a semielectronic product line developed in Italy as a stopgap measure; U.S. products with European adaptations were to be developed for the late 1970s.

Hurd, formerly manager of one of the U.S. regional operating companies, was appointed product vice-president for private-exchange equipment. His mission was similar to Dole's. His first task was to develop a new product-line monitoring process, which was introduced in 1974/75. Hurd recalled the first new product to be monitored closely:

Automatic dialing was a new product concept. We got the services of consultants to determine the number of lines in the memory. There were more in Europe and the Middle East than in the U.S. because of a high concentration of relatives and close friends over a small area. Each area had its own ideas, but we wanted to develop a standard set. So we got an "open project" with broad product-design guidelines that we sent to all area and country managers after a first product review by Mr. Wilson. The area managements reviewed our design, criticized it, and suggested ways to improve it. After revisions, we set a target price and the field people saw customers to give us a rough market estimate. Once we get that feedback we put together a five-year project plan, describing how many sets would be made, where, at which price, and where they would be sold. We then had a meeting with the area V.P.s or their representatives and froze the design.

During the same period our product development team had gone to the factories with the product concept and its specifications to ask whether they wanted to cooperate in the design or were interested in the production. We got at least two locations involved in detailed development. Each factory gave us a proposal outlining its design, the required components, an initial cost estimate, and its target transfer price for the quantity we specified. We compared their proposals and chose one. Then we got a design budget from Mr. Wilson. When the first production units were ready we put them in the field and trained customer-service people.

The product vice-presidents had been able to gain a strong influence in main-exchange switching and private-exchange equipment through their ability to develop and control export sales and through their key role in transferring electronic technology from Northlake to the international subsidiaries. They had thus shown their usefulness for the group as a whole. In transmission equipment there was no such clarity. The clear leading company was in Italy, and it exported a large share of its product already (approximately 60 percent). The standards were sufficiently different and the competencies of the Italian company high enough to make technology transfer from the United States unnecessary. Furthermore, TPO reported to Wilson directly.

Generally, in activities other than export marketing and product development, the responsibilities of product vice-presidents had not developed so clearly. By building into the managerial tools a role for himself as arbitrator for such critical processes as proposal evaluation and factory loading, Wilson had acquired the ability to intervene directly in each contract. Other tools, such as accounting methods and planning and budgeting systems, were not changed, thus leaving the direct responsibility for operations with the area management. The preeminence of the area component was implicitly embodied in the structure of formal processes. That preeminence was moderated, however, by two devices. First, Wilson, as arbitrator in key decisions, had the power to selectively tilt the balance toward the product management component. Second, because informal communications were very important, such selective interventions by Wilson would set precedents, which in the long run would make managers seek informal consensus before moving. More information would flow from the local companies in the consensus-building process.

Such formality also permitted the development of regulating mechanisms. A key problem faced by Wilson was to keep the allocation of power within bounds, to prevent the product managers from being rejected by the geographic managements, but also to limit their power over the operations of the national subsidiaries. Informal communications enabled each side of the matrix to make a stand whenever the balance of power swung too far to one side. Just how far was "too far" depended upon the cognitive differences between the two components. Because of risk-avoidance preference, it was likely that the component feeling a direct threat would make a stand before the balance was allowed to tilt to a point where either political acceptability or overall economic performance would be jeopardized. In other words, one could expect such matrix management to remain relatively balanced between national responsiveness and global integration while retaining some self-regulating capabilities.

The flavor of the relationships was well conveyed by the following description of the evolution of the Telecommunications Group made by the managing director of a European subsidiary:

If we were to have a worldwide P&L by-product line I would leave my responsibilities. We can't have such a P&L be-

cause of the need to coordinate activities locally and because of the political penetration problems. However,
there is a common global responsibility for products at
the corporate level [that is, divisional level in Stamford].
Responsibilities to some extent are a matter of who is
powerful. Mr. Dole is very powerful. First, switching
is narrowly related to development in the U.S. Consequently, Mr. Dole's function is clearly needed. In addition, major proposals are handled at the top level anyway, not here. Second, Mr. Dole's leadership and personality make him a driving force. Switching is a big
game, marketing decisions are critical; for other products they involve much less.

Dole's approach, however, is more to support what goes well
rather than to try to do everything by himself. Still, he has developed
a small staff empire in the United States and elsewhere. Wilson's
role was also essential in maintaining the balance. He could side
with one or the other side according to the issues and give signals
through his handling of conflicts. He also worked to encourage product vice-presidents to adopt an entrepreneurial role where they developed new products and markets for the group as a whole. He discour-
aged them from assuming a controlling or operating role in the operations of the subsidiaries.[2]

Implications

The power-balance mode did not rely on a clear strategy to
respond to the conflict between political and economic imperatives.
GTE attempted to respond to the separateness of individual markets
(Italy, Belgium); in some others it pooled the resources of various
subsidiaries together (for example, to serve the Iranian export order).

Within the organization, the strategy was unclear. The geographic organization favored national responsiveness, but its members
knew they had to rely, at least to some extent, on the technology and
export orders that the product management controlled. Members of
the product organization were quite aware of the need for differentiation and sensitiveness in dealing with government and PTT, but they
strived for uniformity and integration.

Wilson had set the managerial tools in such a way as to:

1. Make the formal responsibility of the geographic management clear, but give much informal influence to the product manage-

ment: this brought their various perspectives to bear as specific decisions without creating direct opposition and rivalry. For instance, had profits been used as a measurement and evaluation tool on both sides, then conflicts would have been more likely.

2. Promote a synthesis: a situation where the two inputs had different identities, perceptions, and priorities, but where each worked for the success of the group as a whole. The reward systems and the lack of set winning career tracks maintained ambiguity and fostered cooperation.

3. Reserve for himself the ability to rule on key decisions: investments and plans, proposals and pricing, plant loading, and scheduling. He could intervene to make sure that neither side of the product-area matrix gained much power over the other. His attention to the process (circulation of documents, composition of meetings) was directed at preserving the balance and making sure that the duality of perspectives embodied in the organization agreed on all significant decisions.

Wilson had been assisted by the nature of the success of the product managers and by their perception of the environment. First, product managers had been able to find their source of influence in bringing success to the whole organization. By going after large, difficult export orders they had also shown their willingness to take more than their share of risks for the total organization. Second, they had been able to relate to the development in Northlake. Third, they recognized the complexity of the environment and the need for a balanced process wherein the necessity of national responsiveness was recognized.

It is possible to argue that an ambiguous balance of power such as that at GTE would tend to maintain its equilibrium in the long run. In a phase of international expansion the product management would gain ascendency over the organization by controlling key factors of success. Similarly, during deep technological changes, the product management would be most needed. Conversely, as technologies, markets, and subsidiaries mature, the importance of national managers is likely to increase and that of product managers to decrease. With maturity, national responsiveness becomes more critical and the national managers face the most significant sources of uncertainty for the organization as a whole.[3] Adjustments to internal relative power thus correspond to changes in the relative weight of economic and technological imperatives (new technology, new market) and of the political imperatives (mature technology, well-established markets).

It remains true, however, that a balance of power seems to be extremely difficult to maintain and manage in the long run. It forgoes the clarity provided by a preferred strategy and a clear direction.

The key danger here is to see the management process degenerate for one or several of the reasons described by Davis and Lawrence.[4] One difficulty is cognitive overload at the apex of the matrix. Wilson had to handle only a dozen key managers, including the heads of central services. Again, as in LM Ericsson or Brown Boveri's heavy equipment businesses, key customer orders or significant decisions were relatively few and far between. A larger matrix in a more complex industry would hardly permit the level of attention to individual decisions that Wilson was able to bring.

In conclusion, the power–balance mode provided most flexibility to deal with decisions in a very differentiated way, yet it afforded top management the possibility to maintain consistency in the stream of decisions as top management could decide whether to give precedence to national responsiveness of multinational integration.

NOTES

1. Adapted from internal GTE documents. For more details, see "General Telephone and Electronics: International Telecommunication Division" (Boston, Intercollegiate Case Clearing House, no. 2, 379–061, 1978).

2. For a description of unsuccessful product management in a matrix and ill-conceived top management role, see Michael Beer and Stanley M. Davis, "Creating a Global Organization: Failures along the Way," Columbia Journal of World Business, Summer 1976, pp. 72–84.

3. For a theoretical treatment of this point, see D. J. Hickson et al., "A Strategic Contingency Theory of Intraorganizational Power," Administrative Science Quarterly 16 (1971): 216–29.

4. Stanley M. Davis and Paul R. Lawrence, Matrix (Reading, Mass.: Addison Wesley, 1977).

10

STRATEGIC MANAGEMENT

The specific company descriptions and analyses made in Chapters 7, 8, and 9 provide a concrete meaning and a set of illustrations to the approach developed in Chapter 6. Initially, we started with a question: How could multinational companies be successful in industries that attract much government attention and the markets for which are state controlled? We then explored the social and political demands created by government influence, first, in general abstract terms in Chapter 2, then in specific details as they apply to telecommunication equipment and electrical power systems, in Chapter 3. We identified and explored the political imperatives faced by the multinational manufacturers of such equipment and systems. We also reviewed the economics of manufacture and the technology of the products, and the consequences of these in terms of oligopoly industry structure and the dynamics of competition. We found that these production economics and technological conditions created very strong pressures for rationalization and integration of production, that is, for moving from a set of semiautonomous subsidiaries catering to their respective domestic markets to a global production network where each subsidiary makes only part of the product line, but for the world market. Generally, however, political imperatives caused by government concerns and interventions made such rationalization and integration impossible. How companies responded to these various conflicting economic and political imperatives seemed to depend primarily on their competitive posture within their industries. It was possible to outline strategic groups determined by two central variables: (1) the mix of market served—mature markets or newer ones (for the company)—and (2) the use of technology by the company—whether the company was a technology leader or a follower.

Finally, the operations and the management of one company in each of the three international strategic groups are described and analyzed in some detail.* Through the various steps in this analysis, we have explored the consistency between the economic and political characteristics of an industry, its structure, the strategy of individual companies, the emergence and identification of strategic groups, the operating patterns found in individual companies, and the managerial tools used by the companies' top management to shape and direct the operating patterns.

Yet, the initial question is not fully answered. The descriptions and analyses in the three preceding chapters show clearly the key role of top management in directing the organization (again, keeping in mind that for GTE top management refers to the product-group level, not the corporate level). They also document the impossibility of clear strategy-structure solutions of the type found in businesses where the economic imperative of global competitiveness leads to clear regional (or global) integration and centralization (Ford in the automobile industry), or in businesses where the diversity between national markets leads to very autonomous national subsidiaries (Nestlé in the food industry).

In this chapter we pause to explore in more detail the managerial difficulties introduced by the key role of top management and the fuzziness of the strategic substance. This exploration is developed in three parts. First, we will analyze the problem of the process of developing a strategy in the telecommunication equipment and power system industries. We will also analyze methods used to maintain consistency among strategic decisions made over time. The key issue here is that of stability: to what extent it is possible for companies in these industries to maintain consistency in the allocation of key resources over time. Second, means of improving the strategic management process and shifting the strategy over time are reviewed. Finally, some problems of diversified multinationals are summarized. In particular, the trade-off between developing a clear strategy for any given business and taking advantage of interdependencies between businesses is explored.

STRATEGIC CONSISTENCY

Alfred D. Chandler defines strategy as "the determination of the basic long-term goals and objectives of an enterprise and the adoption of courses of action and the allocation of resources necessary for carrying out these goals."[1]

---

*The data gathered on each of the three companies were much more detailed than what has been presented here, but the richness of the data had to be reduced to a readable format for inclusion in this book.

The fact that Chandler sees strategy as a process is clear from the above quote; the emphasis is on action, determining, allocating, and so forth.

These tasks, in a large complex organization such as the multinational, are distributed in the organization, as Chester I. Barnard had already noted:

> The formulation of organization purposes and objectives
> and the more general decisions involved in this process
> and in those of actions to carry them into effect are dis-
> tributed in organizations and are not, nor can they be,
> concentrated or specialized to individuals, except in
> minor degree.[2]

.More recently, many authors have elaborated on this point and have attempted to gain an understanding of these processes.[3] Without exploring this body of literature in detail here, it is possible to stress that strategy, as a stream of resource allocation decisions and the shaping of operating patterns over time, is not dissociable from the administrative process that leads to a stream of decisions. This is particularly true in the companies studied in depth here. We have seen already in Chapter 6 that the matrix structures adopted by these companies represent a significant departure from the unidimensional geographic or product structures found in simpler businesses. Whereas unidimensional geographic or product structures embody a single clear strategy, the matrix evidences indeterminacy of decision making.

In order to understand how the companies studied here are managed, one thus has to go beyond their structure and explore how strategy is formulated, as an administrative process. It is useful, in order to gain such an understanding, to disaggregate our view of strategic management into four subdimensions and to review how top management can influence them.

The Dimensions of Strategy in a Multinational Matrix

Perceptions

What is perceived by the individual as most relevant facts is largely a result of past experience, consistency with belief patterns, and influence of other members of the organization and peers.[4] In a matrix, by design, such perceptions are dual. Some managers are more sensitive to the political imperative and to national responsiveness. Some others are more sensitive to worldwide economic competitiveness. In generating data, and in gaining a point of view on the environment of the company, these managers will tend to use different information and develop divergent interpretations. Individuals' views are likely to be internally consistent but different from each other's. Top management will thus be the beneficiary of a dual logic. In other words, data pertinent to key strategic decisions are likely to reach top management through two different filters: managers giving preference to worldwide integration and rationalization and selecting data and interpretations consistent with that preference, and managers giving preference to national autonomy and responsiveness and selecting data and developing interpretations accordingly. For instance, the perceptions and interpretative logic of national subsidiary managers are likely to be influenced by their proximity to officials in the host government's agencies, that of product-oriented managers at headquarters by the overall performance of the company and by proximity to central research laboratories.

Top management could influence the perceptions and interpretations of individual managers in several ways. First, managers' selection could be used to bring the perceptions more closely together or differentiate them. At GTE, selecting former area executives as product managers made the convergence of perceptions easier and gave the product managers a keen appreciation for the other side of the matrix. In a similar vein, Luterbacher at Brown Boveri wanted to use the new "business aggregate" executives in the major national companies to make them cooperate more closely on specific business strategies. The short-term operating orientation of the division managers (who sat on the KSTs) had made them poor vehicles to foster integration. Business-aggregate executives were not promoted from BBC national managers who could be expected to defend jealously the autonomy of their national company, as division managers did in the secondary structure. Instead, business-aggregate executives were hired from companies where responding to the economic imperative was clearly favored, such as Control Data and Honeywell (Control Equipment). Yet, these companies were in industries of sufficient significance to governments to make top executives sensitive to the political imperative. In a different way, LM Ericsson selected area marketing managers as integrators because they had dual perceptions: the interests and idiosyncracies of the area for which they were responsible, and the corporate headquarters' view. Area marketing managers were promoted from headquarters staff members with previous operating line responsibility within the area.

Second, perceptions can be made more homogeneous by the provision of corporate scenarios as working hypotheses. None of the companies studied in depth emphasized this, but the development of common working hypotheses was part of the first stage of the strategic planning process that the Brown Boveri planning staff tried to coordinate among the major national companies.

Third, the patterns of executive socialization can be used to influence managers' perceptions.[5] For instance, at LM Ericsson, no contacts existed between the managers of different subsidiaries, but the management of each subsidiary interacted closely with headquarters. The socialization between subsidiary managers and local milieus (PTT executives, government officials, local businessmen) was balanced by the countervailing socialization between subsidiary and corporate executives. The KPT/KST secondary structure at Brown Boveri was also primarily a mechanism to provide a socialization arena for executives from different national companies.

Finally, the nationality of executives was of some importance. At LM Ericsson, many key subsidiary managers were Swedish expatriates who saw their long-term future in Sweden and attached their loyalties to LM Ericsson as a whole. At BBC or GTE, on the other hand, most subsidiary management positions were filled by local nationals who saw their future and loyalty mainly in national terms. Their socialization in the local environment was also easier; for instance, Koch, president and CEO of Compagnie Electro-Mécanique, was sufficiently "French" to be president of the French association of electrical equipment manufacturers.

In summary, top management can influence the perceptions of managers within the organization, and, to some extent, regulate the differentiation of perceptions between geographic and product executives. This is achieved by managing career paths, providing corporate scenarios as working hypotheses, and influencing patterns of socialization.

Substantive Plans

As we have seen, there can hardly be an overall comprehensive strategic plan for multinationals active in the telecommunication equipment and electrical power system industries. Yet, in order to compete effectively and make resource allocation decisions, some consensus has to be reached on specific decisions. Also, the selection of "relevant data" and the interpretations made of them often lead naturally to the development of substantive plans. A strategy has to be developed, at least in terms of what to do to compete successfully in the industry. Within a matrix, several strategies can be competing for selection and implementation, particularly when the overall strategic preference is unclear. For instance, at GTE, Dole, the product vice-president for main-exchange switching could develop a strategy involving the rationalization of production into a few plants serving the world markets whereas the European area vice-president could consider a myriad of smaller plants, each geared to serve its national market. Their models of how to compete successfully in the telecommunication equipment industry were substantially different.

Top management can influence the substance of plans in several ways. First, and simplest, some central strategic theory can be developed. We have seen that a rigid, across-the-board model of how to compete (for instance, such as that used by Texas Instruments)[6] is hardly suitable in the industry considered here because product, market, and technology diversity are too high and government interventions too uncertain. Yet, it is possible to develop a preferred way of competing. At LM Ericsson it was clear that technological excellence (the AXE system for the current switching equipment generation), efficient centralized component production, comparatively low prices, and "clean" dealing were centrally determined premises to any strategy. Second, repeated support of resource allocation proposals corresponding to a particular strategy can signal very clearly to managers which strategy is "right," without top management getting involved in the explicit formulation of goals and objectives. Again, LM Ericsson provides an example: formally, the company had neither goals nor a statement of objectives, yet top management could signal fairly clearly what was to be done. Signals came early in the definition of specific plans and proposals, through the area marketing managers. Top management influence was also exercised at the review stage, through the budget committee.

Short of influencing the substance of plans directly, top management can structure the process through which they are developed. For instance, by creating worldwide planning teams, such as the KSTs in Brown Boveri, and giving them veto power on the plans of individual units, top management can ensure integration between subsidiaries. Complementary check-and-balance mechanisms, for instance, through functional audits of the subunit plans, may be needed to avoid bargaining and "horse trading." By deciding who initiates plans, and what is included in them, top management can impact their content and the way strategies will be developed. For instance, if national subsidiaries start drawing up plans, interdependencies between products at the national level are likely to be emphasized as a key element of strategy. Conversely, if product-oriented managers draft the plans, interdependencies between countries along any given product lines are going to be emphasized.

Thus, again, as for influencing perceptions of the environment, top management is not without means to determine how specific substantive strategies are developed within the company.

Commitment of Resources

The ability to commit resources to particular projects and plans (for instance, to new products or plant expansion) or to withdraw resources (for instance, divestiture of a subsidiary) provides a measure of actual power in the organization. Insofar as realized strategy (as opposed to intended strategy)[7] is the result of resource commitments, power over the actual strategy derives from such commitments, even if they contradict the agreed-upon substantive plans. Formally, resource allocation is usually tightly controlled at the corporate level. Yet, the reality is substantially more complex than a simplistic view of corporate control would suggest. Joseph L. Bower described in detail the social and political process that leads middle-level executives to commit their judgment and reputation by providing impetus to specific projects and not supporting others. [8]

Top management can influence the commitment of resources by making sure that serious resource allocation conflicts do not get smoothed over at lower levels. For conflicts to be dealt with, they first need to be brought to top management attention. Various means can be used to make sure resource allocation conflicts get attention. Functional managers can be used as mediators between product divisions and national subsidiaries, à la LM Ericsson, to monitor their interface and bring the substance of disagreements to top management attention. Administrative systems and access to the top can also be used to encourage managers, on either side, to voice their reservations with the decisions of the other side of the matrix. When national subsidiary managers at GTE felt decisions made by the product managers would seriously impact their own results, these national subsidiaries could bring the issue to the attention of Wilson. Faced with the need to resolve such conflicts, top management could decide, based on industry experience or on a sense of the integrity of the management process or on a desire to reduce risks. For instance, Lundvall and his central functional staff at LM Ericsson had a deep-enough knowledge of the telecommunication industry to gain an in-depth understanding of most issues and to use their substantive judgment to resolve them. Conversely, at GTE Wilson relied more on risk minimization and process integrity. On technical problems, he trusted more the judgment of product managers; on marketing ones, that of area and country managers. He decided between them based on a sense of which was most likely to decrease the overall risk of a decision. At the same time, he still made sure that both sides could review resource allocation decisions fully. Concretely, he acted on the mechanics of the management process: who gets which documents, sits in which meeting, talks to which customers, and so forth.

In all three companies, it seems that a key element was the decoupling of business risks from personal risks. The debate over resource commitments had to be made with the interests of the company as a whole in mind, not those of a particular subunit or those generated by measuring worldwide product line results. In most cases, the reward and punishment systems were not linked to individual performance but to the results of the organization as a whole. Conversely, at BBC, bringing national division managers who operated in a tight, short-term measurement system to take the interests of BBC as a whole into consideration, through the KST-KPT structure, was next to impossible.

Another element was that the application of tight reward and punishment schemes, without a clear-cut strategy and well-defined rules of behavior, could lead to questionable behavior on the part of subsidiary managers or product managers involved in negotiations with customers. The nature of the customers and the oligopolistic structures of both industries provided opportunities for questionable commissions and payments to intermediaries or kickbacks to customers and for price fixing among suppliers of equipment. *

As a key ingredient of the matrix management in the companies studied was the continuous challenge of decisions by one group or the other, and their active involvement in all decisions, one also needed to dissociate the rejection of one's ideas from personal failure. Substantive conflicts on what was best for the company on a particular issue was not to degenerate into consistent deadlocked opposition between the sides of the matrix. This also called for a dissociation of rewards and punishments from individual measurable performance.

In summary, power over the commitment of resources could thus stay with top management whenever lower levels disagreed. To ensure that such disagreements did not lower the intensity of cooperation and debate on substantive issues, the personal rewards and punishments had to be dissociated from scorekeeping. The key danger was that of "bureaucratic politics" within the organization, with individual managers defending narrowly defined interests.[9] By making sure that disagreements would move up for resolution, and that the facts as seen through several sets of conflicting perceptions and interpretative schemes would be available to top management, a discriminating allocation of power to the geographic or the product side of the matrix could be made. Such allocation can be much more precise

---

*No evidence was found of organized price fixing as had existed in the U.S. domestic power system industry, and such a cartel would probably be more difficult to maintain internationally. Yet, one cannot infer from the fact that this researcher did not see evidence of collusion, that such collusion did not exist, at least for some contracts or some products.

than the sweeping changes in the locus of relative power described by
Prahalad in his study of a multinational active in businesses that do
not attract the same level of government attention as power systems
and telecommunication equipment. [10]

Implementation Authority

In unidimensional structures, the authority structure is the key
element in strategy, and the perceptions, orientation of substantive
strategic plans, and power to commit resources fall approximately in
line with the authority structure. Here, as the lines of reporting relationships and the possible loci of any particular activities (such as
a new product development) are multiple, it becomes important to
assign authority over particular tasks in a precise way. For instance,
at BBC the task of allocating the bids was clearly the responsibility
of the Konzern marketing staffs, but the responsibility for individual
bids, once allocated, was fully with the chosen national company.
Conversely, at GTE things were more ambiguous, many tasks were
left to the cooperation of the area and the product vice-presidents.

By delineating clearly the allocation of authority for specific
tasks and leaving more ambiguity for others, top management could
also influence the way in which specific decisions would be implemented and the extent of top management day-to-day discretion on such
implementation. Such allocation of authority would also determine
the extent and direction of interdependencies between subunits.

One can use the contrast between GTE and Brown Boveri to illustrate this point. At GTE bids were processed, and proposals and
submissions prepared by a central product staff (Dole's staff for
main-exchange switching and the TPO for transmission equipment).
Contracts were then administered centrally and the production of
equipment subcontracted to the various subsidiaries. Operating control over export sales thus remained with the product vice-presidents
and their staff. At BBC, the responsibility for bidding was allocated
to an individual national subsidiary early on. It then prepared its detailed submission and, if it won, was responsible for contract management. Subcontracting was done by the responsible national subsidiary
to sister subsidiaries or to third parties. Such differences in the allocation of responsibility for critical tasks gave the central product
vice-presidents of GTE a much stronger say in determining the direction followed by GTE than that of BBC's central corporate marketing
managers. In sum, the allocation of task responsibilities is a fourth
means for top management to influence the overall direction of the
company. Together with the three dimensions reviewed above, it
provides handles for top management to guide the company. It is important to recognize that within a multinational matrix trying to re-

spond to both political and economic imperatives these four dimensions of the strategic management process—perceptions, substantive plans, commitment of resources, and implementation authority—need to be considered separately, but managed jointly.

Maintaining Strategic Consistency

The "ideal" view of matrix management would be a perfect balance, where all four subdimensions would be aligned, as in Figure 10.1.

Such an "ideal" matrix, however, would easily be subjected to all pathologies described by Davis and Lawrence and summarized in Chapter 6. Furthermore, it would not be possible to maintain consistency in the deployment of resources, that is, to follow any strategy. It thus becomes important to recognize, following Prahalad, that asymmetry in the matrix is needed for strategy to exist. It is also important to recognize that whereas breadth of perceptions and, to some extent, variety of substantive plans are needed to take into consideration the duality of environments, unity in resource commitment and specialization in implementation authority are needed to allocate and utilize resources efficiently. The multinational matrix thus may be sketched as in Figure 10.2.

As we saw in Chapter 6 in abstract, and concretely in the cases of LM Ericsson and Brown Boveri, strategy implies a preference for

FIGURE 10.1

An Ideal View of a Multinational Matrix

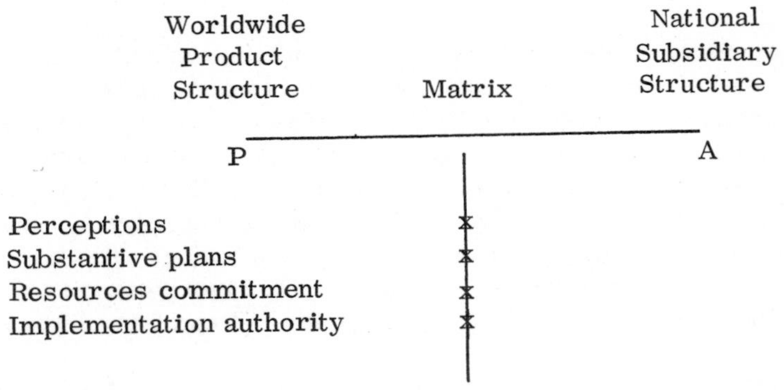

Worldwide Product Structure	Matrix	National Subsidiary Structure
P		A

Perceptions
Substantive plans
Resources commitment
Implementation authority

Source: Compiled by the author.

FIGURE 10.2

A Possible View of a Multinational Matrix

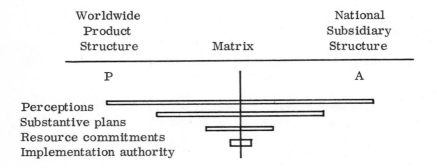

Source: Compiled by the author.

rationalization and integration (and asymmetry in resource commitment and implementation authority toward a centralized product structure) or a preference for decentralized national responsiveness (and
asymmetry in resource commitment and implementation authority toward a rational subsidiary structure). Such asymmetry is a key to
maintaining strategic consistency among decisions. Yet, given the
importance of both the economic and the political environments, and
the differences in relative criticality of either between mature and
newer markets, asymmetry needs to be kept within narrow bounds.
National subsidiary managers can have more power or resource commitments than worldwide product managers, but they cannot have absolute power. The interface for resource commitments is centrally
managed.

Furthermore, as we have seen in Chapter 6, differentiation between functions becomes necessary. The power to commit resources
of product managers is larger for R&D projects than for capacity investments. Differences in power asymmetry between functions also
make the maintenance of an overall balance easier. Similarly, the
implementation responsibility may lay with product managers for R&D,
and national subsidiaries for marketing or manufacturing. The real
view of a multinational matrix thus becomes rather more complex
than that of the "ideal" or of the "possible" ones. It can be sketched
as in Figure 10.3.

For instance, at LM Ericsson marketing (both export marketing
and to some extent marketing to the domestic markets of individual

FIGURE 10.3

A Real View of a Multinational Matrix

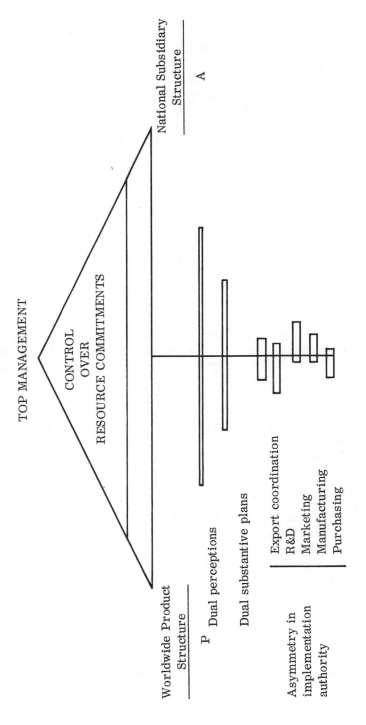

Source: Compiled by the author.

245

subsidiaries) was centrally controlled, whereas at BBC coordination did not go beyond the allocation of export markets or tender offers from customers. Similarly, manufacturing of all components was centralized at LM Ericsson, whereas none was at BBC.

Finally, the various managerial tools described in each of the previous three chapters were also used to maintain asymmetry and check it. For instance, we have seen above how top management could influence the plans by acting on the planning process that generates them. The organizational structure, the information systems, the planning and budgeting processes, the measurement and evaluation criteria, the career paths, and the reward and punishment systems can all be used to influence the balance toward more power to the geographic or the product executives. An abstract treatment of how to use these tools would be beyond the scope of this book. Illustrations are provided in the three company descriptions in the preceding chapters, and some specific examples have been given in the first few pages of this chapter of how top management can use these managerial tools to influence the various dimensions of strategy. We shall not go any further here except to present Figure 10.4, a graphic outline of the scope of strategic management and of the means to provide strategic consistency.

In summary, as shown in Figure 10.4, one can consider strategic management as the use of managerial tools and functional managers to set the balance between geographic and product orientations in the various dimensions of strategy. This is not an easy task. The duality of critical environments makes the simplicity of unidimensional structures where all the components of strategy are aligned impossible. Strategic management in such ambiguous situations is also more demanding; the various managerial tools described here and the ability to differentiate the management of various functions must be developed.

THE CAPABILITY FOR STRATEGIC
MANAGEMENT AND STRATEGIC CHANGE

The Development of Strategic
Management Capability

Top management's ability to direct strategy through the use of managerial tools and functional managers is not a given; it needs to be developed and embodied in the organization. Brown Boveri, among the three companies studied in depth, was in the process of developing such capability. Since 1970, a sequence of administrative changes had been taking place:

FIGURE 10.4

The Scope of Strategic Management

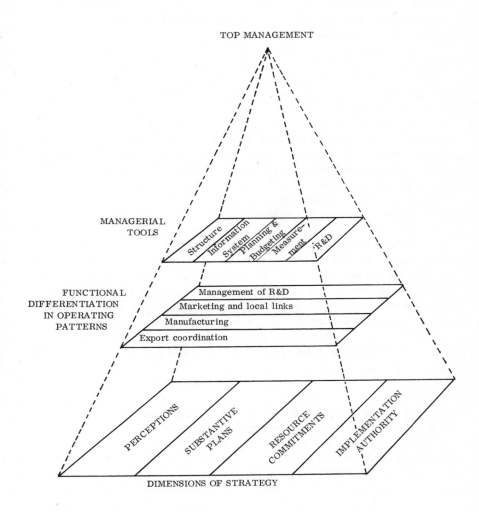

Source: Compiled by the author.

1. The national companies had been reshuffled and divisionalized. Measurement, control, and planning and budgeting systems had been introduced in each company. A management-by-objective evaluation system had been set up.

2. Central staffs, distinct from the Swiss national company, had been created and various processes had been developed to link these staffs to the national companies and composite groups. For instance, integration along functional lines was taking place through the steering committees.

3. Brown Boveri International had been developed as a separate group for expansion into new markets.

4. Product divisions within the national companies had been regrouped into major business aggregates, and business aggregate managers appointed.

5. Efforts had been started to develop worldwide product line and business strategies through the secondary structure. This structure had started to be used to comport the perceptions of national company and corporate executives on specific strategic plans.

6. Attempts had been made to rationalize and integrate the production of some mass-manufactured items that faced international competition; low-voltage apparatus and small electrical motors in particular.

7. The regrouping of medium manufacturing subsidiaries into a distinct group had created pressures to improve their performance.

8. A coordinated strategic planning process was beginning to take place between the French and the German national companies.

9. Efforts were being made to coordinate R&D and preserve the technological leadership of the company.

This mere list shows the immensity of the task tackled by BBC's top management to develop a management capability that would both make the various units more clearly visible from the top and make coordination between these units possible. One can retrace some of the steps taken at BBC and see how they contributed to increase top management's strategic management capability.

The initial step was to create information channels without evoking withdrawal reactions. Next, developing corporate staffs for such activities as control, finance, and planning permitted the adaptation of uniform measurement methods and some commonality between the procedures of the various national companies. Divisionalizing the bigger national companies permitted the introduction of a product portfolio approach to strategic planning at the national level. A series of communication channels and forums were then built up with the development of the secondary organization and of a number of functional steering committees. Top management resisted plans that would have created strong "business committees" (KST) presidents, whose roles in international product management could have been resented by the national companies.

The pyramid of committees was used to acquaint managers with each other and to bring up controversial issues so as to explore reactions to possible solutions. Coordination was fostered first in relatively low-stake activities such as exchange of technical information, purchase of machine tools, and coordination of production methods.

When the existing power structure was affected, moves were slow. Highly talented people were brought into useful corporate staff positions to take care of tasks that did not raise too much controversy, such as exports coordination. Before they asserted themselves, Luterbacher had already signaled the importance of their staff services by relying upon them for advice. Competent outsiders, well-seasoned in international management, were brought in to run businesses where the top management lacked in-depth knowledge. Tight measurement, evaluation, and reward systems were introduced in many national companies to shore up lagging businesses locally before international cooperation was promoted. In businesses such as turbo-generators, where cooperation between national companies already existed informally, it was protected and institutionalized. Where no tradition of cooperation existed, it was left to the new business-aggregate managers to build whatever international links they deemed necessary. So when their interests, perceptions, and solutions to common problems coincided, such as with low-voltage equipment between France and Germany, cooperation developed relatively easily. When the starting positions were less compatible, or when reciprocal trust and esteem did not develop to the same extent between line managers, there was little pressure from the top management of the Konzern to encourage the implementation of coordination schemes that enjoyed only lukewarm support from the management of some national companies. The implementation of small motors production rationalization projects had always stumbled for lack of overall commitment to cooperation, among other difficulties.

By 1976 it was decided that Hummel, the deputy to Luterbacher, would assume leadership of BBC's secondary organization. Managers expected this move to enlarge the role and weight of the secondary organization. Slowly, over a period of six years, Luterbacher and Hummel had woven links among the various national companies and had begun to create a central staff service to build a managed group of companies. They had played a difficult balancing game, relying upon what existed (the strong management of the national companies), while changing it. Slowly, managers had started to adhere to new procedures, to adopt the central planning guidelines, to share their experiences, and so on. The key role of the managing committee had permitted them to rely upon the local companies' top management while intervening in the local companies' activities at the same time.

For Luterbacher and Hummel, managing had meant selecting the department heads for the corporate staff services, signaling their importance to the line managers by relying upon the advice of staff departments, deciding the membership of the KSTs, approving the appointments of business aggregate managers, establishing the agenda for the managing committee meetings, and leading the discussions. Except for two critical areas, nuclear energy and the choice of a U.S. partner, they had had little direct involvement in substantive business decisions. Financial decisions of some magnitude (for instance, how to react to the one-year compulsory import deposit in Brazil), however, were the domain of Luterbacher. The elaboration of the financial guidelines for strategic planning in each of the national companies was also his responsibility. It was expected that Hummel would stir up the secondary organization, making it into a decision-making body. His long experience in successfully coordinating turbogenerator activity would be of considerable help. Many managers hoped that such effective and informal coordination could be developed for other businesses involving several of the national companies.

For Wilson at GTE, developing a strategic management capability had been simpler. Introducing product managers and starting with main-exchange switching had provided a means to carry out the transfer of technology to the European subsidiaries and to start a worldwide expansion effort. Because the product managers could rely on the United States as their source of technology, and because they had been able to log in export sales on their own, they immediately acquired "weight" sufficient to develop their strategy function. Managing, for Wilson, had meant settling disputes between the product and the area sales of the matrix either substantively, by deciding what to do, or administratively, by deciding which side would have the power advantage for the task at hand. Managing also meant making sure that information flowed easily and that it was shared. Concretely, it meant deciding who would sit in what meetings, who he would see on trips abroad, what his agenda would be, how the various managers below him would keep him informed, and who he would tend to trust for certain types of decisions and information.

For Lundvall, at LM Ericcson, managing meant using the functional managers as arbitrators and feeding them enough information to keep the group closely knit and each member well abreast of the activities of the others. When disputes erupted between foreign subsidiaries and domestic product divisions that could not be resolved by the functional managers, he would then intervene.

One key element for all three top managers was their closeness to the point where conflicting perceptions, substantive plans, and pro-

posals for resource allocation would converge. Being at the point
where heterogeneous information converges gives one power over
managers who have only one point of view and partial information.
This position was used very consciously by functional managers at
LM Ericsson to control both the subsidiaries and the product divisions.
It was also used by Wilson at GTE. Hummel, through his role in
leading the secondary organization, would put himself in a position
where conflicting information, schemes, and proposals converge.

The quality of the information that reached the top and the way
in which it was used were important for top managers to exercise
their choice and rule over differences of opinion in a constructive way.
The use of administrative tools by top management can thus be seen
largely in terms of gaining the right information and using it for
motivating and directing lower-level managers. Often the extent and
the quality of the information possessed by one manager will suffice
to give him ascendency over others in the organization. He will thus
gain a stronger influence in certain decisions. This process was used
to differentiate the locus of relative power between functions in all
three companies. The extent and quality of the information was narrowly related to the measurement system used. What was measured
and how, and what comparisons were made, served to channel the attention of managers toward specific variables and areas. The "green
booklet" on plant performance against expectation, circulated among
the LM Ericsson subsidiaries, clearly signaled the importance of efficient operations. The development of common accounting methods
for the European subsidiaries of GTE to share the profits of the export
contracts was not a neutral requirement. It made it possible to compare the various plants in terms of economic efficiency.

The measurement system could also be used to signal the priority and quality of information. So long as national companies could
cook up development budgets, including whatever information the local
management wanted to include, the central allocation of R&D funds
could not work.

Individual measurement and the definition of criteria for success
also showed what was critical for managers in various positions.
Each manager would have a different set of critical areas defined for
him and was figuratively issued a set of red flags to wave when things
went wrong in any of these critical areas. By carefully defining territory of each manager and also by selectively outlining some overlaps
and leaving others ambiguous, top management could instill a check-
and-balance mechanism into the organization. Such a balancing mechanism was used explicitly at GTE: whenever a manager felt his position would be too adversely affected by a decision, he would wave a
red flag toward the top and take a stand against the decision. For instance, an individual investment that would substantially decrease the

average profits of a subsidiary was critical to the subsidiary manager, though it might be desirable from the point of view of the product manager. If the subsidiary manager decided to take a stand
it was unlikely that the product manager would want to get into a fight.

In summary, by signaling what information was more important
and what outcomes more desirable (or detrimental), the measurement
system could very finely differentiate the locus of relative power between types of decisions and channel the decision processes with great
precision.

But one aspect of the development of a strategic management
capability has been developed above: the use of information systems
by top management to further their own understanding of their business and their ability to exercise choices based on substance and to
influence lower-level managers. Again, one could take the other
managerial tools and analyze how they could be used. Such an exercise, however, would be relatively fruitless, as the idiosyncracies
of each situation would tax the generality of such an approach.* It
remains true that in any particular situation for an individual firm in
the two industries studied here, it is likely that the various managerial tools need to be used purposefully to manage a balance between
the economic and political imperatives. The more developed these
tools are, the easier defining and stabilizing a balance is likely to be.

The Process of Strategic Change

The ability for smooth strategic change, internally and externally, was a major concern for top managers in all three companies.
The murky nature of the conflict between political and economic imperatives and the unpredictability of national governments' reactions
called for series of small incremental changes, none of which would
be drastic enough to become a political issue in the host countries.
Because governments could control their activities and because testing was not possible, MNCs did not engage in sweeping moves or innovative behavior. They were "muddling through," probably more
than most other companies.[11] The complex overlay of managerial
tools corresponded to the need not to affect the status quo abruptly,
or in any visible way.

---

*It is important to stress here again that my objective is not to
articulate a set of general empirical propositions about the firms but
to develop a language system and some categorizations that are useful
to understand the management process of individual firms and to intervene to improve its capabilities.

This external discomfort was echoed internally by relatively delicate balances of influence. As physical operational integration was not possible, much managerial interdependence had to be developed to protect the unity of the company. One way to develop such subtle interdependence was to use very rich and complex managerial tools. These tools provided both stability and possibility for change. Sweeping reorganizations would not have provided for the internal evolution needed to match the external "muddling through." The development of new administrative procedures, while gradually discarding older ones, permitted a slow realignment of the organization to take place over time. It also enabled top managers to decide on what types of decisions should come up to them without changing the perceptions of managers too much.

Strategic change thus took the form of gradual changes made in the managerial tools, to result,· in turn, in changes in the dimensions of the strategy and in changes in the operating patterns. Again, sophisticated managerial tools within the matrix were thus needed to effectuate such changes smoothly so they would not disrupt relationships with the governments in host countries. The central difficulty here is that the political imperative is not explicit. For instance, a company may want to start to rationalize some production, instead of manufacturing all equipment on a "local-for-local" basis. If it seeks clearance from the involved governments before it moves, rationalization may be denied. If it starts rationalizing some production, it may get by. If it moves to full rationalization, it may lose markets for good. Concretely, this means that strategic change has to be incremental and reversible, to test host governments' and customers' reactions to a change in the status quo before making it irreversible.

Beyond this general conclusion, examples drawn from the data support Prahalad's findings.[12] First, use of key individuals can create a strategic shift. For instance, at Brown Boveri, the hiring of business aggregate managers who had a successful experience in integrated rationalized companies provided a catalyst to integrate and rationalize the production of some mass-produced items between France and Germany. Second, standardization of plants provided a way to increase the power of product managers and shift toward an economic strategy. We have seen this at work in GTE, with the partial standardization brought about by the need to fulfill export orders from several European plants. Third, communication among executives and career paths can be used, as we have seen with LM Ericsson and earlier in this chapter. Changes in patterns of career paths and promotions can lead to changes in perceived interest and loyalty and to shifts in the relative importance of geographic and product executives in providing rewards to junior lower-level managers. Fourth, changes in information systems can be used, as we have seen. Finally, reporting relationships can be altered to change the authority structure.

In summary, the same managerial tools are used for shifting the balance between product and geographic executives as are used to maintain the balance at any given point. In both cases the existence of a strategic management capability, through the refinement and explicit use of these managerial tools, is essential.

STRATEGIC CONSISTENCY IN A DIVERSIFIED MULTINATIONAL

So far, the argument developed in Chapter 6 and pursued in this chapter, as well as the descriptions and analyses of Chapters 7, 8, and 9, have not addressed the issue of product diversity. Table 5.10, at the end of Chapter 5, left one with a sense of the significance of product diversity within both the telecommunication equipment and the electrical power system industries. Quite obviously, the relative importance of the political and economic imperatives varies among product lines. Thus, it should not come as a surprise that within the same MNC some businesses will face very different managerial demands. Consequently, one is quite likely to find in the same company some businesses where decentralization and national responsiveness prevail, and others where integration and economic efficiency are given precedence. For instance, at Brown Boveri, turbogenerators clearly call for national responsiveness whereas small motors call for rationalization.

Problems are likely to arise when there exist interdependencies between these businesses. Interdependencies are of various kinds. They can be technical, with common technologies among several businesses. For instance, PABX technology is similar to that of main-exchange switching equipment, yet in main exchange the political imperative is permanent, whereas in PABX freer economic competition is becoming the rule. Interdependencies can also derive from vertical integration; for instance, BBC's turnkey contracts involve a whole range of equipments. Interdependencies can also be external. BBI's managers were frequently told, "We are willing to import your power stations, but what about your creating a motor plant in one of our depressed areas to generate employment and offset the trade deficits that importing your other products would create?"

A first approach to the difficulties of product diversity was to differentiate the management of individual businesses within the matrix. A Brown Boveri manager commented:

> We should differentiate simple mass-manufactured series products from more complex ones. A basic question remains how to organize in pursuing our business activities

for some businesses where a worldwide product strategy
can be developed, for instance, small motors. For some
other equipment it would not make sense, they are too much
dependent upon national customers. In fact, the small
series products require a "company within the company"
approach, throughout.

There were growing pressures to differentiate the management
of BBC's three major business aggregates so that the series products
and industrial systems businesses could be managed through a product-oriented structure. It was clear that rationalization of production and the growth of cross-shipments would not be possible in the
foreseeable future for heavy equipment and rolling stock. It was also
clear that competitiveness in the small series products could only be
maintained by extensive integration, and probably by the transfer of
some production to developing countries. To manage the simple con-
trol-devices business a multinational strategy had been developed between BBC-Mannheim in Germany and Compagnie Electro-Mécanique
in France. It involved the integrated management of the product lines
worldwide and, in particular, the closing of workshops in Germany
and the opening of assembly plants in Brazil and Singapore. Rationalization of small motors production was under way in the same spirit.

In a similar fashion ITT-Europe was spinning off its PABX
product line from "group 9" (the main-exchange switching product
group, run collegially by the heads of the various major national ITT
companies) to the Business Systems Group (BSG).* The BSG was
more strongly directed from the European headquarters in Brussels
than was "group 9." Over time, the PABX business became increasingly managed from Brussels as functional and product staffs developed. Production of specific types was allocated only to certain countries that would export to other ITT companies. This move met some
opposition from the national ITT managers, some of whom resented
their lesser influence. At both BBC and ITT the development of
strong competitors, either operating internationally integrated networks of plants (Leroy-Somer in motors, IBM in PABXs) or selling
from low-wage areas (Eastern bloc motors, Southeast Asian PABXs),
created such pressures that it forced the divorce of these openly competitive businesses from the businesses where the political imperative
remained dominant.

---

*Though ITT was not one of the companies studied in depth in the
research, some information was obtained about it from a variety of
sources. This example is used here because it is particularly significant.

At ITT the BSG provided a logical new home for the PABX business, whereas at BBC the changes in perception, plans, and power needed to shift to an economic strategy for businesses where government influence was less had to be started from scratch. This was a difficult process. The problem was that operational integration of the various national companies had been sought directly without first achieving integration through corporate managerial tools or building a strong functional coalition to support integration. Moreover, top management had not shown much support for the project manager, whose status could not counterbalance that of the division managers in the national companies.

The drive to rationalize motor production started as a staff report to the managing committee. The report suggested, as a first step, to specialize production between the four producing companies in Switzerland, Germany, France, and Italy. The plan, however, was to be partly implemented under the direction of the marketing staff manager for the product line. The Swiss company, for which the standard low-voltage motors were a low-profit, low-growth business, gave up production to shift resources to more profitable businesses. Italy was to be a major beneficiary of the shift, whereas France was recognized as the technological lead house. Unfortunately, conditions changed quickly. A sudden market upturn in Europe led to undercapacity. The Italian plant expansion could not get started fast enough, so the German company decided not to specialize production as projected. A cost-cutting program in Germany, coupled with full capacity utilization, turned around the German division, previously scheduled for production cuts, whereas mounting start-up losses and inefficiencies plagued the Italian company. Export potential, meanwhile, was lessened by fierce price competition from Soviet bloc and Far Eastern suppliers, thus affecting adversely the power base of the marketing manager. In the end, the plan was only very partially implemented.

A second proposal, drafted in 1975, was then dropped. It suggested the creation of a separate motor company, operating internationally as a single, separate profit center. Such a company would have been entirely independent from the national companies, though it would use the nationally established sales organizations for the marketing of its products. Though the wisdom of moving toward a centralized system in small motors was intellectually well recognized, the plan was deemed managerially impossible: spinning off the motor activity would have been seen as a dangerous precedent by national company managers.

In 1976 it was decided to try to deal with the reorganization problem at the level of business aggregate managers. One of them commented on the situation:

The project manager was given complete responsibility but not commensurate power. The organization to some extent is paralyzed. He should implement the production and development rationalization project, monitor the results, and further coordinate export sales. In fact, his coordination is not concrete enough to take hold, without the power to manage the motor activity. Two years ago the weaknesses and the need to deal with that project from a higher level were already known. The overall scheme could not work because its management was not at the convenient level. Divisions managers worry about the efficiency of day-to-day operations in their country. We should have an overall competitive strategy against Leroy or Siemens, but we lack consensus on such a strategy. Our plans still are extrapolations of the past. In that motor business a number of countries now have access to the technology. This means that high in the company someone should think in terms of future industrialized countries, and should be able to direct the activities in terms of presence in some key countries. The need to pick up the project at a higher level is obvious. Now the Algerians and the Egyptians start manufacturing their own motors, and the Russians sell right here 30 percent below our prices.

The example above illustrates both the difficulty of effectuating a strategic shift when central managerial tools are not well developed and the need to differentiate strategic management among businesses in a diversified multinational.

Assuming the successful differentiation of strategic management among businesses, the issue of interbusiness coordination remains open. One approach is functional coordination across businesses. The functional steering committees at BBC were attempting to provide such interbusiness coordination. Planning processes could also force an explicit recognition of interdependencies between businesses. Various planning committees can be set across businesses. Yet, the available data suggest that managing interdependencies between related businesses and at the same time attempting to provide strategic direction and consistency for individual businesses is very difficult.

It may well be that for strategic management purposes the various businesses should be considered as if they were separate. Several companies, ITT for instance, established clear market mechanisms internally for allocation of resources and determination of transfer prices. It appears that top management must accept, as a trade-off, the complexity of a joint strategy for multiple businesses with the complexity of developing managerial tools for imparting strategic consistency to individually related businesses. This has several significant implications. First, in order to provide strategic consistency to a business, some of the interdependencies among businesses may have to be consciously ignored. Second, top management must constantly make an effort to evaluate the "worth" of interdependencies in strategic terms.

A partial answer may be to manage just the most critical interdependencies. This is in essence what ITT did in shifting PABX from the Telecommunication Equipment Group to the Business Systems Group, recognizing that the most critical interdependency now involved marketing rather than technology. Over time, the most critical interdependencies may shift and evolve, reflecting changes in the competition, economies of manufacture, and the political imperative.

CONCLUSION

In this chapter, after the descriptions provided in Chapters 7, 8, and 9, the analysis started in Chapter 6 has been pushed a little further, with the focus being on strategic decisions and their consistency over time in a given business and across businesses in the diversified multinational. The use of the managerial tools described in previous chapters has been explored and a general framework of top management guidance developed. This general framework was derived from the data gathered on LM Ericcson, Brown Boveri, and GTE. Its quality can be tested only by applying it to other multinational companies in industries where both the economic and the political imperatives are significant, and seeing whether it furthers one's understanding of the management of these companies.

We can end this chapter on a more pragmatic note. It remains that managing the conflict between political and economic imperatives is an inordinately difficult undertaking. This leads to the question, For the sake of strategic clarity and administrative simplicity, should multinationals stay away from industries where both imperatives are extremely important?

NOTES

1. Alfred D. Chandler, Strategy and Structure (Cambridge: Massachusetts Institute of Technology Press, 1962), p. 14.

2. Chester I. Barnard, The Functions of the Executive (Cambridge, Mass.: Harvard University Press, 1938), p. 187.

3. For a summary see, for instance, Joseph L. Bower and Yves Doz, "Strategy Formulation: A Social and Political Process,"

in Strategic Movement, ed. Charles Hofer and Dan Schendel (Boston: Little, Brown, 1979).

4. See, for instance, Peter L. Berger and Thomas Luckmann, The Social Construction of Reality (New York: Doubleday, 1966). Also, John D. Steinbruner, The Cybernetic Theory of Decision (Princeton, N.J.: Princeton University Press, 1974).

5. See C. K. Prahalad, "The Strategic Process in a Multinational Corporation" (D.B.A. diss., Harvard Business School, 1975).

6. Steve Hart, "Texas Instruments Shows U.S. Business How to Survive in the 1980s," Business Week, September 18, 1978, p. 66.

7. Henry Mintzberg, "Patterns in Strategy Formation," Management Science 24 (May 1978): 934.

8. Joseph L. Bower, Managing the Resource Allocation Process (Boston: Harvard Business School Division of Research, 1970).

9. This behavior is described by Graham Allison in Essence of Decision (Boston: Little, Brown, 1971).

10. Prahalad, "The Strategic Process."

11. Charles Lindblom, "The Science of Muddling Through," Public Administration Review 19 (1959): 79–88.

12. Prahalad, "The Strategic Process."

11

IMPLICATIONS

The research reported in this book represents an effort to further the understanding of how some multinational companies respond to the conflicts between economic and political imperatives. The goal was not to develop general empirical propositions but to improve our understanding of individual companies. The goal was to develop a framework allowing the treatment of each multinational company as an individual case and improving the understanding of that case.

The goal of this chapter is to make the findings more useful. The language used in describing the data and conceptualizing the findings is already using variables that managers can use to think about their organization, so the translation of findings into a managerial language is not critical. This chapter will summarize the implications of the findings. First, implications for management will be drawn, then implications for further research, and, finally, implications for public policy.

IMPLICATIONS FOR MANAGEMENT

For the Management of a Single Business

The research confirmed that the ability to cooperate closely with state-owned customers and government agencies in a variety of different countries is a critical success factor for multinational manufacturers of telecommunication equipment and electrical power systems. This led to a need for flexibility, adaptation, and responsiveness at the national subsidiary level. Such need was most easily served by a decentralized managerial mode leaving almost complete autonomy to the national subsidiaries.

The research also confirmed that the intrinsic difficulties of the technologies used in telecommunication and power systems, the large economies of scale and experience in production, and the significant economies of aggregation in R&D in both industries created a need for centralization of R&D and integration and rationalization of production in large efficient plants serving the world market. Such rationalization was usually made impossible by the insistence of state-owned customers that the equipment they purchased be manufactured locally.

It was found that the extent of government control over the markets and the scope of government intervention went beyond the usual view of government intervention. The usual issue-oriented view of government intervention was found inadequate here, that is, instead of government's desire for control being driven by separate issues (employment protection or balance-of-trade equilibrium), it was found to be of an all-encompassing nature. Consequently, the usual approach to multinational government relations was found wanting: it failed to capture the extent and depth of the interaction between host governments and multinational companies. To capture adequately this interaction, one had to consider the strategy, structure, and management process of the firm. The ability of a company to cooperate with national government agencies and state-owned customers and maintain its multinational competiveness is by and large determined by its operating patterns. In turn, these patterns evolve over time as the result of a seldom fully articulated strategy that is embodied in the use of specific managerial tools.

One key finding was that the ambiguity created by the duality of imperatives (political and economic) made it extremely difficult to preserve the clarity of strategy, structure, and managerial process. As a consequence, the clear unidimensional product or geographic structures were not suitable in these two industries. Companies had to manage both the product and the geographic dimensions. Some form of matrix management was usually adopted to manage these two dimensions simultaneously. At GTE the matrix nature of the organization was explicitly recognized; at LM Ericsson and Brown Boveri the management displayed matrix characteristics, but the formal primary structure remained nonmatrix.

In turn, the clear and simple analytic economic strategy that is usually prescribed by the supporters of a substantive strategic planning approach was found nearly impossible to develop and implement in these firms.[1] The business policy approach, because it incorporates explicitly an assessment of the firm's administrative capability (resources, distinctive competence), comes closer to capturing what was seen here than the corporate planning view that assumes complete organizational plasticity.[2] If strategy and strategic planning are not possible, then how is strategy developed?

First, one must recognize that, in the companies studied in depth, strategy can only be expressed as a preference—a preference for national responsiveness and decentralization or a preference for global economic competitiveness and centralization. As described in Chapter 5, the choice of preference for global economic competitiveness or national responsiveness is largely a function of the mix of markets served (in terms of maturity) and of the technology level of the firm's products (in comparison with competition). The logic of this choice of national responsiveness or global economic competitiveness was derived from the intensive study of three firms. In a later stage, data of a general nature were obtained on ITT, Philips Telecommunication Industries, Westinghouse's power group, and ASEA in Sweden.* Though the data were not detailed enough to lend themselves to such detailed analysis as that of LM Ericsson, Brown Boveri, and GTE, they supported the argument.[3] ITT, well established in large, mature markets, had a number of very autonomous national telecommunication equipment subsidiaries. Each operated in its host country much in the same way as BBC's national companies. Some had accommodated outside shareholders. Conversely, Philips was centralized and found it quite difficult to penetrate well-established markets in Europe, or rapidly maturing ones (Brazil, for instance). It was only in countries where local production was not an issue (such as Saudi Arabia) that Philips was successful. We have already seen, in the description of the French situation, that Westinghouse was approaching Europe as an integrated multinational and faced many serious problems. Similarly, what data were available on ASEA suggested that as the company engaged in manufacturing activities in more countries, its tight central control through worldwide product divisions based in Sweden was submitted to increasing stress.

Second, if comprehensive strategic planning or policy formulation is impossible, and if management has to be content with some form of administrative coordination, how is consistency maintained?

To gain an understanding of strategy under conditions of ambiguity it was found helpful to disaggregate the notion of strategy, as a process, into four subdimensions. These are: managers' perceptions of their environment, the formulation of substantive plans, the power to commit resources, and the authority to implement decisions. An implication of this breakdown into subdimensions is that top management must raise questions concerning the quality and location of these dimensions. We can argue, for instance, that the perceptions ought to be dual—some managers perceiving the environment through a worldwide product management lens, others through a national subsidiary or regional headquarters lens. Differentiation of perception

---

*Two of these firms had initially declined to cooperate fully in the research but provided some data.

is helpful, and it can be managed. On the other hand, it can be argued that, if top management is to effectively mediate between geographic and product executives, the power to allocate corporate resources (and not just the project proposal rubber-stamping ritual) must remain with corporate executives. Conversely, the authority to implement decisions has to be delegated and decentralized. So a first step, to analyze and improve the strategic management of a multinational company such as those studied here, is to analyze the dimensions of strategy and the location of the various activities. Is the substance of plans principally determined by product managers or by national subsidiary managers? Does the current planning process lead to an effort to decrease differentiation or to encourage it? At what stages in the process? Are the answers to these questions consistent with the preferred strategy?

Beyond disaggregating strategy into specific components, it is also possible to consider the various functions in the business separately. In some functions (such as marketing) national companies may enjoy much autonomy, whereas some other functions (such as R&D) may be run centrally. Allocation of resource commitment power and implementation authority can thus vary among functions. Furthermore, the overall balance and the ability to maintain consistency can be served by the use of strong functional managers as mediators. Such functional managers have no a priori commitment to a national subsidiary or to a worldwide product management orientation. Their power is not based on control or authority but on expertise, and possibly on personality qualities that can make them good integrators.[4] Another implication of the research is thus the importance of functional managers when the trade-offs between product and geographic executives are unclear and shifting from decision to decision.

Some simplification can also be brought by distinctions among subsidiaries. Quite clearly, a key element is that large subsidiaries in mature markets are to be managed very differently from recently established ones in developing countries. The formal system of assigning individual manufacturing subsidiaries to specific categories, according to the extent of support and control from Stockholm, was an explicit recognition of these differences by LM Ericsson. Similarly at BBC, the BBI companies, the medium manufacturing subsidiaries, and the major national companies were treated quite differently in strategic and administrative terms.

Consistency can also be maintained through use of managerial tools, from the structure to the reward, punishment, and promotion system. Top management can audit each of these systems, looking at how they influence specific decisions, and for inconsistencies. For instance, a desire to give managers a diverse and extensive international experience cannot lead to action unless the promotion system rewards intersubsidiary mobility of managers.

It remains true that consistency is not to be maintained or strived for across the board. Because the political imperative and the economic imperative are both critical but often conflicting and contradictory, complete consistency is impossible. By nature, strategic ambiguity will remain and some unclear administrative coordination will prevail over a well-defined strategy. One can argue that dissent and differences of opinions among managers are of the essence of management in industries where both the political and the economic imperatives are critical.

How, exactly, to use the various administrative tools is a question that seems to defy generalization. One has to admit that no empirical generalization, which would be applicable to a broad set of multinational companies, is possible. Yet, these tools provide a general categorization that is helpful in thinking about managerial action. These tools are helpful because they apply to action, provide certain information, encourage and elicit certain types of behavior, shape the perceptions of self-interest of individual managers, force the full recognition of interdependencies, and are useful to bring issues to top management's attention.

One implication that is simple, but not trivial, is that for top managers in such government-influenced industries as telecommunication equipment and power systems an in-depth experience of the industry, acquired over a lifetime, is helpful. The control difficulty here is that of top management as an arbitrator between product and geographic executives. The evidence of the research is that, for instance, the experience of Hummel or Lundvall was extremely useful for them in deciding on the substance of conflicts. Wilson at GTE faced a slightly more difficult situation, as his experience in the telecommunication equipment industry was more limited.

It remains true that the management of such businesses is comparatively difficult. Because of the ambiguity and potential conflicts in responding to the economic and political imperatives, decisions cannot fall easily into well-structured chains of means-end relationships. The principles of hierarchy and authority have to be relaxed, and zones of uncertainty and ambiguity left around specific decisions. For instance, at LM Ericsson much ambiguity surrounded the reporting of subsidiaries to the corporate office and the role of the area marketing managers. Similarly, at Brown Boveri the role of the secondary structure and its importance could lend itself to contradictory interpretation. Finally, at GTE, Wilson purposefully left the allocation of decision responsibility between product and geographic executives undefined and forced them to cooperate on all key decisions. Ambiguity and conflicts needed to be checked at the same time as they strived. The differentiation along functional lines provided for some checks and limits in ambiguity. Similarly, each managerial tool could be used rigidly or flexibly to facilitate differentiation and ambiguity or to limit them. An example from another company, ITT, is helpful here. At ITT the reporting, measurement, and evaluation systems are absolutely similar throughout the company; no ambiguity or differentiation exists. Conversely, though, the reporting structure is often unclear; it can be easily changed without managers showing much commitment to the organization chart. Finally, differentiations are possible within individual tools. The determination of transfer prices between, say, domestic divisions and foreign subsidiaries is usually part of the budgeting exercise. For accounting purposes a certain transfer price can be used, a different one for measuring the subsidiary performance, and a third for deciding on where to locate capacity expansions. The ambiguity can be increased or decreased by making such accounting and measurement variations explicit or by letting them be ambiguous.

Practically, my argument is that it is useful for managers to consider all of these elements explicitly and to fine-tune the use of managerial tools in each particular situation. Of course, there is a point where the complexity of the management process may not make it worthwhile to pursue the further refinement of these tools. One has to accept that, short of the administrative simplicity found in businesses where governments do not significantly limit multinationals' strategic freedom, the type of management process described here and its implications are only second best. In fact, many diversified companies carefully elected to stay clear of businesses so closely government-influenced as telecommunication equipment and electrical power systems.

Implications for the Diversified Multinational

The first implication for a diversified multinational is the need to recognize the intrinsic complexity of managing such government-influenced businesses as telecommunication equipment and power systems. We have seen already that Westinghouse faced serious problems by not fully recognizing these difficulties. A typical analysis following Westinghouse's problems was:

> Since 1972 the American group became as modest as it could be. . . . "Flexibility" now replaces the grand strategy. There is no attempt any more to create a PWR club to counterbalance GE's BWR club. "The strategy of Westinghouse can change from one month to the next" is the prevalent attitude in Brussels, and the motto now in all European countries is the same as in Belgium: "We want to in-

tegrate ourselves into the local scene by being good industrial citizens. . . ." The acceptance of minority equity positions (Framatome) or even of mere technical cooperation agreements (as with Steam Generator in Sweden), general program agreement with GEC in the UK, cooperation with Cockerill for development: Westinghouse now plays on all registers at once, case by case, with a typical Anglo-Saxon pragmatism.[5]

Conversely, we have seen Brown Boveri's small motor business suffer dearly from competition, and its assimilation to the more closely government-controlled businesses BBC's top management knew best delay the rationalization efforts in the business.

A second straightforward implication involves the problems faced in running businesses closely influenced by host governments. Any simple structure is likely to run into trouble. Entrusting such businesses to autonomous national subsidiaries is likely to lead to loss of economic competitiveness in the long run; assigning them to worldwide business groups is likely to lead to short-term political acceptability and responsiveness problems.

The first danger is well illustrated by the experience of GTE in the main-exchange switching business in Europe. One of the company's executives commented:

> In switching we had originally been a leader, but when the Crossbar system came about no need was felt; our domestic sales were still satisfactory with the Strowger. Up to a few years ago the area management was running its largely autonomous unit. All business decisions were left to the area management. We had not much of a position in switching: our international sales were insignificant; we had only domestic markets; with the development of Crossbar we were no longer competitive internationally. There was little competence in switching, no experience, and a need to rebuild a marketing organization when our electronic switching systems were developed by the domestic unit in the U.S. The difficulty we faced was how to develop an international effort in switching. The organization had not the capability to marshal resources and talents. We needed one man to head the drive and develop a product line strategy to get back into the worldwide switching market.

Conversely, the management of some companies was keenly aware of the difficulties of a product-oriented organization in the in-

dustries studied here. Gilbert Jones, chairman of IBM-World Trade
Company, stressed:

> As soon as you cross the border from data processing to
> telecommunications everything becomes political. We are
> not interested in the number of jobs per se, but in technol-
> ogy problems. In the public sector you deal by political de-
> cisions not by economic balance and common sense. The
> technologies are converging between telecom and computers.
> The difficulty in both lies with component technology. The
> question for IBM is whether a company can protect its own
> technology. The answer is "yes" in data processing, "no"
> in telecommunications so far. The governments are right:
> they do not want you to have anything you can withhold.
> The safest way is to require you to give away all that you
> know to a local company. We would not accept a telecom-
> munication equipment joint venture in which we would, have
> to provide the technology. Telecom companies could use
> it to set up new competitors in data processing. [6]

It was also clear that PTTs and governments would in all likelihood attempt to break IBM's integrated worldwide network of manufacture and require complete local production, were IBM to enter
the main-exchange business. IBM had successfully entered the PABX
market in Europe and Brazil. Sophisticated equipment revolving
around the IBM 3750 large-size PABX was sold in great numbers in
Europe. It was considered very unlikely that IBM would enter the
main-exchange business. Jones, however, expected the economic advantages of electronic telephone to be such that:

> Government policies will have to shift to the advantages of
> high technology instead of short-term employment and con-
> trol. The cost of a line is going to decrease to $100 with
> time division. Governments cannot distort economic deci-
> sions too much just to protect low-productivity jobs.

In summary, the management of large diversified companies
has to recognize the specific managerial requirements of high-technology businesses narrowly controlled by host governments. As these
requirements are more complex and cognitively taxing than those of
the management of other businesses, their management should not
only be separate but also, in all likelihood, should require more complex forms of administration than businesses under less direct government influence.

A third significant implication for a diversified multinational active in telecommunication equipment or electrical power systems is

the potential for interbusiness linkages by host governments, and the weakening of the overall bargaining position of the firm vis-à-vis host governments. Governments can use their market power in one business (telecommunication equipment or power systems) to gain advantages in other businesses. For instance, as we have seen, Brown Boveri often was asked to use light, easy-to-manufacture equipment as an offset to turbogenerator imports. Similarly, GTE could be asked to set up a television-set plant in some Latin American country in exchange for main-exchange equipment orders. The "worth" of its activity in closely government-influenced industries must be assessed by the diversified multinational, in comparison with the overall loss of bargaining power in negotiations with governments across the spectrum of its businesses.

Similarly, as we saw in Chapter 10, the worth of internal interdependencies between businesses must be assessed. Because of their strategic ambiguity, businesses closely influenced by governments are likely to prevent strategic clarity in related businesses. For instance, an electronic components business could be managed either as a source of telecommunication components or as a separate business in its own right. GTE's corporate management was absolutely clear on this: each business group had to be treated separately. Sylvania (the electronic component group of GTE) supplied part of International Telecommunication Group's needs; but neither group was under pressure to increase the internal flow. Similarly, great autonomy was left to GTE's International Telecommunication group to set up its own subsidiaries, with little coordination with the other groups, so there was not a strong "Mr. GTE" in any country. This made government linkages between products more difficult as they had to be dealt with at the corporate level. On the contrary, Brown Boveri was much more willing to link its various businesses internally and to use them jointly in dealing with host governments. For instance, it had taken over an ailing Canadian motor manufacturer to save jobs in Canada in the hope of furthering its position on public large equipment orders.

In conclusion, there are strong arguments for a diversified multinational not to invest in businesses that are closely influenced by the governments. By staying clear of them it can protect a measure of external strategic freedom and internal strategic clarity and also keep its management process relatively simple.

IMPLICATIONS FOR RESEARCHERS

A central implication for research that can be drawn from this effort is the need to be industry- and firm-specific in researching strategic management problems. The kind of strategy structure research done by Stopford and Wells seems to go into as much detail as possible and still remain an empirical work aimed at developing general propositions. Yet, as for the nitty gritty of individual business strategy, of managerial tools, or of operating patterns, the managerial content of the Stopford and Wells research is relatively low. Researchers thus face a difficult trade-off between managerial content and comparability and additivity. In the research reported in this book, the choice has clearly been to be industry- and firm-specific, to attempt to develop an understanding of the specifics of management problems, and to propose a language and a framework to describe and conceptualize them. In this process the attempt to develop general, empirical propositions of the nature of those found in the natural sciences has been forgone.

The framework was developed by using detailed analyses of three companies. In a second stage it was applied to data from several other companies in the same two industries. One central difficulty was to get cooperation from several direct competitors in the same industry. Yet, enough information could be gathered on firms such as ITT, Philips, Westinghouse, or ASEA to check that the framework could be used to interpret and conceptualize their management problems.

Another implication is the usefulness of relating the industry structure and competitive patterns to the managerial structure and managerial tools of individual companies in the industry. Typically, research has focused on the overall industry level or on the internal management of firms; seldom has it focused on both simultaneously. In the research reported here it was found very useful to understand both the internal management of the firms and the dynamics of competition between firms and to use them to clarify each other. The basic premise of this approach is that in oligopolistic industries, where the major competitors are a handful of large complex firms, the strategy of the firm can only be conceptualized as a pattern in decision making over time. Thus, for a researcher who also is interested in intervention possibilities, it is important not only to try to attempt to gain an understanding of the firm's strategic behavior as an observed output to which the researcher assigns a logic but also to gain an understanding of the processes within the firm that are likely to shape individual decisions. This is why much attention was devoted to the managerial tools used by the firms internally. Attention to internal processes was found all the more important as the duality of critical environments, and the strategic ambiguous characteristics of these firms made an imputation of strategy from observed decisions more difficult. In other words, it is much easier to understand the management of a firm that has a clear-cut strategy, such as IBM or Texas Instruments for instance, than it was to understand the management of the firms studied here.

The question of generality beyond the two industries studied here has not been addressed. This research does not pretend to generality beyond these two industries. It may be that other industries are characterized by a similar interaction between the economic and the political imperatives, but no efforts have been made to compare the findings with data on other industries. The definition of broad categories, operating patterns, and administrative tools, and the findings on functional differentiation, the use of functional managers, and the development of managerial tools to manage along several dimensions simultaneously are sufficiently general to be applied to other industries. There is no reason to believe that such conceptualizations would be useful only in the two industries studied here, but their applicability or usefulness beyond these two industries is untested.

IMPLICATIONS FOR PUBLIC POLICY

In this book no effort has been made to assess the wisdom of government policies as they affect the two industries. Whether government intervention and control result from market failure, or from an adjustment desire, or from other reasons has not been explored in detail. The costs and benefits of intervention and of various national policies in this respect have not been analyzed. Yet, the research has shed some light on issues of relevance for public policy.

First, it is important to recognize that public policy to affect multinational corporations is often based on a myth. The myth has two different versions, one economic and the other administrative. The economic version is that of unitary rational actors. The point that complex organizations do not make decisions in a way whereby the assumptions of decision theory would hold true is well known of decision scientists. Yet the myth of the MNC as an economic agent maximizing long-term profits survives. The administrative version is that of a technostructure of bureaucracy as popularized by John K. Galbraith.[7] The reality is substantially more complex. The global unitary rational actor or the tight technostructure hierarchy assumptions are equally misleading. For successful intervention in a process, it is important to gain an understanding of its dynamics and of the leverage points to change them. Decisions by multinationals are the output of a complex process influenced by the diverse variables described in this book. A straightforward implication is that regulators and government officials would be in a better position to influence the outcome of multinational companies' decisions if they gained some understanding of the processes through which these decisions are reached and if they could influence the participants in the process.

One key element here is the building of a national coalition around the MNC subsidiary. One can think of a subsidiary managing director as a link between two different coalitions (the multinational company and the national industry and government groups) who trades dependencies between the two. Not only is it important to recognize the cultural dimensions of this linkage but also its content. In other words, governments can try to make the subsidiary less dependent upon the multinational headquarters and more dependent upon the host country environment, so that the dependency trading process is unbalanced in favor of the host country and the subsidiary becomes more responsive to the host country than to the MNC headquarters. Various linkages—for instance, joint R&D work between subsidiary and national state research centers or universities or the selective support of the government for export sales—can tilt the balance in favor of the host country in sensitive functions where patterns of relative power between product and geographic executives are not well set. Another means used by some governments is to induce diversification of the subsidiary into industries wherein the strengths of the multinational parent are of little use. This policy has been used by India, with some success.[8]

Second, one implication of this research is that companies are likely to respond quite differently to similar government demands according to the strategy these companies have chosen. For instance, ITT was quite willing to develop a number of variants of its Metaconta SPC-exchange system to incorporate nationally produced electronic components and processors. Conversely, LM Ericsson resisted attempts to incorporate locally produced electronic components in countries such as Brazil or France. In an opposite way, government could know that the pressure for financial results applied to ITT subsidiary managers might lead some of them to more ethically questionable behavior, for instance, in their dealings on new export markets, than, say, LM Ericsson's subsidiary managers who were not submitted to such strong pressures from headquarters. In short, the cost of any given national demand on a company was likely to be perceived by its managers in terms of departure from the chosen strategy of the company. Thus LM Ericsson, which placed great emphasis on technological excellence, was more likely to resist demands that would weaken its technology than was ITT, which competed by fostering the integration of national subsidiaries into the host countries. In negotiating with multinationals, gaining an understanding of the strategy of the company, of the difficulties it would face in managing what would result from accepting government demands, and of precedents in the same company is important for government officials assessing the bargaining posture of the company.

Third, it is important to note that government-multinationals bargaining is not necessarily a zero-sum game, as many adversaries of the multinationals would like to frame it. What factors are key to a multinational for maintaining its competitive advantage in the industry and what a government demands are not necessarily contradictory. In many cases it is possible for a multinational to yield on some issues and points and gain an advantage in a given country without compromising its overall economic competitiveness worldwide. Only a careful effort, made in good faith, to approach negotiations in a constructive way can sort out the real conflicts from the issues that can be resolved to mutual satisfaction.

Finally, and most important, the whole issue of regulation and government ownership deserves review. The overall trend in both industries has been toward national consolidations and MNC expropriations. In large, mature countries, consolidation and rationalization have developed along national lines: for example, KWU in Germany, Alsthom–Atlantique–CEM in France, the consolidation of the French telecommunication equipment industry, and pressures in the United Kingdom to merge ITT's subsidiaries into the national producers. In newer countries, as soon as the markets were large enough and the current technology available locally, great pressures have been applied for MNCs to divest. For instance, in Brazil, Argentina, and Mexico the foreign ownership in the local industry decreased. Whether the observed predominantly nationalist response is outdated and solves yesterday's problems is an open question.

There is ample evidence that the economies of scale and experience in heavy electrical equipment production are such that national consolidation in Europe still leaves considerable untapped potential economies of scale. In fact, only a few plants, worldwide, would be needed to serve the market in an efficient manner. The same is apparently true of telecommunication equipment, though the economies of scale seem to be less. On the other hand, the move to electronic switching and digital coding blurs the distinction between the telecommunication and data processing industries. Both the data processing and the electronic switching industries are dominated by a handful of multinationals. Furthermore, technological changes in electronics and nuclear engineering are likely to be faster and more complex than in the technologies they replace, thus making it more difficult for national suppliers to catch up technologically between product generations.

The growing economies of scale in manufacture and the increasingly fast pace of technological change thus put to question the policy of national champions and national autonomy clearly evident in countries such as Brazil, France, Germany, and the United Kingdom. The cost of controlling the suppliers is growing.

A related emerging issue, created by the convergence between telecommunication and data processing technologies, is that of the very nature of telecommunication networks. A conventional origin to government intervention was the combination of a natural monopoly argument with the strategic and economic importance of the telecommunication industry. Yet, as the conventional telephone share of the telecommunication industry decreases, with the surge in data transfer and computer links, and as the basic switching and long-distance transmission technologies evolve, the natural monopoly argument is eroded. With miniaturized electronic switching, optical fibers, and long-distance microwave transmissions, and the segmentation of the market for telecommunication services among customer sets with very different needs, the traditional PTT monopoly is at least questionable.

So, in conclusion, it may well be that both in terms of the evolution of the technology and of the changes in the nature of the demand for telecommunication services the current government policies toward the telecommunication industry are outdated.[9]

What future there is for the multinationals in both industries is a key question. The evidence suggests that the extreme government interest in nuclear energy issues, the close involvement of government in new nuclear reactor technologies, and its desire to preserve a national capability in nuclear electrical engineering are likely to leave little room for BBC, the only true multinational in heavy electrical equipment. In telecommunications the situation is less clear. A key problem for companies such as LM Ericsson or ITT is the danger of being squeezed between "national champions" supported by their own governments and the leaders of the data processing industry, IBM in particular. What impact the convergence of the data processing and telecommunication technologies will have on industry structure and on the multinational companies studied here is likely to depend on the future of IBM, both in terms of regulation and possible breakup and in terms of IBM providing the degree of national responsiveness demanded by governments.

NOTES

1. In this field the central work remains that of George A. Steiner. See, for instance, George A. Steiner, Managerial Long Range Planning (New York: McGraw-Hill, 1963); and idem, Multinational Corporate Planning (New York: Macmillan, 1966).

2. The key work in this field remains Kenneth R. Andrews, The Concept of Corporate Strategy (Homewood, Ill.: Dow Jones-Irwin, 1971).

3. See my working paper, "Strategy and Structure in Fragmented Worldwide Oligopolies" (Boston: Harvard Business School, 1979).

4. Paul R. Lawrence and Jay Lorsch, Organization and Environment (Boston: Harvard Business School, Division of Research, 1967).

5. Michel Turin, "Les dessous de la Stratégie Américaine en Europe," Entreprise 9-71 (April 19, 1974): 24.

6. Research interview, March 8, 1976.

7. John K. Galbraith, The New Industrial State (New York: New American Library, 1967).

8. Summary results of a research carried out by C. K. Prahalad at the Indian Institute of Management are reported in C. K. Prahalad and Yves Doz, "Strategic Management in Diversified Multinationals" (Paper presented at the International Institute of Management Conference on the "Functioning of the Multinational Corporation," West Berlin, Germany, December 10-12, 1978).

9. The research described here did not focus on these issues. As the research work was being completed, the researcher learned of several projects in a start-up phase. Among several, two can be mentioned as particularly promising: Gary Jordan's work for the Swedish PTT at the Institute of International Business, the Stockholm School of Economics, and Jürgen Müller's projected study of the "Communication Equipment Industry in Europe" at the University of Sussex (Brighton) in the United Kingdom.

INDEX

ABOUT THE AUTHOR

YVES L. DOZ, Assistant Professor of Business Administration at the Graduate School of Business Administration, Harvard University, is a specialist of strategic management research in large multinational companies.

Before joining the Harvard University faculty, Professor Doz taught Business Policy and International Management at the Centre d'Enseignement Superieur des Affaires in Jouy en Josas, France, and consulted for multinational corporations. During his doctoral studies at Harvard University, Professor Doz specialized in the clinical study of management processes within large complex organizations. His dissertation, of which this book is an extension, was completed in 1976.

Professor Doz is researching and writing in the fields of business policy and multinational management.